VOLUME XIV

HIGH SCHOOL ENCYCLOPEDIA

in 20 Volumes

Pilgrims • Rafter

GOLDEN PRESS • NEW YORK

FIRST PRINTING, 1961

Library of Congress Catalog Card Number: 61-13292

© Copyright 1961 by Golden Press, Inc. Designed and produced by Artists and Writers Press, Inc. Printed in the U.S.A. by Western Printing and Lithographing Company. Published by Golden Press, Inc., New York.

Illustrations from GOLDEN BOOKS © 1951, 1952, 1953, 1954, 1955, 1956, 1957, 1958, 1959, 1960, 1961 by Golden Press, Inc.; and from the Basic Science Education Series (Unitext), published by Row, Peterson and Company, Evanston, Illinois, © 1941 by Row, Peterson and Company.

THE GOLDEN
HOME AND

THE GOLDEN HOME AND HIGH SCHOOL ENCYCLOPEDIA, while sufficiently comprehensive and detailed for family use, has been created principally for students at the high school level.

The aim of this reference work is twofold: first, to serve the student's immediate need for authoritative information on a wide range of subjects, and, second, to set forth and explain the many areas of knowledge, so that a student may explore them and thus more competently plan his educational future.

Arranged alphabetically in twenty volumes, here are thousands of full, accurate entries, written and reviewed by experts. The text is abundantly illustrated with full-color photographs and paintings.

Designed to complement the high school curriculum, this encyclopedia offers help with assignments and valuable guidance in the use of other reference tools —dictionaries, atlases, and various library materials. Extensive cross-references and a complete index direct the reader quickly to the information he seeks. A special feature of this work is the sound career information it offers in scores of job and professional fields.

Among the many subjects encompassed in these volumes are the newest developments in science, from microbiology to radioastronomy; fine arts and literature; history and government; religion and philosophy; the physical world, its plants and animals; the social sciences; invention and industry. Four-color maps and latest census figures contribute to an up-to-date view of the world, its continents, nations, and peoples.

Every care has been taken to make *The Golden Home and High School Encyclopedia* lively and stimulating, without sacrifice of accuracy. It is the hope of the editors that these volumes will be used with both advantage and pleasure.

PILGRIMS, or the first of the Puritans to come to New England, originally lived in southeastern England. Persecuted for their beliefs by the English king and the powerful churchmen he favored, they fled to Holland, where they settled in Leiden in 1609. The group grew, but many members became dissatisfied because they were rather poor, their children were growing up as Dutchmen, and they wished to be independent. Therefore, with the help of a Puritan London merchant, part of the Leiden group obtained a charter from the Virginia Company permitting them to settle in the New World. In the summer of 1620 they sailed for England, where more people had been recruited for the settlement. After some disagreements with their financial backers and trouble with one of their ships, they sailed in the *Mayflower* in September. Before landing in Massachusetts two months later, they drew up the Mayflower Compact to govern themselves. Then they settled nearby at what is today Plymouth, Mass. See MAYFLOWER.

PILGRIM'S PROGRESS, a religious allegory written by John Bunyan and published in 1678. It told the story of Christian's journey from the City of Destruction to the Celestial City. During his trip Christian encountered such characters as Mr. Worldly Wiseman, Good-Will, Sloth, Simple, Presumption, Formalism, Hypocrisy, Discretion, Prudence, Piety, Charity, Faithful, and Knowledge. He passed through such places as the Slough of Despond, the Valley of Humiliation, and Vanity Fair.

Bunyan published a second part in 1684, in which Christian's wife, Christiana, and her children make the same perilous pilgrimage from the City of Destruction to Heaven.

Brown Brothers

This is an artist's conception of the first Sunday that the Pilgrims spent in America. The first winter was so severe that over half the Pilgrims perished.

Myles Standish is shown below behind an Indian guide at the head of his small Pilgrim army. Standish, an employee of the Pilgrims, did valuable service in organizing their defenses.
Brown Brothers

Brown Brothers

PIN AND NEEDLE, general terms for small pieces of bone, ivory, thorn, and metal used for fastening objects together, for piercing small holes, for carrying and guiding thread, and for many other manufacturing purposes. In general, a sewing needle is made with an eye at one end.

The earliest steel needles with eyes were probably used by the Chinese and were carried westward by the Moors. In the 14th century needles were made in Germany, and a century later they were made in England. Needles were made laboriously by hand, and their manufacture became an important industry.

John Bunyan wrote many of his works, including the first part of the great religious allegory *Pilgrim's Progress*, while serving a prison sentence for unlicensed preaching.

In the 18th century mechanical methods of manufacture were originated and improved until the process became entirely mechanical.

Needles are made of different materials according to their purposes, such as chromium and stainless steel surgical needles. There are special kinds of needles for many kinds of sewing, such as that done on carpets, shoes, and sails. Many types of sewing machines require special needles. Fine hand-sewing needles are made chiefly in England, but all sorts of machine needles are made in the United States.

Although the first pinmaking machine was not invented until 1824 by the American Lemuel W. Wright, the manufacture of pins was a flourishing industry by the 17th century in England.

PINE, a coniferous, evergreen tree, any member of a genus containing approximately 80 species, most of which are in the North Temperate Zone. Nearly all the species are distinguished by continuous trunks and possess whorls of branches at successive levels. The leaves of pine are of two kinds. The primary leaves are spirally arranged and reduced to small, dry bracts. They bear in their axils the conspicuous, needle-like leaves, which are in clusters, usually of two, three, or five. The cones are the reproductive organs of the pine. Some cones of a pine tree bear seeds; other cones of the same tree bear the pollen that fertilizes the seeds. Most pines mature their seeds in two years; a few require three years. The seeds are liberated from the cones in autumn of the year of maturity. A few, as jack pine and loblolly, retain seeds in the cones, to be opened by such outside conditions as fire. Cones of different species vary greatly in shape and size. Their length ranges from 1 inch to nearly 2 feet.

More than 35 species of pine are native to North American forests, the most numerous ones being the yellow pine and the white pine. Mugo pine is usually a prostrate shrub; some pine species grow only 15 or 20 feet high; others grow from 100 to 250 feet high.

Various species of pine are of considerable economic importance. Southern pines in the United States are resinous, yielding turpentine, tar, and other valuable products. The furniture industry uses a considerable amount of pine wood, and pine is an important source of pulp for paper. The pines are among the most attractive evergreens; they furnish decorations in the form of cones, branches, and Christmas trees.

Ponderosa Pine

Pitch Pine

Pinyon Nut

Pinyon Pine

Lodgepole Pine

Eastern White Pine

Hawaiian Pineapple

PINEAPPLE, one of the most delicious of tropical fruits. It really is not a single fruit but rather a collection of many small, undeveloped fruits that have grown together in one solid, juicy mass. The pineapple plant is from 3 to 6 feet tall. It grows from the ground as a tuft of long, narrow, spiny-edged, grayish-green leaves, in the center of which is borne the pineapple itself, which is topped by another tuft of quite small leaves. Each shoot of the pineapple plant bears fruit only once. Subsequent fruits develop on shoots that branch from the first one. The pineapple family also includes the ornamental bromeliads and Spanish moss, an epiphyte that, seen in the tropics and the Gulf States, grows thickly along the branches of many trees.

The pineapple is native to South America, specifically Brazil and probably Paraguay. Some 300 years ago it was taken both to Europe and to the Orient and is now grown to some extent in most of the tropical regions of the world. About four-fifths of the world's pineapples, however are raised at present in the Hawaiian Islands. The West Indies, Mexico, and the Malay region are also important producers of the fruit. Pineapple is marketed both fresh and canned. Canning was begun in Singapore in southeastern Asia shortly before 1900. Soon thereafter it was started in Hawaii, where it has since become a very large industry. Pineapple crops have steadily increased to take advantage of the market that canning has given to the Hawaiian fruit.

PING-PONG. See TABLE TENNIS.

PINKERTON'S NATIONAL DETEC-TIVE AGENCY is the world's largest and oldest private detective agency. Its founder formulated a code of ethics that still governs much of the private-detective business. Pinkerton detectives guard businesses and industrial plants, social affairs, conventions, and athletic events. They may be used to investigate burglaries, to check up on charge-account applicants, or to check on the courtesy and efficiency of employees. In the past Pinkerton detectives caught train robbers, outlaw bands, famous jewel thieves, and counterfeiters. The agency also served during the Civil War as the first U.S. government secret service.

The Pinkerton Detective Agency was founded in 1850 in Chicago by Allan Pinkerton. Among the agency's first clients were railroads. In January, 1861, Southern sympathizers threatened one of these railroads, whose lines were strategically located, with sabotage if war broke out. The railroad had Pinkerton investigate, and he discovered a plot to assassinate Lincoln en route through Baltimore to his inauguration in Washington, D.C. Lincoln's route was changed and the assassination averted. When war began, General George B. McClellan, formerly vice-president of the Illinois Central Railroad and employer of Pinkerton, used the agency's services to spy out the size and movements of Southern troops, since there was no government espionage system at the time. When McClellan was disgraced for his failures to attack the Confederate armies, Pinkerton resigned with him.

From 1866 the Pinkerton agency supplied guards for struck industrial plants. This service was given up after the Homestead Steel strike (1892), during which workers opened fire on the detectives, believing that they had been imported to take the workers' jobs.

PINOCHLE, a card game for two, three, or four players. Almost nothing is known of the origin of the game, but, under various spellings, it has appeared in game books since about 1864.

In the basic two-hand game a 48-card pack is used—2 each of the A, K, Q, J, 10, and 9 in each of the four suits. The rank of the cards is (from high to low) A, 10, K, Q, J, 9. Twelve cards are dealt to each player, three at a time. The 25th card is turned face up as the trump card. The remainder of the pack is placed face down on the table as the stock. If the trump card is a 9, the dealer immediately scores 10 points. The object of the game is to score points by melding, by winning counting cards in tricks, and by taking the last trick.

The play from the 1st trick through the 12th is known as the early play, and these rules apply: The players may lead any card they wish and do not have to follow suit nor trump. A trick containing trumps is won by the higher trump; a trick in which there is no trump is won by the higher card of the suit led. If two cards of the same suit and rank are played to the same trick, the card led wins it. After each trick is won, and before another card is led, the winner draws the top card of the stock, and his opponent takes the next one. Thus each player still has 12 cards before each lead. All melded cards are placed on the table face up. They are considered still part of the hand and may be played at any time. A dix (9 of trumps) may be exchanged for the trump card by either player at any time. The winner of the 12th trick shows the card he draws from the stock. The other player then takes the last card (the trump, or the dix which has taken its place). Each player then picks up all his melded cards from the table.

The following play, from the start of the 13th trick to the taking of the final trick, is called the later play. During this part of the game these rules apply: Any card may be led, but the opponent must follow suit if able. If he has none of that suit, he must play a trump if he can. When a trump is led, the opponent must play a higher trump if he has one.

At the end of the deal each player adds up the points he has won in tricks on the basis of the following count: each ace, 11; each ten, 10; each king, 4; each queen, 3; each jack, 2; last trick, 10. The 9 has no point value in tricks. To get his score for the deal this trick total is then added to the player's score of points made for melds. Each deal may be considered a separate game, or the game may be set at 1,000 points. If both players reach 1,000 points on the same deal, the winning score is reset at 1,250 points.

PIONEERS is a term that describes the settlers of uncultivated and undeveloped country. They, unlike explorers, prospectors, and fur traders, establish permanent settlements. They come to the land they open on their own initiative rather than through state planning. They usually work without benefit of hired help.

Pioneers have been especially important in the histories of the United States, Canada, and Israel. The first pioneers in what is now the United States were the New England Pilgrims and Puritans. The country was developed by a constant push of pioneers westward. Pioneering is still going on in Alaska. Pioneering in Canada was at first largely subordinate to the fur trade and was never quite as important a factor in the development of the country as it was in the United States. Gradually the French established perma-

Daniel Boone leads a group of American pioneers westward through Cumberland Gap.
Washington University—Courtesy TIME

Nebraska State Historical Society

Plains pioneers lived in sod houses built of thick prairie sod tightly woven with grass.

PIPE, an instrument for smoking tobacco. It consists of a bowl, in which the tobacco is burned, and a stem, through which the smoke is drawn. The bowl is usually made of wood and the short stem of plastic. Pipes are also frequently made of clay, such as meerschaum, or of metal.

Pipe smoking was probably introduced into England by Sir Walter Raleigh, who learned the practice from North American Indians. Many Indian tribes made the smoking of the calumet, or peace pipe, a kind of ceremonial treaty. The clay pipe and the corncob pipe are well-known varieties. Immense porcelain pipes, often highly decorated, were formerly used by the Germans. The oriental hookah is the largest pipe used. This pipe has a long, flexible tube, and the smoke while passing through this tube is cooled by water in which the tube rests.

Pipes are made of a variety of materials and in many different styles.

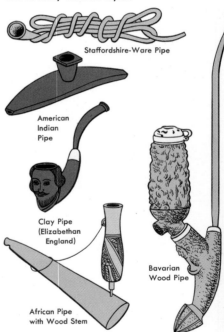

Staffordshire-Ware Pipe

American Indian Pipe

Clay Pipe (Elizabethan England)

Bavarian Wood Pipe

African Pipe with Wood Stem

nent pioneering settlements along the St. Lawrence River, and before 1800 English pioneers had established fishing and lumbering settlements, similar to those of New England, in the maritime provinces. However, more typical pioneering activity occurred in what is now Ontario after 1800, when farmers took up land and hewed farms out of the woods. Widespread pioneering in the great western Canadian breadbasket occurred only after 1900.

Pioneers, wherever they came from and whenever they lived, were dissatisfied with their lives at home and hoped to make better lives in the new uncultivated lands. Some—like the Puritans of New England, the Dukhobors who came to western Canada from Russia, and the Mormons who settled Utah—came to escape religious persecution. Others—like many of the Scots, the Irish, and the English who pioneered in Ontario and other parts of Canada after 1800—came because of economic distress at home. In addition, some of the pioneers in the United States moved from more settled areas because of financial failure or because the soil was worn out.

Life was usually hard for pio-

neers. In wooded areas, such as Ontario and much of the eastern United States, it sometimes took years for a farmer to clear his land completely. Other pioneers had long trips, and in the case of some pioneers going to the west coast of the United States they had deserts or high mountains to cross before they reached their land. Pioneer homes, whether log cabins (as in the eastern United States and Canada) or sod huts (as on the Great Plains of the United States), were poor, and pioneers often suffered from loneliness.

Pioneering has been of equal, if not greater, importance in the development of present-day Israel, for pioneering agricultural settlements formed the basis on which the state was built. The pioneers of Israel, however, have differed from those of Canada and the United States in that their purposes in pioneering have been political and social as well as personal. The pioneering movement has been an intimate part of the Zionist movement; the pioneers have gone on the land explicitly to build the state. They have settled in cooperative settlements because they hoped in this way to build a better society.

These two stone pipes, with wooden stems decorated with quillwork, were made by the Sauk and Fox Indians of North America.

Museum of the American Indian—Heye Foundation

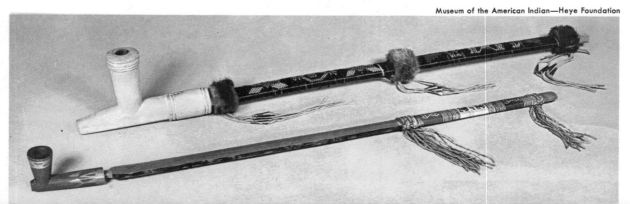

PIPE AND PIPEFITTING. A pipe is a hollow, cylindrical object for containing the flow of fluids, such as oil, water, steam, gas, and the like. Pipe is also widely used for carrying loads in construction, as in scaffolding. Pipes are made of a multitude of materials such as clay, asbestos cement, cast iron, wrought iron, steel, copper, brass, lead, plastic, glass, and rubber compositions. Each kind of pipe has its own special methods of fitting. For example, cast-iron pipes are commonly joined with oakum and lead and various kinds of bolted unions, some of which even permit flexibility. Steel pipe fittings are generally threaded, while copper pipe is either threaded or joined with a flange and flaring tool. Pipe varies from $\frac{1}{8}$ inch to 7 feet in diameter. Among engineers *tube* refers to a part of a machine while *pipe* refers to a conveyer of liquids or gases over a distance.

In choosing pipe and in fitting it together one should determine just what the pipe is expected to do in terms of holding pressure, in resisting frost and corrosion, and in sustaining horizontal and vertical strains. One should also consider the ultimate use of the material to be carried through the pipe. For example, lead pipe splits when subjected to high pressure and freezing, is completely rustproof, must be sustained by hangers or similar devices every foot or two, and is excellent for carrying off waste water, but it should not be used for a water-supply line. Copper and brass pipe and pipefittings are inferior to iron in some areas where the water is loaded with chemicals. Copper and iron fittings may corrode when brought together in a simple joint. Fittings should be chosen and pipe should be reamed so as to provide smooth inside joints that will not block the flow of liquids nor permit the building up of deposits that will clog the line.

Pipefitting need not be limited to the engineer and the plumber. With a pipe vice, a pipe cutter, and threading equipment anyone can build a workbench frame threaded into a floor flange that can be bolted to a cement or wooden floor. Or a cellar-stair rail can be bent to exactly the right shape and held securely to the wall by the use of threaded tees that screw into a small floor flange. With a supply of 1-inch heavily galvanized iron pipe and the necessary fittings a jungle gym may be built that can be enlarged, cut down, or moved in pieces without loss of strength.

PIRACY, robbery on the high seas. However, pirates were always more than robbers. They had close connections with general trade, the slave trade, smuggling, privateering, and war. Until the middle of the 19th century, lines between these occupations were vague.

Pompey the Great, the Roman general of the 1st century B.C. who conquered, robbed, and enslaved millions of people, achieved spectacular fame by suppressing pirates in the Mediterranean Sea. A thousand years later the coasts of Europe were ravaged by shiploads of Vikings, whom the settled people and traders called pirates. Actually, the Vikings were peoples expanding along the sea routes.

Five hundred years later the Elizabethan sea captains, like Sir Francis Drake, attacked the fleets of Spain and plundered the Spanish centers of wealth. Drake and Raleigh were pirates backed by their queen, but they were also slave catchers, smugglers, privateers, and officers in the queen's navy. Their enormous profits taken from the Spaniards, who had robbed the Aztecs, were divided with the English queen and her courtiers. In those days all ships that went to sea carried cannon, muskets, and cutlasses, not only to defend themselves against pirates, but also to do a bit of plundering on their own account if they met a smaller vessel. In general, pirates respected the flag and the sailing papers of their own nation and their nation's allies. For example, English pirates rarely robbed English or Portuguese ships, but French and Spanish ships were

always fair game. Pirate loot was frequently smuggled into enemy ports at a high profit.

The necessities of orderly international trade and the development of international law brought piracy to an end about the middle of the 19th century. However, in 1896 Captain Joshua Slocum, while sailing alone in the sloop *Spray* off the African coast, was chased by a pirate who dismasted himself by crowding on too much sail.

Sir Henry Morgan (about 1635-1688) was a successful English pirate and colonial administrator. As a boy he was kidnaped from Bristol, England, sold as a slave in the Caribbean Sea, joined Edward Mansfield's buccaneering expedition against the Spaniards, and, when Mansfield was killed, was elected "admiral" by the pirates. He collected immense booty by seizing many Spanish ships and towns and became possibly the greatest of all pirates by his capture, looting, and utter destruction of the town of Panama in 1671. A year later he returned to England, was knighted by King Charles II, and was sent back to the Spanish Main as lieutenant governor of Jamaica, where he continued as a pirate chief.

Captain William Kidd (about 1645-1701) was a New York real estate owner and sea captain, who in 1695 was backed by the king of England and his Whig lords to go to sea as a privateer to capture pirates and French ships. His voyage of 1696 and 1697 to the Indian Ocean is still a mystery. He attacked no pirates but neither did he take any English vessels. He seized three ships, all

Below are the raiders Sir John Hawkins, Sir Francis Drake, and Thomas Cavendish. At right are some of the Spanish coins they took.
Greenwich Hospital Coll., National Maritime Museum, Greenwich, England

Gold doubloon

Silver cob

The notorious Blackbeard, above, was finally slain by Lieutenant Robert Maynard.

sailing under French papers, which at the time was perfectly legal. When Kidd was brought to trial for piracy, the court hid the papers, and they remained hidden in the Public Record Office in London for 200 years. He was hanged not for piracy but for the alleged murder of one of his mutinous crew. Captain Kidd seems to have been the victim of political intrigue among the Whigs and Tories of the English court when those gentlemen were growing rich on the profits of slaving, piracy, privateering, war, and trade with India.

Captain Kidd's famous buried treasure seems to have been largely the product of literary imaginations. Actually, his loot disappeared under the hands of the Admiralty officers in the West Indies and on the New England coast.

Blackbeard, or Edward Teach (? -1718), was an English licensed privateer during the War of the Spanish Succession, but after the Treaty of Utrecht he continued the war on his own account. In the *Queen Anne's Revenge,* 40 guns, he plundered ships indiscriminately off the coasts of the American colonies until an English sloop of war forced Blackbeard's ship aground. With pistol and sword the English captain slew Blackbeard, cut off his head, and lashed the bloody trophy to the sloop's bowsprit.

PIRANDELLO, LUIGI (1867-1936), Italian dramatist and novelist, was born in Girgenti (now Agrigento), Sicily. Soon after completing his education at the University of Bonn, in Germany, he settled in Rome, where he commenced his literary career; he was supported by an allowance from his father. In 1897 circumstances forced Pirandello to take a position as a high school teacher, a position he held for the next 24 years. The success of his play *Six Characters in Search of an Author* permitted him to leave the teaching profession and to dedicate his life to the Italian theater. Shortly after the production of *Henry IV* Pirandello established his own theater in Rome and at the head of a troupe toured Europe and America. Other plays include *Right You Are, if You Think You Are; As You Desire Me;* and *Better Think Twice About It.* Marked by a grim humor and a pessimistic view of human hopes and attitudes, Pirandello's plays exerted a strong influence on the post-World War I drama. His novels, which include *The Outcast* and *The Late Mattia Pascal,* as well as his short stories, which number in the hundreds, also attained widespread popularity. Pirandello received the Nobel prize for literature in 1934.

Galileo used the Leaning Tower of Pisa for his famous experiments with falling bodies.

PISA, LEANING TOWER OF. This famous Italian Romanesque bell tower is 179 feet high. Begun in 1174, it was not completed until 1350. Today the tower is world famous for being 13 feet off the perpendicular, an effect sometimes thought intentional but more likely the result of the subsidence of soil, causing a sinking of foundations.

Pisces commemorates the legendary escape of two gods, Venus and Cupid. While walking beside a river one day, they saw the giant Typhon approaching. To escape they jumped into the river, where they changed themselves into fish and swam to safety.

PISCES, or the Fishes, is an inconspicuous constellation of the zodiac between Aries and Aquarius. It contains many faint stars of fourth and fifth magnitude but none brighter. One of the fishes may be found near Andromeda and the other near Pegasus. Two faint lines of stars connect the fishes in a V-shape. The vernal equinox is located in this constellation. Pisces is visible in the evening sky from midnorthern latitudes between September and January.

PISCIS AUSTRINUS, or the Southern Fish, is a small southern constellation south of Aquarius. Most of its stars are faint, but it contains one first-magnitude star, Fomalhaut, the only brilliant star in a wide area of this part of the sky. Fomalhaut is visible in the evening sky from midnorthern latitudes between September and November.

Piscis Austrinus is often pictured as a fish with its mouth opened toward the falling spout of water from the jar of Aquarius, the Water Carrier, in an adjoining constellation. The brilliant star Fomalhaut marks the position of the fish's mouth.

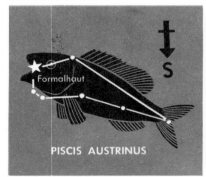

These dueling pistols and loading accessories were made in France about 1840.

PISTOL, a small firearm designed to be fired by one hand. It probably originated either in Italy or in Germany about 1550. At first pistols were muzzle loaded and made as single-barreled and double-barreled weapons, in principle resembling the ordinary firearms of the day. The modern pistol is a precision-built device composed of about 72 different parts, some machined to tolerances of less than $\frac{1}{1,000}$ inch. It differs from the revolver in that ammunition is inserted in a clip into the butt. Such automatic pistols are constructed so that the force of recoil, after each shot, is utilized to open the breech, extract the empty bullet shell, cock the pistol, and reload it, making it ready to fire the next time the trigger is pressed. Pistols are used by police, by the military forces as sidearms, and by private persons for sport or for protection. The standard U.S. service pistol is a .45-caliber, automatic, recoil-operated weapon having a magazine holding seven cartridges.

PISTON, the movable end of a cylinder, whose effective volume is changed by a moving piston. Moving pistons remain in such firm contact with cylinder walls that only a very small amount of liquid or gas can pass the piston of an engine. Pistons are essential parts of steam engines, internal-combustion engines, and some compressors and pumps.

Steam engines have disk-shaped or conical pistons. Internal-combustion engines use trunk pistons, which have a skirt and a head de-

signed to withstand high temperatures and high pressures. The skirt provides support for the sideways thrust on pistons exerted by the connecting rods of the engine and helps align the piston with the cylinder. A trunk piston also carries the piston pin, or wristpin.

Most piston heads have a flat surface. Some are specially shaped for use in special cylinders. Piston heads may be saucer shaped, domed, or of very irregular shape.

Piston rings fit in grooves cut into the head or skirt of a piston. The rings have a short gap on one side. They are made of springy metal. Piston rings may be concentric or eccentric. The rings press against the cylinder walls as the piston moves and keep the cylinder sealed. Some pistons also have oil-scraper rings that prevent too much oil from coating the cylinder walls.

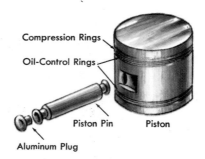

Compression Rings

Oil-Control Rings

Piston Pin

Piston

Aluminum Plug

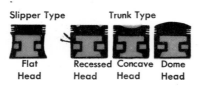

Slipper Type

Trunk Type

Flat Head

Recessed Head

Concave Head

Dome Head

The airplane-engine piston assembly above is both light in weight and extremely rigid.

PITCH is the attribute of a pure tone, primarily determined by the frequency of the vibrations of its sound waves perceived by the listener. The greater the frequency of vibrations (expressed in cycles per second) the higher the pitch of the tone and the higher its relative position on the musical scale. In addition to frequency, sound pressure (loudness) also determines pitch. Assuming constant frequency, an increase in sound pressure causes a decrease in pitch. In music the standard pitch (also known as the philharmonic pitch) for tuning instruments is based upon an A (above middle C) of 440 cycles per second. See MUSICAL SCALE; SOUND.

PITCHBLENDE is a variety of the mineral uraninite. It is one of the ores of uranium and is also a source of radium.

Pitchblende is an oxide of uranium. Its theoretical composition is UO_2. Pitchblende is always partially oxidized, and its actual composition is somewhere between UO_2 and U_3O_8. Pitchblende contains small amounts of lead, rare earths, nitrogen, radium, helium, and argon. Pitchblende usually contains some thorium, and there may be as much thorium as uranium in a sample. The lead present is the stable product of radioactive disintegration of some of the original uranium and thorium. Radium is present because it also is a product of the disintegration of uranium and thorium. Argon and helium are both decay products.

Pitchblende is a brownish-black or greenish-black mineral that often has a dull, pitchlike surface. Pitchblende is usually found in fine-grained masses that sometimes look like grapes stuck together. The specific gravity of a sample may be from 6.5 to 9.7. Any piece of pitchblende feels unusually heavy for its size. Pitchblende is radioactive, and a Geiger-Müller counter or other detector of radioactivity will respond to its presence.

Pitchblende is most often found in veins of sulfide minerals and is associated with ores of silver, lead, cobalt, bismuth, and nickel. A famous deposit of pitchblende is at Jachymov, Czechoslovakia. Radium was discovered in pitchblende from the mines there. The Shinkolobwe mine in the Katanga province of the Congo Republic is a large producer of pitchblende. Canada has several areas where pitchblende is mined: the shores of Great Bear Lake, in Northwest Territories; the Beaverlodge Lake region, Saskatchewan; and the Blind River area, Ontario.

A sample of pitchblende from a mine in Saxony, in Germany, is pictured below.

PITCHER PLANT, the name given to members of several genera of carnivorous plants. They possess green, pitcher-shaped leaves that contain a fluid capable of digesting insects and the bodies of other small animals. Their carnivorous aspect is associated with the soils in which they grow. Such soils are deficient in certain substances, and the plant obtains these from the juices of the animal life it traps. See PLANT, INSECT-EATING.

PITT, WILLIAM (1759-1806), English statesman, second son of William Pitt, earl of Chatham, was prime minister of Great Britain during the French Revolution and the Napoleonic Wars. He was born near Bromley in Kent and was educated at Pembroke Hall, Cambridge. He began his political career in 1781, when he was elected member of Parliament for Appleby. His oratorical and administrative skills were quickly recognized, and in 1782 he became chancellor of the exchequer and leader of the House of Commons. In December, 1783, before his 25th birthday, he was named prime minister. He also held the offices of first lord of the treasury and chancellor of the exchequer. He remained in power until 1801, one of the longest terms of office in British history.

Before the outbreak of war with France in 1793 Pitt accomplished a number of lasting reforms in financing the public debt, reducing customs duties, and administering India, where the political control was transferred from the East India Company to the government. Pitt could do nothing about the badly needed reform of Parliament, and after 1793 all internal policies were subordinated to the necessity of opposing the French wars of conquest. He dealt with the troubled affairs of Ireland by pushing through Parliament the Act of Union (1800). The radical policies and propaganda of the French revolutionary government frightened the educated classes in England, and Pitt's government resorted to severe measures to suppress all speech and action directed toward political reform. On the Continent he organized coalitions to oppose French expansion, and, with the aid of Nelson's naval victories, saved England from conquest. To complete his Irish policy he advocated Catholic emancipation, and when the king proved unalterably opposed to it, Pitt resigned in March, 1801. After the Treaty of Amiens failed to preserve the peace, Pitt returned to office (May, 1804). He formed another European coalition with Russia and Austria. When this was destroyed by the battles of Ulm and Austerlitz, Pitt was completely broken by the disasters. He retired to his villa at Putney and died less than two weeks later.

PITTSBURGH is situated in southwestern Pennsylvania, at the junction of the Monongahela and the Allegheny rivers, which here form the Ohio River and the city's "Golden Triangle" area. Because of its favorable location to coal and iron deposits, transportation facilities, and labor supply, Pittsburgh has long been one of the leading cities of the United States in the manufacture of iron and steel products. It has earned the nickname of the "Steel City." Other important manufactures include coke, aluminum, plate glass, cork, clay products, and electrical supplies. A nearby atomic-energy plant furnishes power to many of the city's industries. Pittsburgh is Pennsylvania's second largest city, with a population, in 1960, of 604,332.

Pittsburgh has leading educational institutions, such as the University of Pittsburgh, Duquesne University, and Carnegie Institute of Technology. Points of interest include Carnegie Institute, with its library, museum, and music hall; Buhl Planetarium and Institute of Popular Science; the Zoological Garden; Schenley Park, containing the Phipps Conservatory; and the Fort Pitt Blockhouse, built in 1764 and the only pre-Revolutionary building in the city. Also of interest is the Mellon Institute of Industrial Research, where many new industrial processes have been developed.

In the foreground of this view of Pittsburgh is a part of the city's mill section, which is concentrated on the low river flats. At the left, background, is the University of Pittsburgh's Cathedral of Learning, an imposing symbol of Pittsburgh's cultural life.

USDA

The site of a strategic frontier post in pre-Revolutionary War days, Pittsburgh's famed "Golden Triangle," at the confluence of the Allegheny (left) and Monongahela (foreground) rivers, is the city's major business and financial district.

Pittsburgh occupies a picturesque site, the ground rising eastward from the river flat to the hills. The southern shore of the Monongahela River presents a precipitous, rocky bluff, hundreds of feet high, whose top affords a splendid view of the city.

Fort Duquesne, built here by the French in 1754, was later taken by the British and renamed Fort Pitt. Virginia subsequently claimed the territory, but in 1780 jurisdiction over it was vested in Pennsylvania. The village that had risen around Fort Pitt was incorporated as a borough in 1794 and as a city in 1816.

At the end of World War II an extensive urban redevelopment program was begun in Pittsburgh. Several elaborate parks were opened; many blighted areas were cleared and developed; and a large number of buildings and parking garages were erected in the "Golden Triangle," a part of the city's main business district. The success of smoke-control measures made Pittsburgh's well-known nickname of the "Smoky City" virtually obsolete.

PITUITARY GLAND, a gland located at the base of the brain. The gland is made up of two main lobes, the anterior lobe and the posterior lobe. It is considered to be the master gland of the endocrine system and has a number of specific functions. Among its functions are the secretion of hormones that affect the thyroid, gonads, adrenals, and other glands of internal secretion. It also controls growth, maturation, and reproductive processes.

Courtesy of Pittsburgh Chamber of Commerce

PIZARRO, FRANCISCO (1471?-1541), the conqueror and first governor of Peru, was born at Trujillo, Estremadura, Spain. Little is known of him until 1510, when he sailed with other adventurers for America. Pizarro was with Balboa when the Pacific Ocean was discovered, and in 1519 he settled for a while in Panama. In 1524 he formed an alliance with Diego de Almagro, another adventurer, and Fernando de Luque, a priest, in an enterprise to make new discoveries and conquests in the south. On their first voyage they heard of the Peruvian Empire but were too small a force to make any settlement. In 1528

This is a painting of the battle between the armies of Pizarro and Almagro.

The Bettmann Archive

Pizarro returned to Spain, and in the following year he was given the right of conquest and government in Peru.

In 1531 Pizarro, with an army of fewer than 200 men, landed in Peru at the end of an Incan civil war. The Inca, Atahualpa, greeted him with friendliness. On a visit to the Spanish camp Atahualpa was seized by Pizarro. The enormous ransom asked for Atahualpa's return was paid, but the Inca was nevertheless treacherously executed (1533). War between the Spanish and Incan forces resulted in a Spanish victory, and in 1535 the conqueror built a new capital at Lima. A quarrel now occurred between Almagro and Pizarro regarding the limits of their territories. The battle that resulted in 1538 was won by Pizarro, who had Almagro executed. Later, a group of Almagro's supporters plotted against Pizarro and assassinated him in his palace at Lima.

Pizarro never learned to read or write. He was cruel, treacherous (even to his friends), and ignorant; his one outstanding virtue was courage.

Pizarro's half brother Gonzalo, who had accompanied him in his conquest, set himself up as governor in 1546 but was not recognized by the Spanish government. A new governor was sent from Spain and Gonzalo, whose soldiers deserted him, gave himself up and was executed in 1548.

PLAGIOCLASE, a general name for feldspar minerals rich in sodium and calcium. The plagioclase feldspar series of minerals includes a sodium aluminum silicate, a calcium aluminum silicate, and several sodium calcium aluminum silicates. The sodium aluminum silicate member of the series is called albite. The calcium aluminum silicate member is anorthite. The other members of the series, in order of decreasing sodium content, are oligoclase, andesine, labradorite, and bytownite. Plagioclase feldspars are commonly found as irregular grains and cleavable masses in igneous and metamorphic rocks.

Most specimens of plagioclase feldspar are colorless, white, or gray. They have a glassy or pearly appearance. Labradorite or andesine may show a play of blue or green as a specimen is slowly turned. Plagioclase feldspars are harder than a steel knife blade. A plagioclase feldspar has two cleavage directions (planes along which the mineral breaks smoothly). The angle between the cleavages is about 94 degrees. Plagioclase feldspars can often be distinguished from other minerals by the striations present on a fresh cleavage surface. A mass of plagioclase is usually made up of a large number of thin crystals. Individual crystals may be distinguished by the differences in orientation of the striations.

The members of the plagioclase series are difficult for the amateur to distinguish from each other. A good guide to the type of plagioclase present in a rock is the rock itself. Granites, syenites, rhyolites, trachytes, and pegmatites often con-

Here are three minerals in the plagioclase feldspar series. At the upper left is a sample of albite. The fine parallel striations on the cleavage surface are typical of all plagioclase feldspars and show, in this sample, that albite twinning is present. At the lower left is anorthite. Directly above is a sample of labradorite, in which a play of color, blue and green, can be seen.

tain albite. All these rocks are light-colored igneous rocks and contain light-colored minerals. Igneous rocks with a greater proportion of dark minerals, such as monzonite, granodiorite, andesite, and diorite, commonly contain oligoclase and andesine. Dark, heavy igneous rocks, such as gabbro, contain labradorite and bytownite. Anorthosite is a rock composed almost completely of labradorite or bytownite. Some metamorphosed limestones and some very dark igneous rocks contain anorthite. The plagioclase feldspars are common in some metamorphic rocks.

The plagioclase minerals are extremely abundant and are found in many parts of the earth. A few specimens of plagioclase minerals are used as semiprecious stones. Some plagioclase feldspar is used in the manufacture of ceramics.

PLAIN, an expanse of generally low-lying territory with little relative relief, as distinguished from a tableland or plateau. The Great Northern Plain extends, with one break in the Ural Mountains, from the shores of the Atlantic nearly to Bering Strait and from the Arctic Ocean to the Caucasus and the Altai Mountains. It extends over about 4,500,000 square miles. Among its various subdivisions are included the North German Plain in Europe and the Siberian Plain and the Kirghiz Steppe in Asia. In the Western Hemisphere are the great Central Plains and the Atlantic Plain of North America and the great South American Plain, which is estimated to occupy four times as great an area as the mountainous parts of that continent.

A wheatfield on the West Siberian Plain
Marilyn Silverstone—Nancy Palmer Photo Agency

PLANCK, MAX (1858-1947), a German physicist, born at Kiel, who established the basis of the quantum theory of the radiation of energy. He began his lifelong study of physics at the University of Munich at the age of 16 and later studied at the University of Berlin, where in 1879 he wrote a doctoral thesis on thermodynamics. He was professor of theoretical physics at the University of Kiel from 1885 to 1889 and at the University of Berlin from 1889 to 1926.

Early in his career Planck conducted research on thermodynamics and energy radiation. His research on the radiation of energy from black bodies culminated in 1901 in a treatise called *The Law of Radiation*, in which he established the foundation of the quantum theory. He proposed in his contributions to this theory that the energy of light, X-rays, and other radiations does not flow continuously like a stream. Instead, this energy consists of discrete units called quanta, whose activities in some important respects resemble those of particles of matter. His contributions to the quantum theory exerted an influence on modern physics comparable to that of Albert Einstein's theory of relativity.

In 1918 Planck was awarded the Nobel prize in physics. In 1930 he became president of the Kaiser Wilhelm Society, a scientific society in Berlin, which since has been renamed the Max Planck Society.

PLANET. The word *planet*, derived from the Greek root meaning "wanderer," was used prior to the 13th century to denote those celestial objects (other than meteors and comets) that were observed to be in motion relative to the stars. Before the 15th century seven objects were considered to be planets: Sun, Moon, Mercury, Venus, Mars, Jupiter, and Saturn. With the advent of the heliocentric hypothesis of the structure of the solar system in the

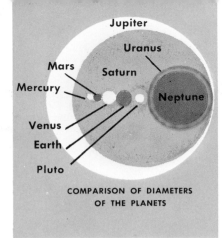

COMPARISON OF DIAMETERS
OF THE PLANETS

Jupiter and Saturn account for 95 percent of the combined volume of all the sun's planets.

16th century the sun and the moon were no longer considered planets, but the earth was. Since the application of the telescope to astronomical observation three additional planets (Uranus, Neptune, and Pluto) and over 1,000 asteroids (small planets with orbits between Jupiter and Mars) have been discovered. The term *planet*, as used in modern astronomy, denotes any celestial body (except comets and meteors) that revolves about a star and that shines by reflected sunlight.

In spite of the fact that many of the sun's planets are larger than the earth, their distance from earth is so great that they appear as bright stars. In fact, of the planets Mercury, Mars, Jupiter, Venus, and Saturn only the last shines less brightly than does the brightest star, Sirius. Uranus, Neptune, and Pluto, on the other hand, are relatively faint. In general, under good atmospheric conditions a planet does not appear to twinkle, as does a star. However, this rule is not infallible. Certain identification can only be made by observation by means of a telescope. Through a telescope planets (with the exception of Pluto and the asteroids) appear distinctly disk shaped. Stars appear as points of light, no matter how much magnification is used.

The planets have been classified in several ways. Nine of them—Mercury, Venus, Earth, Mars, Jupiter, Saturn, Uranus, Neptune, and Pluto—are known as the principal, or primary, planets. Their satellites are sometimes called secondary planets, and the asteroids are known as minor planets. Classified as inferior planets are Mercury and Venus, whose orbits lie closer to the sun than Earth's. Planets called superior are Mars, the asteroids, Jupiter, Saturn, Uranus, Neptune, and Pluto with orbits outside Earth's. A different classification involving only the nine principal planets lists Mercury, Venus, Earth, and Mars as inner planets, the rest as outer planets. The inner planets are also called terrestrial planets because of their similarity to Earth in size and mean density. Pluto is classed as terrestrial because of its similar size. The remaining four planets—Jupiter, Saturn, Uranus, and Neptune—are known as the major planets. They are much larger than the terrestrial planets, but also much less dense.

At present no star besides the sun is known to have planets revolving around it. However, some astronomers consider it likely that many other stars may have planetary systems. (See SOLAR SYSTEM.) We are so far from even the nearest other star that any light reflected from a possible planet would be indistinguishable from the glare of the star itself. Radio telescopes, however, could distinguish radio signals from such planets, and one is already in use for the detection of such signals. (See LIFE BEYOND THE EARTH.) Also, certain stars show a slight wobble in their motion through space, which could conceivably indicate the presence of a heavy planet revolving around the star.

Special positions of other planets, inside and outside earth's orbit, are identified below relative to a line from earth to sun.

Both inferior planets Venus and Mercury appear at times as morning and as evening stars.

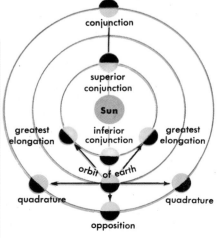

The Morrison Planetarium in San Francisco contains over 100 projectors and several hundred lenses, which produce the appearance of the sky on a domed ceiling. An artificial city skyline adds to the realistic effect.

PLANETARIUM, an apparatus or mechanism for exhibiting the movements of the planets and other members of the solar system, also the structure housing such apparatus. Particularly after the acceptance of Copernicus' heliocentric hypothesis scientists attempted to build models of the solar system that would show planetary motion, orbits, and the relative sizes of planets. Such planetaria consisted of globes of various sizes, which represented the components of the planetary system. In the early 18th century an especially elaborate planetarium of this type was built for Charles Boyle, 4th Earl of Orrery. Ever since, a device of this sort has been called an orrery.

In recent years the term *planetarium* has come to be more closely associated with the type developed during the early 20th century at the Carl Zeiss Optical Works in Jena, Germany. The Zeiss planetarium consists of a stereopticon apparatus that projects points of light, representing the heavenly bodies, onto the inside of a domed ceiling, which represents the celestial hemisphere. Rotation of the projector reproduces the movements of the stars and planets as they appear in nature. In a large planetarium the dome may be 80 feet in diameter. The first planetatium of the Zeiss type, built at the Deutsches Museum in Munich, Germany, was opened in 1925. The Adler Planetarium in Chicago, opened to the public in 1930, was the first of the Zeiss type in the United States.

A present-day Zeiss planetarium can project over 9,600 stars. The sky may be shown as it would appear from any point on the surface of the earth.

PLANT. Almost 350,000 different species of plants have been discovered and classified. These species vary in size and form from certain single-celled bacteria that are about $\frac{1}{50,000}$ inch long to giant redwood trees, which may become more than 350 feet tall and have a trunk diameter of 30 feet. Plants also vary as to their constituent parts, or organs. Although certain brown seaweeds, called kelps, may become more than 100 feet long— as large as trees—they nevertheless differ fundamentally from trees in not having true roots, stems, or leaves.

Despite their many differences all plants have in common certain characteristics. Some of these characteristics are also possessed by animals. The bodies of plants, like those of animals, consist of one or many minute cells. Each cell contains the unique living substance called protoplasm. Plants, like animals, carry on metabolism, a complex of chemical processes by which life is maintained. One vital metabolic process is assimilation, or the transformation of nonliving organic foods into living protoplasm. Another vital metabolic process is the chemical disintegration of foods and the accompanying release of their latent chemical energy, which then can be utilized by the organism in movement, growth, and reproduction. Both plants and animals are capable of growth, which results from food assimilation and involves in multicellular organisms a numerical increase of cells. Both plants and animals are capable of reproduction; each species produces offspring like itself. Plants, as well as animals, are characterized by irritability, or sensitivity to environmental stimuli. Many plants respond to such stimuli as light, moisture, heat, or pressure by movement of their parts or by chemical change.

Other characteristics common to all plants are not possessed by animals and serve to distinguish plants from animals. Most plants can manufacture their own food from carbon dioxide and water by means of photosynthesis, which will occur only in the presence of light. The green pigment chlorophyll, which imparts to plants their green color, is an essential agent for photosynthesis. Animals cannot manufacture their own food. The cell walls of most plants contain cellulose and serve as an interconnected framework that supports the plant and makes it firm. The cell walls of most animals lack cellulose. Except

for some bacteria, most plants are incapable of locomotion, whereas most animals are capable of locomotion. Most plants continue growing beyond maturity, whereas most animals cease growing at maturity. The branches, twigs, and roots of most trees and shrubs usually continue to grow throughout their lives. The maximum size and mature form attained by most species of plants are much more variable and depend more upon environmental conditions than those attained by most species of animals.

Although many plants—including algae, fungi, mosses, and ferns —do not reproduce by means of seeds, seed plants nevertheless dominate the vegetation of the earth today and are more important to man than these other plants. Angiosperms, or flowering plants, are one of the two types of seed plants. The structure and functions of a typical angiosperm will be described.

PLANT ORGANS

The typical angiosperm consists of roots, stems, leaves, and flowers. The roots, stems, and leaves are regarded as organs because, like the organs of animals, they perform one or more related functions that are essential to the organism. A flower is not a single organ but a group of organs whose function is reproduction by means of the development of seeds. Roots, stems, and leaves are further regarded as vegetative organs because, not being involved in the development of seeds, their functions are to maintain the life of the plant and enable it to grow.

The principal functions of the roots are to anchor the plant in the soil, to absorb water and dissolved minerals from the soil and conduct them upward into the stems, and to conduct water and manufactured foods downward from the stems. In some plants the roots also store food for future use by the plant. Many plants have a relatively thick primary root, from which several thinner branch roots extend sideways. Arising from the roots are numerous tiny root hairs, through which most of the absorption of water occurs. The tip of each root, called the root apex, consists of special cells called meristem cells, whose division and growth cause the root to lengthen. See ROOT.

The primary functions of stems are to produce and support leaves and flowers, to conduct water and dissolved minerals upward from the roots, and to conduct manufactured foods downward from the leaves to other parts, where they are assimilated. The stems of most plants also store foods for future use. Those of some plants contain chlorophyll and can manufacture foods by means of photosynthesis. Stems vary greatly in size and texture. The slim, green, supple ones of herbs are one type, while the trunks and branches of trees are another type.

Stems are divided into alternating nodes and internodes. A node is the point on a stem from which a leafstalk and leaf will develop. An internode is the space between two nodes. A bud frequently forms in the upper angle between a leafstalk and the stem. A bud also frequently forms at the tip of each stem or twig. These buds produce new stems. Some of the new stems bear only leaves; others bear only flowers; still others bear both leaves and flowers. See STEM.

The primary function of leaves is to manufacture food from carbon dioxide and water by means of a complex chemical process called photosynthesis. In most plants the food that is manufactured is a sugar called glucose. The raw materials of photosynthesis are carbon dioxide, which is absorbed into the leaves from the air, and water, which is absorbed into the roots from the soil and conducted to the leaves. Photosynthesis can occur only in the presence of light, the primary source of light being the sun. During photosynthesis the energy of light is converted into the chemical energy of foods. Chlorophyll, the green pigment that exists in most leaves and that imparts to them their green color, absorbs light and also participates in the production of sugar. Another function of leaves is transpiration, or the evaporation of water into the air.

The leaves of most angiosperms are broad, flat, and thin. Those of some gymnosperms, such as pine and spruce trees, are needle shaped. Ramifying through most leaves are minute veins, which conduct water and dissolved minerals into the leaves from the stems and manufactured foods from the leaves to the stems. See LEAF.

The function of flowers is the formation of seeds for reproduction. The organs that constitute a complete flower are sepals, petals, stamens, and a pistil. The sepals, which resemble small green leaves, enclose and protect the other floral organs while they are at the bud stage. The primary function of the petals is to attract bees or other insects by means of their sweet-

tasting nectar, their fragrance, and their colors. The stamens produce pollen grains, in which the male reproductive cells, or sperms, are later developed. The enlarged base of the pistil is called the ovary. Within the ovary are the ovules, each of which contains a female reproductive cell, or egg.

After pollen has been transferred by insects or wind from stamens to pistil, the sperms of the pollen grains unite with, or fertilize, the eggs within the ovules of the ovary. After fertilization of the eggs the ovules develop into seeds, the ovary develops into the fruit that encloses and protects the seeds, and the sepals, petals, and stamens usually wither and die. See FLOWER.

CELLS AND TISSUES

A flowering plant is composed of millions of microscopic cells, which range in diameter from $\frac{1}{250}$ to $\frac{1}{2,500}$

inch. Each cell is a mass of living protoplasm enclosed by a nonliving wall, which usually contains cellulose, the substance that makes wood so hard and strong. The protoplasm, which is a viscous liquid, is differentiated into a central nucleus and a surrounding cytoplasm. The nucleus controls most of the activities of the cell. Cells are the units of plant function; within them occur photosynthesis and all of the other physiological activities that maintain the life of the plant.

Cells differ greatly in structure and function. A group of cells of similar structure that performs essentially the same functions is called a tissue. Different tissues performing different physiological functions constitute a division of labor in a plant. Some of the tissues that compose a flowering plant are the meristematic tissue, the epidermal tissue, the xylem, and the phloem.

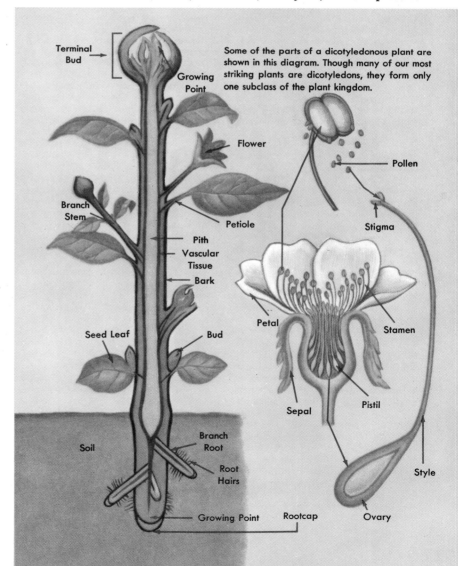

Some of the parts of a dicotyledonous plant are shown in this diagram. Though many of our most striking plants are dicotyledons, they form only one subclass of the plant kingdom.

Terminal Bud
Growing Point
Flower
Pollen
Branch Stem
Petiole
Stigma
Pith
Vascular Tissue
Bark
Petal
Stamen
Seed Leaf
Bud
Sepal
Pistil
Soil
Branch Root
Root Hairs
Style
Growing Point
Rootcap
Ovary

Meristematic tissue is growth tissue and is found in buds and root tips, between the bark and wood of trees and bushes, and in other parts of a plant where growth occurs. Growth results from the division and consequent numerical increase of meristematic cells. The meristematic tissue between the bark and wood, or xylem, of tree trunks and branches is called cambium and causes them to grow in diameter.

Epidermal tissue, which is usually only one cell thick, forms the surfaces of leaves, flowers, fruits, and young stems and roots. Epidermal tissue prevents moisture from escaping from the aboveground portions of a plant and protects them from parasites.

Xylem tissue, which lies inside the cambium of stems and which exists also in roots, conducts water and dissolved minerals upward through roots and stems into leaves, flowers, and fruits. Xylem tissue serves also to support and strengthen stems; it is the same as the wood of tree trunks and branches.

Phloem tissue, which lies just outside the cambium of stems, conducts manufactured foods downward from the leaves through the stems and into the roots. Phloem tissue also has a supportive function.

PHYSIOLOGICAL ACTIVITIES

Complex physiological activities occur within plants as within animals. These activities maintain the life of a plant and enable it to grow and reproduce. Some of the important physiological activities of a typical flowering plant are the absorption of water and dissolved minerals, photosynthesis, digestion, respiration, protein synthesis, and protoplasm synthesis.

All water utilized by a plant is absorbed from the soil by the roots. Dissolved minerals of the soil are also absorbed by the roots along with the water. These minerals, which include the elements potassium, phosphorus, sulfur, calcium, iron, magnesium, and zinc, are absorbed in the form of compounds such as nitrates, sulfates, and phosphates. Nitrogen also is absorbed from the soil in the form of nitrates.

After being absorbed, the water with its dissolved mineral and nitrogen compounds is conducted upward through roots and stems to the leaves. Carbon dioxide enters the leaves from the atmosphere. By means of photosynthesis the water and carbon dioxide react chemically in the presence of chlorophyll and light to form the sugar called glucose. The energy of light is transformed into the chemical energy of the glucose. See PHOTOSYNTHESIS.

In most plants the newly formed glucose is converted immediately into starch, which remains in the leaves until nighttime. During the night, after photosynthesis has ceased, much of the starch, which is insoluble in water, is converted back into sugars, which readily dissolve in water. This conversion of an insoluble food into a soluble one is termed digestion. Some of these dissolved sugars are then conducted to various parts of the plant, where they enter the cells and are united with oxygen, or oxidized. During oxidation the stored chemical energy of the sugars is released so that it can be utilized by the plant in growth, reproduction, movement, and other vital activities. The oxidation of sugars and the release of their energy is termed respiration.

Some of these sugars are synthesized into proteins, which always contain nitrogen from the absorbed nitrates. Proteins also frequently contain sulfur and phosphorus from absorbed mineral compounds. The proteins may then be assimilated into the plant cells and synthesized into the living protoplasm that composes them.

REPRODUCTION

Angiosperms and other seed plants are capable of both sexual and asexual—or vegetative—reproduction. Many of the plants that occupy a lower position in the evolutionary scale are not capable of sexual reproduction, and none of them produce seeds. The phenomena involved in the sexual reproduction of a typical angiosperm will be described.

The male reproductive cells, or sperms, develop within pollen grains, which in most flowers are minute yellow particles that collectively resemble yellowish dust. Pollen grains are produced within anthers, which are the enlarged uppermost portions of the stamens of a flower. When an anther has matured, it opens, and the pollen grains are exposed. They then are transferred—in most angiosperms by insects, chiefly bees, but in some by wind—to the stigma, which is located at the top of the pistil of a flower. Self-pollination is the transfer of pollen from an anther to the stigma of the same flower or of another flower on the same plant. Cross-pollination is the transfer of pollen from an anther to the stigma

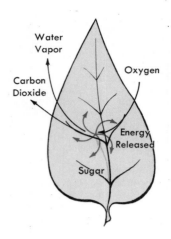

of a flower on another plant. See POLLEN AND POLLINATION.

After being deposited on a stigma, each pollen grain produces a tube called a pollen tube, which grows downward through the slender style of the pistil, into the ovary that forms the base of the pistil, and then into an ovule that is attached to the inside of the ovary. The pollen tube finally penetrates the embryo sac that is enclosed by the ovule. Within the pollen grain is a minute body called a generative nucleus that enters the pollen tube and, while moving downward through it, divides mitotically to form two male reproductive cells, or sperms. The two sperms then continue to move downward through the pollen tube until they enter the embryo sac, within which is the female reproductive cell, or egg. One of the sperms then unites with, or fertilizes, the egg. The single-celled fertilized egg, or zygote, then undergoes many successive mitotic divisions to form the plant embryo.

After fertilization the ovule develops into the seed that contains the embryo. The ovary enlarges to become the fruit that encloses the seed or seeds. After the seeds and fruit have matured, the fruit splits open or disintegrates and releases the seeds. If a seed alights in the proper soil, it may remain dormant for a while and then germinate, or sprout. Germination involves the growth of the embryo within the seed, the splitting of the seedcoat, and the emergence of the embryo from the seed. The tiny embryo grows into an adult plant, and reproduction has been accomplished. See GERMINATION.

In the asexual, or vegetative, reproduction of an angiosperm the new plant does not develop from a seed. Instead, it develops from a

...st annual plants are herbs. ...bs remain small in size, and ...r stems are usually slender ...green and contain little or ...tough, woody tissue. Annuals ...after one growing season.

Perennials include all trees and shrubs and many herbs. Stems and leaves of perennial herbs die each winter but are regrown during the next growing season. Their roots remain alive during winter.

Biennial plants do not produce flowers and seeds until their second growing season. Only stems, leaves, and roots—which are termed vegetative organs—develop during the first growing season.

runner, bulb, tuber, or other part of the parent plant.

IRRITABILITY

All flowering plants and many other plants can react by movement of their parts to external stimuli, such as light, moisture, gravity, temperature change, touch, or chemicals. Most plants have no specialized sensory structures like the eyes or ears of animals. Sensitivity to external stimuli is a property of most of the cells of a flowering plant. All portions of leaf blades are sensitive to light; all plant organs react to moisture and temperature change.

A common type of responsive movement in flowering plants is tropism, which is the bending of a stem, root, leafstalk, or flower stalk in response to certain external stimuli. The bending of a stem or leafstalk toward the light is called a positive phototropism. The bending of a root away from the light is called a negative phototropism. The upward bending of a stem away from the earth's gravitational force is called a negative geotropism. The downward bending of a root toward this force is called a positive geotropism.

A tropism is caused by a difference in the rate of growth of different parts of a stem, leafstalk, or root. For instance, if one side of a stem receives less sunlight than the opposite side, the less illuminated side grows faster than the more illuminated side, causing the growing stem and its attached leaves to bend toward the sun. This unequal growth rate results from an unequal distribution of a growth hormone through the tissues of the stem. Tropisms and other responsive movements enable plants to adjust as advantageously as possible to their environments. For instance, the bending of a stem toward the sun enables the leaves to receive as much light as possible for photosynthesis. See PLANT KINGDOM; TROPISM.

PLANT, ANNUAL, BIENNIAL, AND PERENNIAL. Plants may be classified into three groups according to the length of their lives. The first group contains annual plants, whose span of life is completed within one year. The second group contains biennial plants, whose lifespan is completed within two years. The third group contains perennial plants, which live for more than two years.

Annual plants spend the greatest part of their lives, which extends from spring to late summer or autumn, in growing roots, stems, and leaves. Later they reproduce themselves by growing flowers, fruits, and seeds, and by scattering the seeds. Reproduction consumes so much of an annual plant's stored food that it dies soon thereafter. Corn, marigolds, sweetpeas, and soybeans are familiar annuals, which also include many other flowers, vegetables, and weeds. The stems of most annual plants are slender, green, and soft. They seldom become thick, hard, and woody.

Deciduous biennial plants spend their entire first year growing roots, stems, and leaves. During autumn they shed these leaves, and their stems wither and die. However, life remains in their roots, and when spring arrives, biennials grow new green stems and leaves. Later during their second year they produce flowers and provide for reproduction by maturing and scattering seeds. Soon thereafter they die. Familiar biennials are carrots and beets. Most biennials have slender, soft, green stems.

Perennials include all trees and bushes and some smaller plants, such as the tulip, the rose, and the iris. Some perennials live only a few years, while others, like oak, cypress, and redwood trees, may live for over 100 years. During the first few years of their lives perennials do not produce seeds. They devote themselves entirely to growing large roots, trunks, and branches. Later they produce and scatter seeds each year for the remainder of their lives. Deciduous perennials of the Temperate Zones shed their leaves each autumn and cease growing during winter. However, they produce new leaves and resume their growth each spring. Most perennials grow to larger size than do annuals or biennials. Perennial trees and bushes develop thick, hard, woody trunks and branches.

PLANT, AQUATIC, a plant whose habitat is either the sea or fresh-water lakes, ponds, streams, or swamps. Many aquatic plants, such as the algae, or seaweed, of the sea, are entirely submerged in water. Some aquatic plants, such as reeds, bulrushes, and water lilies, have only their roots and the lower portions of their stems submerged in water while their leaves and flowers grow above or on the surface of the water.

Most aquatic plants of the sea are various kinds of algae. The smallest and most abundant marine algae are single-celled diatoms. Each tiny diatom is enclosed in a hard, brittle shell made of silicon. Diatoms are free floating and range in color from green to golden brown.

Fresh-water aquatic plants like the herb *Philotria* can be grown in a small indoor aquarium.

They usually float singly but sometimes form colonies. Seaweed consists of both red and brown algae. Red algae, which are multicellular, grow in the form of ribbons, ferns, or miniature branched shrubs. Ranging in length from a few inches to 2 or 3 feet, red algae are most abundant in warm tropical seas. Most species are attached to submerged rocks, but a few are free floating. The hue of the Red Sea is imparted by red algae that grow plentifully in it during certain seasons of the year. Brown algae include certain species called kelps, which are of great size and complex structure. Some kelps of the Pacific Ocean attain a length of 200 feet or more and are differentiated structurally into parts that resemble roots, stems, and leaves. These parts, however, are not true roots, stems, or leaves since, unlike them, they are not differentiated as to physiological function. The kelps are attached to submerged rocks by

Some green and red algae (above) are branched and fernlike. Sargassum (below, top and bottom) occurs widely in warmer seas.

Bruce Hunter, American Museum of Natural History

Sargassum (left and below) is a brown alga of the Sargasso Sea. A blue-green alga is shown above.

Rockweed (below, left) is a coastal alga. Air bladders (below, right) grow on some algae.
Bruce Hunter, American Museum of Natural History

Helen Cruickshank, National Audubon Society

Raymond F. McAllister

Courtesy of Ford Motor Company
The roots of a water lily are anchored in the mud at the bottom of a pond.

their rootlike parts, which are called holdfasts. Brown algae grow most abundantly in the cold waters of the North Atlantic, North Pacific, Arctic, and Antarctic oceans. They grow in shallow water near the coast and along the tide-washed shore. Some brown algae float unattached in huge masses at or near the surface of the ocean, far from shore. The Sargasso Sea, located in the Atlantic Ocean east of the West Indies, is a mass of free-floating brown algae that extends over an area of about 500,000 square miles.

Various algae also inhabit bodies of fresh water. Blue-green algae, which are single celled and extremely primitive, grow together in long filaments or slimy masses in stagnant ponds or streams. Green algae, which are both unicellular and multicellular, unite to form threads or filaments that impart to ponds and streams a brilliant-green hue. (See SEAWEED.) In fresh (not salt) water, such as ponds, lagoons, or slowly moving streams, small floating plants of the duckweed family may completely cover the surface. They are flowering plants not related to the algae.

PLANT, INSECT-EATING. Plants, like animals, can be carnivorous. Certain plants, which are called insectivorous or carnivorous plants, catch insects and digest them as part of their daily diet. Most insectivorous plants are small flowering ones that live chiefly in bogs. Their leaves are modified into organs for trapping and digesting insects.

One type of insectivorous plant, called the pitcher plant, has leaves that are shaped like tubes or pitchers and that contain a digestive fluid. An insect, attracted by an agreeable odor and by the colors of a pitcher-shaped leaf, enters the leaf and crawls downward over many downward-pointing hairs that line its inner surface. If the insect tries to crawl back, these hairs prevent it from doing so. Soon it falls into the fluid and is drowned. Then it is digested and assimilated into the cells of the leaf, just as it might have been digested and assimilated in an animal's stomach.

The leaves of other insectivorous plants, such as the Venus's-flytrap, have teeth or hairs that entrap the insect and a sticky liquid in which it becomes glued. Then the insect is digested by juices secreted from glands.

Because the swampy soil in which they grow is deficient in certain foods essential to them, insectivorous plants must eat insects in order to obtain these foods. Even though these plants possess chlorophyll and can manufacture their own food by photosynthesis, they still must supplement their diet by eating insects. Insectivorous plants either secrete their own digestive fluid, or else they possess bacteria that secrete it.

Insectivorous plants grow in bogs of both tropical and temperate regions, including North America. They occasionally also capture tiny crustaceans, amphibians, and mammals, but never larger ones.

PLANT, MICROSCOPIC. Some plants are so minute that they are visible only through a microscope. Bacteria, which are single-celled plants, range in diameter from about $\frac{1}{10,000}$ to $\frac{1}{50,000}$ inch. They are scarcely visible under the high power of a standard microscope and should be examined under a microscope with a magnification of 1,000 diameters or more. Bodies of water, the air, the soil, and foodstuffs contain many bacteria; the bodies of animals and of other plants are virtually teeming with them. They are more numerous and widespread than any other organism. The microscopic study of bacteria is extremely important because some of them inflict dreadful diseases on man, while others perform services that are beneficial to man or even necessary for the continuance of his life.

Pathogenic bacteria inflict on man such diseases as pneumonia, diphtheria, typhoid fever, tuberculosis, streptococcus throat infection, and scarlet fever. These bacteria inhabit the mouth, stomach, intestine, bloodstream, and body tissues.

The leaves of insectivorous, or carnivorous, plants are modified in various ways for snaring, holding, and digesting insects.

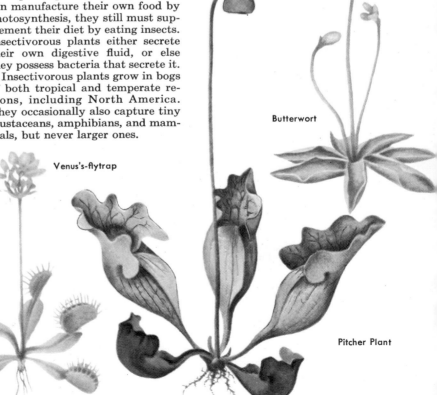
Butterwort
Venus's-flytrap
Pitcher Plant

Sundew

Spiral Bacteria, or Spirilla

Rod-Shaped Bacteria, or Bacilli

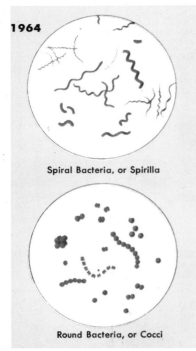

Round Bacteria, or Cocci

An important service performed by beneficial bacteria is the decomposition of dead animals and plants so that their constituent nitrogen and phosphorous can be returned to the soil in the form of nitrates and phosphates. These minerals can later be assimilated again by new generations of plants. Nitrogen-fixing bacteria, which adhere to the roots of alfalfa, clover, and other legumes, extract nitrogen from the atmosphere and change it into nitrates, which are added to the soil. Nitrates are essential for the growth of all

crops. Other beneficial bacteria ferment fruit juices to form alcohol and vinegar, assist in the ripening and flavoring of certain cheeses, and ferment fodder to produce ensilage.

Some single-celled algae are of microscopic size. However, they are relatively larger than bacteria and are visible through a low-powered microscope. Microscopic algae collectively constitute the green scum or film that sometimes forms on the surface of stagnant ponds or streams, along their shores, and on submerged rocks. Other microscopic green colonial algae constitute the mosslike scum that sometimes covers the north sides of tree trunks or rocks when they are damp. Diatoms are microscopic single-celled, free-floating algae that abound in the oceans. Each diatom is enclosed in a hard, brittle shell that is composed of silicon. When diatoms die, their shells fall to the ocean bottom and collect by the billions to form rocklike layers of diatomaceous earth that may become hundreds of feet thick. See BACTERIA.

PLANT, POISONOUS. Although many wild plants are edible and delicious, some are poisonous and must be avoided by both human beings and animals. Poisonous plants are of two kinds: those that poison the system when swallowed and those that irritate the skin upon contact.

The noxious plants most likely to be eaten by human beings are poisonous mushrooms, popularly called toadstools. Some wild poisonous mushrooms closely resemble wild edible ones. Many people have died from eating poisonous mushrooms that were gathered in field or forest on the assumption that they were edible ones. Mushroom lovers should not risk eating wild mushrooms unless they are expert in distinguishing edible from poisonous ones.

People, especially children, occasionally eat poisonous wild berries or fruit because they are prettily colored and sometimes resemble edible ones. The egg-shaped fruits of the Jimson weed, which grows abundantly in vacant lots, will poison children who eat them. Horse chestnuts should not be eaten, especially when green, because their fresh seeds contain a strong poison. Although mistletoe seems harmless because it is associated with the traditions of Christmas, its white berries have fatally poisoned children. The bright-red berries of a certain vinelike species of nightshade, a member of the potato family known for

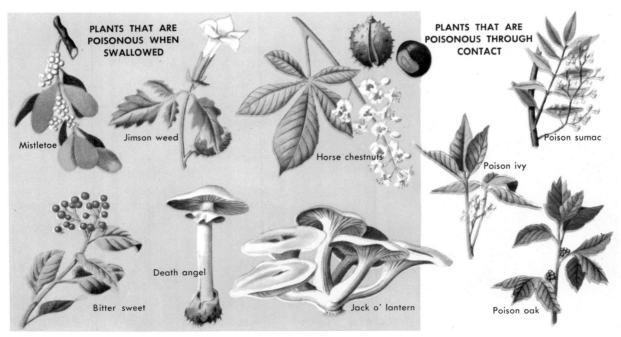

PLANTS THAT ARE POISONOUS WHEN SWALLOWED

Mistletoe

Jimson weed

Horse chestnuts

Bitter sweet

Death angel

Jack o' lantern

PLANTS THAT ARE POISONOUS THROUGH CONTACT

Poison sumac

Poison ivy

Poison oak

centuries as deadly nightshade, have often poisoned unwary persons who took a fancy to them. However, if properly compounded and administered in very small doses, the poisons extracted from plants like these are effective medicines for certain ailments.

Poisonous plants that irritate the skin upon contact include poison ivy, poison oak, and poison sumac. Although they usually do not cause death, these plants can cause the skin to itch and burn so severely that the victim must be hospitalized. Since they grow in woods, in open fields, and beside lakes and streams, they often poison persons who have not learned to identify them. See POISON IVY.

PLANTATION LIFE IN THE SOUTH.

Plantation life, characterized by its great cotton, sugarcane, and tobacco fields and its slave labor, did not become common in the South until the 18th century. The owners of 17th-century Virginia tobacco farms worked them with the help of indentured servants. There were some Negro slaves, but the indentured servants were the most important source of labor. Neither were there any great colonial mansions. The average house was a 1½-story frame dwelling. The Carolinas survived during the same period by means of small tobacco farms in the north and logging and fur trapping in the south.

The large plantation and slave labor became common in Virginia and South Carolina around 1800. In Virginia a fall in the price of tobacco made large plantations necessary for profitable tobacco growing, and new British restrictions on the importation of indentured servants caused the colonists to turn to slave labor. At the same time rice and indigo were introduced into South Carolina. These crops, flourishing in malaria-filled swamplands, required a working force immune to malaria. African slaves were again the answer to the problem.

With the invention in 1793 of the cotton gin, which separated the cotton strands from the seeds, cotton growing became immensely profitable; and the plantation system spread from South Carolina and Georgia westward through Alabama and Mississippi, through parts of Louisiana and Tennessee, and into Texas. All this became known as the Cotton Kingdom. Parts of the South grew other crops, such as tobacco and sugarcane, but these too used the plantation system. In

Heilman—Monkmeyer

The majority of plantation owners could not afford to live in as fine a mansion as this one. Such mansions were generally set in the midst of broad acres of pasture, woods, and plowed fields, far from neighboring houses. Gardens, lawns, and groves lent shade and comfort in the warm climate. Owners of such houses were leaders in their neighborhoods.

a few parts of the South, particularly in North Carolina and the Appalachian Mountain areas, small farms and free labor were the rule. The farmers of these areas were usually poor and resented the plantation and slavery systems. These were the people who caused what is now West Virginia to break away from Virginia at the outbreak of the Civil War.

One reason for the rapid spread of plantations was that the type of farming practiced spoiled the land. By about 1820 many old Virginia plantations were supported either by the sale of slaves or by their owners' newer plantations farther west. Another reason was the increased demand for cotton from the textile mills of England and New England, where improved machinery had enlarged the production capacity. The profits of Southern plantation owners went to purchase more land to replace wornout land and to buy more slaves, for the death rate among slave infants was so high that slaves had constantly to be imported. Thus, with the growth of the Cotton Kingdom, chances for eliminating slavery from the South disappeared.

Plantations ranged in size from a few acres to 2,500 or more acres and in number of slaves from one or two to a hundred or more. The owners of the few large plantations controlled most of the wealth and power. Only these plantations had the beautiful mansions commonly associated with Southern life. Owners of medium-sized plantations of 100 to 400 acres had from 10 to

40 slaves and led plain, hard-working lives, but they too were part of the ruling class. The owners of the smallest and poorest plantations were most numerous and raised half the cotton crop. The life of these farmers was hard, and their houses were little more than log cabins.

The slaves lived on the plantation in small houses or huts provided by their owner. He also provided their food and clothing, although sometimes the slaves had their own small vegetable plots. They worked in the fields, in the house, and as carpenters and blacksmiths. Treatment of slaves varied widely. However, punishments were limited by the necessity of not disabling workers. One of the greatest cruelties of the slave system was the separation of husbands and wives and parents and children through slave sales.

With the development of the Cotton Kingdom differences between North and South became more marked. The North, which did not have as much rich farmland as the South, developed its businesses and industries. The South, because of the plantation system and slave labor, failed to do so and became dependent upon the North for manufactured products. Resentment of this dependence was shown in Southern opposition to tariff legislation sponsored by the North. This resentment also contributed to the growing breach between the two sections over the slavery issue. The result was the Civil War and the destruction of both slavery and the plantation system.

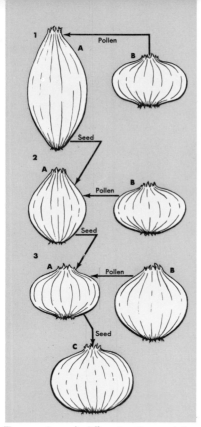

The crossing of different onion varieties

PLANT BREEDING

PLANT BREEDING, the development of new and better plant varieties by means of seed selection and hybridization, or crossbreeding. Men have been breeding improved varieties of plants by means of seed selection since the beginning of agriculture thousands of years ago. Seed selection involves the sorting of the best individuals of a generation of plants from all inferior ones and the sowing of seeds from these superior individuals only. The next generation of the plant will probably contain a greater proportion of superior individuals. but many inferior ones will still persist. Again the inferior ones are rejected, and only seeds from the superior ones are sown. Each subsequent generation contains proportionately more superior individuals until, after many generations of seed selection, a superior new variety of a plant species has been bred from the original inferior variety. In ancient times improved varieties of wheat, barley, and other grains and of lettuce and carrots were developed through seed selection. In more recent times improved varieties of cabbage, beans, peas, oranges, lemons, and cherries have been developed by seed selection. Before the discovery of crossbreeding most new, improved varieties of vegetables, fruits, and flowers were developed by means of seed selection.

The primary objective of plant breeding is the development of larger, higher yielding, more nutritious, and better flavored varieties of vegetables, fruits, and grains and the development of larger, differently colored, or differently shaped flowers. Another objective of plant breeding is the development of varieties that can resist diseases and that can endure adverse climatic conditions, such as drought, excessive moisture, heat, or cold. Rapid growth and early maturation of crops are also objectives of plant breeding.

Hybridization is the crossbreeding of two different but closely related plant varieties or species in order to produce a new variety in which desirable qualities of both parents are combined. For example, one variety of corn might bear especially large ears with numerous kernels but be unable to resist diseases. A different but closely related variety might bear small ears with few kernels but be able to resist the same diseases. If these two varieties were crossbred, the resulting hybrid variety of corn might combine the desirable qualities of both parents by bearing large ears with numerous kernels and by being able to resist diseases. Since all varieties of corn are of the same original ancestry, it is easy to cross them to produce new varieties. Since 1930 most of the corn grown in the United States for feeding livestock has been of the hybrid type. Hybrid varieties of corn can yield from 60 to 80 bushels per acre, whereas in former times ordinary varieties yielded no more than 20 to 40 bushels per acre.

Many new, improved varieties of fruits, vegetables, and flowers have been crossbred from two different but closely related varieties or species. Techniques of crossbreeding were used by the famous U.S. horticulturalist Luther Burbank. He crossbred the plum and apricot to produce a unique hybrid called the plumcot. By crossbreeding he also developed the Shasta daisy, a pitless plum, a thin-shelled walnut, a hybrid of the squash and pumpkin, and a spineless cactus for use as fodder. See HYBRIDIZATION.

PLANT COLORS. The predominant color of nature is green. Throughout spring and summer the leaves of most trees and shrubs, most blades of grass, and the stems of many herbs are green. This color is imparted to them by a green pigment called chlorophyll. The chlorophyll is contained within microscopic bodies called chloroplasts, which lie within the cytoplasm of the cells of leaves, grass blades, and stems. Chlorophyll is involved in photosynthesis, the process by which carbon dioxide and water react chemically to form a sugar called glucose. See CHLOROPHYLL.

Besides chlorophyll the chloroplasts also contain a yellowish pigment called xanthophyll and a yellowish-orange pigment called carotene. Because these pigments exist in relatively small amounts, they are usually masked by the chlorophyll, and leaves usually appear green. However, leaves with larger amounts of these yellowish pigments may appear yellowish green or light green.

In spring the glowing colors of plants delight the eye. The blue ajuga in the foreground below blends richly with the red-leaved shrubs and green trees behind.

Gottscho-Schleisner

Courtesy of Ford Motor Company

The girl above is planting petunias in a home garden. Children can best learn to appreciate the colors of flowers and leaves by cultivating plants themselves.

This huge philodendron was cultivated indoors in a pot. The plant is supported by a steel rod, which is surrounded by sphagnum moss. The stems are intertwined through the moss. Potted philodendron grows rapidly.

The red, yellow, and orange hues of many flowers and of certain vegetables and fruits are imparted by pigments called carotenoids. The carotenoids are contained within microscopic bodies called chromoplasts, which also lie within the cytoplasm of the cells. The orange color of the carrot is imparted by carotenoid pigments.

The blue, purple, lavender, and red hues of other flowers are caused by pigments called anthocyanins. The red of garden beets, the purple of certain cabbages, and the blue or purple of certain grapes are also caused by anthocyanins. Anthocyanins are soluble in water and may be found either in the cytoplasm or dissolved in the central vacuole of the cell.

The yellow and gold autumnal hues of some deciduous trees result from the decomposition of their chlorophyll during late summer and autumn. The yellowish pigments xanthophyll and carotene decompose more slowly and, when no longer masked by chlorophyll, become apparent to the eye. The red autumnal hues of the leaves of hard maples, sumacs, and other deciduous trees and shrubs result from the formation of anthocyanin pigments. Sudden decreases in temperature are thought to be one cause of their formation.

Courtesy of Ford Motor Company

PLANT CULTIVATION involves all of the measures necessary for the successful growth of agricultural crops, including fruits, flowers, and vegetables.

Certain crops are grown in certain areas in the world because of their requirements as to climate, moisture, and soil. Temperature, length of day, and rainfall or availability of water are probably the most important factors of climate affecting plants. For example, since bananas require tropical temperatures throughout the year and large amounts of moisture, they can be grown only in tropical, high-rainfall areas. Corn, or maize, native to South America, cannot be grown successfully in Norway because there are too few warm days there to allow the corn to mature. Apples, on the other hand, cannot be grown in tropical regions because they need a cold period during the year so that the plants can undergo a period of dormancy. Without this dormant period they will not flower and fruit. The seasonal change in length of day in the temperate regions has a profound effect on the flowering and fruiting of such plants as soybeans and chrysanthemums. This response to day length limits the areas in which these crops may be grown. Few crops grow on deserts, not entirely because of high temperature or poor soil, but because of lack of water. Once water is available abundant crops of certain plants can be grown in deserts.

Certain soils are best for certain crops, but through the proper use of fertilizers most soils will produce a wide range of crops. Soils may be poor because of too much moisture, as in a swamp. After the swamp is properly drained, it will produce good crops. Soils may be poor because they lack plant residues, called organic matter. If crops that provide large quantities of organic matter are grown for several years and this matter is plowed into the soil, these soils are greatly improved.

Plants of importance for food, fiber, or flowers have been improved down through the centuries. This improvement has come about largely through plant selection. Seed from the best plants is saved for next year's plantings. In 1866 reports were published concerning experiments made by an Austrian monk, Gregor Johann Mendel; the rediscovery of these reports about 1900 led to modern scientific plant breeding. Since this time plant improvement has been spectacularly speeded up.

Methods of sowing and harvesting by mechanical means developed in the past century have greatly increased man's ability to produce more and better plants. Weed control by mechanical cultivators and chemicals and the discovery of chemical nutrients are but two examples of the rapid progress in scientific plant cultivation.

This coffee tree was grown in a barrel containing mica and dissolved mineral salts.
Wilson & MacPherson Hole

PLANT GEOGRAPHY

MAP SHOWING ORIGIN OF OUR COMMON VEGETABLES

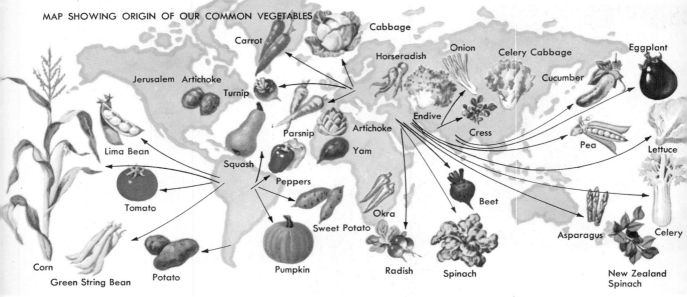

Carrot · Cabbage · Horseradish · Onion · Celery Cabbage · Eggplant · Cucumber · Jerusalem Artichoke · Turnip · Endive · Cress · Pea · Lettuce · Parsnip · Artichoke · Yam · Squash · Peppers · Beet · Lima Bean · Tomato · Okra · Asparagus · Celery · Corn · Sweet Potato · Radish · Spinach · New Zealand Spinach · Green String Bean · Potato · Pumpkin

MAP SHOWING ORIGIN OF OUR COMMON FRUITS

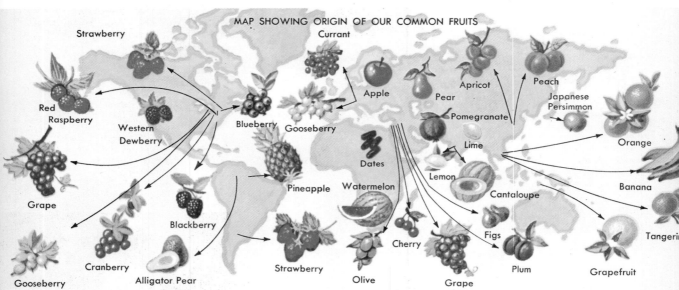

Strawberry · Currant · Apple · Apricot · Peach · Japanese Persimmon · Red Raspberry · Pear · Pomegranate · Orange · Western Dewberry · Blueberry · Gooseberry · Lime · Grape · Dates · Lemon · Banana · Pineapple · Watermelon · Cantaloupe · Tangerine · Gooseberry · Cranberry · Blackberry · Cherry · Figs · Grapefruit · Alligator Pear · Strawberry · Olive · Grape · Plum

MAP SHOWING ORIGIN OF OUR COMMON FARINACEOUS SEEDS

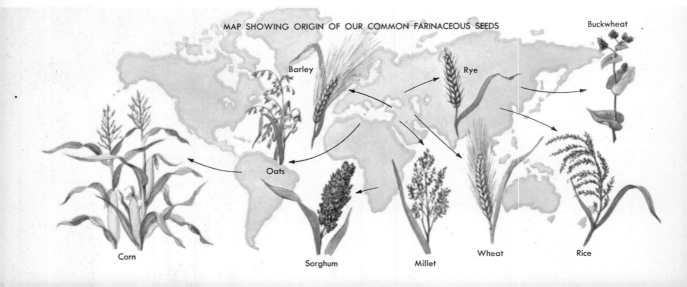

Buckwheat · Barley · Rye · Corn · Oats · Sorghum · Millet · Wheat · Rice

PLANT GEOGRAPHY is the study of the distribution of all species of plants throughout all regions of the earth. Most species of plants are adapted to limited environmental conditions and will perish if placed in an unfavorable environment. Therefore, most species are limited in their natural geographical distribution to those relatively few regions of the earth that possess the environmental conditions to which they are adapted. Although few if any species can grow naturally in every geographic region of the earth, some are adapted to a relatively wide range of environmental conditions and can grow naturally in many different regions. Some of the conditions that limit the geographic distribution of plants are intensity and daily duration of sunlight, rainfall, temperature, humidity, seasonal variations in these, soil content, elevation, and topography.

The native forests of New England consist chiefly of hemlock and pine trees, which are coniferous evergreens, and of birch and maple, which are deciduous. The native forests of states bordering the Gulf of Mexico consist chiefly of yellow pine, bald cypress, live oak, and magnolia trees, all of which are evergreens. The native forests of the mountains of Oregon and of northwest and west-central California consist chiefly of redwoods and sugar pines, which are coniferous evergreens. Redwoods are adapted to so limited a range of environmental conditions that they do not grow naturally outside of this region.

On the prairies of Kansas, Nebraska, and the Dakotas trees grow only in widely scattered clumps. The dominant native plants here are grasses, including buffalo grass, grama grass, and western wheat grass. Treeless prairies of grasses exist also in Argentina, in the Orinoco River basin of South America, and in South Africa. The vegetation of the arid and semiarid desert regions of Utah, Nevada, New Mexico, Arizona, and southern California consists chiefly of cacti, sagebrush, greasewood, and creosote bush. Parts of the Sahara in northern Africa are too dry and hot for the growth of any plants whatsoever.

The vegetation of the tundra of northern Canada and Alaska is exceedingly sparse and never grows tall. It includes lichens (such as reindeer moss), dwarf willows, and certain hardy rhododendrons. Greenland, northern Scandinavia, and Siberia are also regions of tundra.

The most dense and varied vegetation grows in the tropical rain forests and jungles of regions where high temperatures and heavy rainfall persist throughout the year. Tropical rain forests exist in Central America, the Amazon Basin of South America, India, Indonesia, equatorial Africa, and on some South Pacific islands. Tropical rain forests include hundreds of different species of trees, shrubs, vines, flowering herbs, and epiphytes, or air plants, which are not rooted in the soil but dangle loosely from trees. These forests are frequently so dense as to be impassable to men.

PLANT KINGDOM, the term employed to designate all plants, both those that are living today and extinct ones that inhabited the earth during the remote geologic past. The plant kingdom is vast and extremely diverse. Botanists have discovered and classified almost 350,000 different species of plants. Some of these species differ greatly from others in size and external form, in the number and character of their organs, in means of reproduction, in physiological activities, and in habitat. On the basis of their similarities and differences all members of the plant kingdom are divided into many subgroups.

The two largest and most comprehensive of these groups are the subkingdoms Thallophyta and Embryophyta. The Thallophyta include algae, fungi, and bacteria, all of which are relatively primitive and of relatively simple structure. All thallophytes lack true roots, stems, and leaves. Most of them lack vascular tissue for the conduction of fluids. The Embryophyta include mosses, ferns, gymnosperms, and angiosperms, or flowering plants. Embryophytes are relatively advanced in the evolutionary scale and of relatively complex structure. Most of them have true roots, stems, and leaves and also vascular tissue for the conduction of fluids. All embryophytes accomplish reproduction by producing tiny multicellular embryos that develop into adult plants. Thallophytes do not produce embryos; they accomplish reproduction by other means.

The subkingdom Thallophyta includes several phyla, some of which consist exclusively of algae. All algae possess chlorophyll and can manufacture their own food by means of photosynthesis. The various algal phyla are often designated by their color. Blue-green algae, most of which inhabit fresh-water lakes and streams, are minute unicellular organisms that sometimes are grouped together in colonies. Blue-green algae reproduce asexually by means of fission or spores. Brown algae, which inhabit the oceans, are multicellular. Some of them are extremely large and of complex structure. Certain kelps may attain a length of 200 feet or more and have parts that superficially resemble roots, stems, and leaves. Brown algae reproduce both asexually and sexually. Red algae, which are multicellular, seldom exceed 3 feet in length. Chiefly of marine habitat, they may be ribbonlike or may resemble ferns or feathers. Red algae reproduce both asexually and sexually. See ALGAE.

One thallophyte phylum consists solely of the Euglena, which are microscopic, unicellular organisms inhabiting fresh-water ponds. The Euglena are sometimes classified with the Protozoa of the animal kingdom because some of them ingest food particles through a gullet, as do some protozoans. However, the Euglena are plantlike in that they possess chlorophyll and carry on photosynthesis. See EUGLENA.

All fungi lack chlorophyll and cannot manufacture their own food by means of photosynthesis. They are either parasites that obtain their food from the tissues of other living organisms, or else they are saprophytes that obtain their food from nonliving organic matter. Fungi reproduce both asexually and sexually. They reproduce asexually by means of budding, spore formation, and fragmentation. Most fungi are injured or killed by sunlight and grow fastest in darkness or dim light. Fungi include about 75,000 different species, most of which are multicellular.

Molds are saprophytic fungi of various colors that grow upon and digest bread, oranges, lemons, meat, cheese, and other stored foods and wood, paper, and leather. Molds flourish in warm, moist, dark places.

Some mildews are parasitic fungi that grow in white or gray powdery patches upon the leaves of potatoes, roses, lilacs, and grapes. Other mildews are saprophytes that form upon cloth, paper, or leather stored in damp, dark cellars. They emit a musty odor. Rusts and smuts are parasitic fungi that grow upon the stems and leaves of wheat, oats, corn, barley, and other plants and injure them extensively.

Yeasts are unicellular fungi that live either as parasites on living tomatoes, beans, and other plants or as saprophytes in nonliving foods.

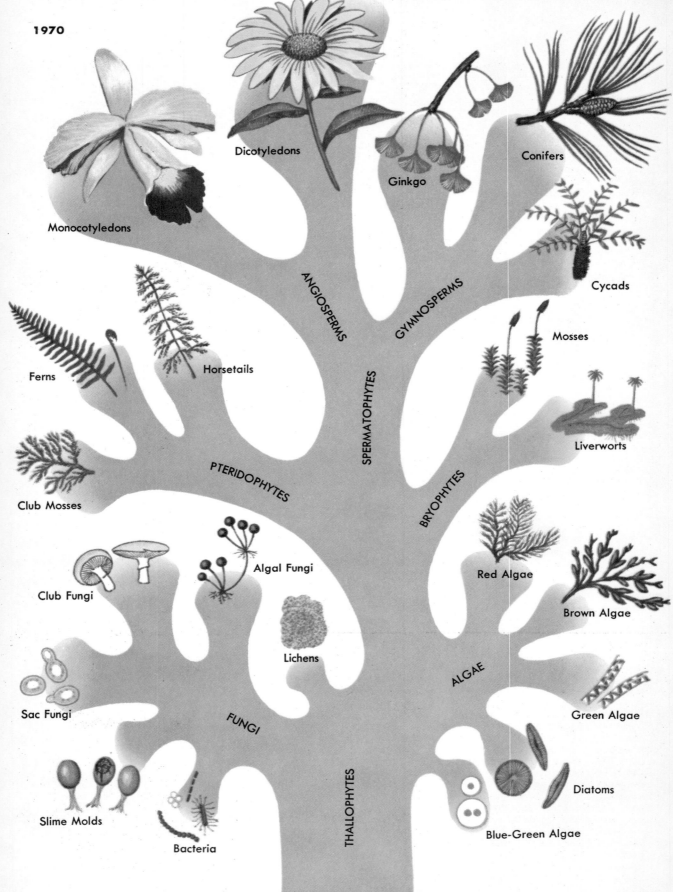

1970

Monocotyledons

Dicotyledons

Ginkgo

Conifers

Cycads

ANGIOSPERMS

GYMNOSPERMS

Mosses

Ferns

Horsetails

SPERMATOPHYTES

Liverworts

Club Mosses

PTERIDOPHYTES

BRYOPHYTES

Club Fungi

Algal Fungi

Red Algae

Brown Algae

Lichens

ALGAE

Sac Fungi

FUNGI

Green Algae

THALLOPHYTES

Slime Molds

Diatoms

Bacteria

Blue-Green Algae

ANCESTRAL PROTOPHYTES

One kind of yeast when put in bread dough forms bubbles of carbon dioxide, which cause the dough to swell, or rise.

Mushrooms are among the largest fungi. Toadstool is the popular name for poisonous mushrooms. Mushrooms are saprophytes that grow in moist soil, in decaying tree stumps, and sometimes on the bark of living trees. They obtain nourishment from decaying vegetation in the soil or from dead, decaying wood. Puffballs are similar to mushrooms except that they are round or pear-shaped instead of umbrella-shaped. See FUNGUS.

Bacteria are unicellular plants of extremely small size; few of them are longer than $\frac{1}{25,000}$ inch. Since they lack chlorophyll and cannot photosynthesize their own food, most bacteria are either parasites or saprophytes that must live in and obtain their nourishment from either living or dead organic substances. Their habitats are the bodies of living animals, including the mouth, digestive tract, and bloodstream; the bodies of living plants; dead bodies; animal excrement; the soil; the air; the ocean and bodies of fresh water; and unrefrigerated meat, vegetables, and other foods. Bacteria inhabiting excrement and the dead bodies of animals and plants cause their decay; those inhabiting unrefrigerated foods cause their decay. Certain bacteria that inhabit the living human body cause diseases such as pneumonia, tuberculosis, and diphtheria. Bacteria are thought to be the most widely distributed of all organisms.

Most bacteria inhabiting liquid mediums accomplish locomotion by moving the hairlike flagella that extend from their bodies. Most bacteria reproduce asexually by fission, which is the division of their single cell into two halves, each of which then grows to adult size. Although bacteria have sometimes been classified with the fungi, they more often are regarded as a distinct phylum. See BACTERIA.

The subkingdom Embryophyta includes mosses, ferns, gymnosperms, and angiosperms.

Mosses are among the few embryophytes that lack true roots, stems, leaves, and vascular tissue for conducting fluids. The green carpets or clumps of moss that grow on moist, shaded earth or on shaded tree trunks are actually compact masses of tiny individual moss plants. See MOSS.

Ferns, like gymnosperms and angiosperms, have true roots, stems, and leaves and also vascular tissue for conducting fluids. The embryos of ferns, unlike those of gymnosperms and angiosperms, are not enclosed within seeds. Although almost all ferns are shrublike, a few resemble small trees. The leaves of many ferns are compound and extremely long. Ferns are most numerous in humid tropical and subtropical regions. They thrive in moist, shaded locations. Much coal was formed from ferns that lived many millions of years ago. See FERN.

Gymnosperms occupy a higher position in the evolutionary scale than ferns but a lower one than angiosperms. Gymnosperms and angiosperms produce seeds, within which their embryos are enclosed. The seeds of gymnosperms are naked; they are not enclosed by fruits as are those of angiosperms. Gymnosperms number about 725 living species. The most numerous living gymnosperms are the conifers, or cone-bearing trees and shrubs, most of which are evergreen. Conifers include the pine, fir, spruce, cedar, cypress, hemlock, and redwood trees. The leaves of most conifers are needlelike or scalelike. Most conifers are native to the cooler regions of the Temperate Zones and to cool, mountainous regions of the tropics. Other gymnosperms are the ginkgo, or maidenhair tree, and the relatively primitive cycads, which resemble ferns. See GYMNOSPERM.

Angiosperms, or flowering plants, occupy the highest position in the evolutionary scale of plants. Angiosperms, which are the largest group in the plant kingdom, number about 250,000 species. Angiosperms are the only plants to produce flowers, parts of which are reproductive organs. The seeds of angiosperms are enclosed by fruits.

Angiosperms are classified as either monocotyledons or dicotyledons. The embryos of monocotyledons have only one cotyledon, or seed leaf (an organ for food storage), whereas those of dicotyledons have two seed leaves. Monocotyledons, which number about 50,000 species, include grains (wheat, corn), grasses, lilies, tulips, bananas, and palm trees. Dicotyledons, which number about 200,000 species, include oaks, elms, apples, roses, beans, potatoes, and daisies. See ANGIOSPERM; PLANT.

A branch of plant science known as plant taxonomy handles the detailed classification of plants according to their similarities and differences. See TAXONOMY.

PLANT NUTRITION. Plants, like animals, must be nourished by foods in order to sustain life. However, unlike animals, most plants cannot ingest as food the tissues of other organisms. Instead, most plants must manufacture their own foods from inorganic substances—principally water, carbon dioxide, and minerals.

Green plants manufacture their own food from water and carbon dioxide by means of photosynthesis. The green color of these plants is imparted to them by chlorophyll, a chemical that is necessary for photosynthesis. Light, chiefly sunlight, is also necessary for photosynthesis. To obtain their two primary nutrients, water and carbon dioxide, green chlorophyllous plants must be rooted in soil that receives sufficient moisture and must be exposed to an atmosphere that contains sufficient carbon dioxide.

The green chlorophyllous plants that carry on photosynthesis include angiosperms, gymnosperms, ferns, mosses, and algae. Fungi and most bacteria, which do not contain chlorophyll, cannot photosynthesize food. They obtain food by living as parasites or saprophytes upon or within the bodies of other plants or animals.

The first product of photosynthesis in most green plants is a sugar called glucose. However, in most plants this glucose is immediately converted into starches, fats, proteins, and sometimes oils and other sugars. Plants digest these starches, fats, and proteins, assimilate them into their own cells, and transform them into living protoplasm.

Besides carbon, hydrogen, and oxygen, proteins contain nitrogen, sulfur, and often phosphorus. These last three elements enter a plant from the soil in the form of minerals that are dissolved in water. The water with its dissolved minerals is absorbed from the soil through the roots of a plant. Nitrogen is absorbed in the form of potassium nitrate and sodium nitrate. Sulfur is absorbed in the form of sulfates and phosphorus in the form of phosphates. Plants convert the nitrogen, sulfur, and phosphorus of these inorganic minerals into organic proteins.

Other nutrient elements required by plants are potassium, calcium, iron, magnesium, boron, zinc, manganese, copper, and probably silicon, aluminum, and molybdenum. These elements likewise are absorbed from the soil in the form of inorganic mineral compounds that are dissolved in water. Plants dissociate these elements from their minerals and combine them with the proteins and other organic foods that are assimilated into the plant cells.

If plants cannot obtain all of these nutrients in the proper proportions, they may die, be stunted in growth, or produce leaves, flowers, or fruits of deficient size or quality. Most plants require a much greater proportion of nitrogen, potassium, and phosphorus than of iron, magnesium, zinc, or some of the other nutrient elements. They require only the slightest traces of manganese, copper, boron, and aluminum. Soil that does not contain all of these nutrient elements in their proper proportions must be enriched by the proper fertilizers. Nitrogen-fixing bacteria that live on the roots of alfalfa, clover, or other legumes are of great value in adding nitrogen to the soil. See NITROGEN FIXATION; PHOTOSYNTHESIS.

PLANT PRODUCTS. Plants are the source of thousands of products that we use every day. Perhaps the most familiar plant products are foods—vegetables, fruits, grains, sugars, starches, spices, and nuts. From grains are made breads and cereals. Sugar comes principally from sugarcane, which belongs to the grass family, and from sugar beets, which are closely related to the common red garden beet. Maple sugar and sirup are obtained by boiling the sap of the sugar-maple tree. Honey is really flower nectar that undergoes a slight chemical change within the bodies of bees and then is stored in their hives. Commercial starch, which usually is packaged in powdered or granulated form, is obtained from corn, rice, potatoes, wheat, cassava, and the stem of the sago palm. Coffee, tea, and cocoa—our three most popular beverages—are obtained from plants. Pepper, cinnamon, nutmeg, cloves, ginger, vanilla, and many other spices also come from plants.

Plants are the source of cotton, linen, and many other fibers that are woven into cloth. Linen is woven from fibers of the stem of the flax plant. Hemp fibers, which come from the stalks of a plant closely related to the banana, are braided into rope and woven into canvas. Jute fibers, which come from the stalks of another tropical plant, are woven into burlap bags and made into twine.

Lumber for construction is obtained from many species of trees. Softwood trees (chiefly pine, spruce, and aspen) are the source of the pulpwood that is ground, soaked, and chemically treated to make paper.

Rubber is made from latex, a viscous, milky juice that is secreted within the trunk of the Pará rubber tree, which is native to the Amazon Basin of Brazil. Latex from certain other tropical trees is made into guttapercha, a pliable rubber-like substance that, however, is only slightly elastic. Guttapercha is manufactured into golf balls, dental molds, and temporary dental fillings. Chicle, the basic ingredient of chewing gum, is made from the latex of still other tropical trees.

Tannin, which is used to tan cowhide and other animal skins, is extracted both from bark, such as that of the hemlock or the chestnut oak, and from leaves, such as those of the sumac bush. Tanning skins preserves them and turns them into the soft, pliable substance known as leather. Plants are also the source of indigo and other dyes that are used to dye cloth.

Resins, which are sticky, viscous liquids that exude from the bark of pine, fir, and other evergreen trees, are the basic ingredients of varnish. Turpentine, which is distilled from pine resin, is used commercially as a paint solvent. Rosin, which is the residue from the distillation of turpentine, is an ingredient of several products, including linoleum, oilcloth, printer's ink, and composition roofing.

Many medicines come from herbs and other plants. Digitalis, which is employed as a heart stimulant, is extracted from the leaves of an herb called foxglove. Quinine, which is used to treat malaria, comes from the bark of the tropical cinchona tree. Other plant medicines are the narcotics morphine and cocaine and the laxatives senna and cascara.

Cellulose, which is obtained chiefly from wood, can be converted into an essential ingredient of many im-

PLANT PRODUCTS

Foods obtained from plants include grains (corn, wheat), fruits (apples, bananas, dates), vegetables (lettuce, carrots, beans), beverages (coffee, cocoa), and spices (pepper, cinnamon, nutmeg).

Fibers obtained from plants include cotton, flax (which is made into linen), jute (which is made into twine, cordage, and burlap bags), and hemp (which is made into rope).

Lumber for the construction of buildings of all types is the most important product obtained from trees. Vast quantities of softwood timber are converted every year into pulpwood, the raw material from which paper is made.

Rubber is manufactured from the milky latex secreted by the tropical Pará rubber tree. Turpentine and other resins are obtained from pine, fir, and other evergreen trees.

Chicle, the chief ingredient of chewing gum, is obtained from the latex of a tropical tree. Tobacco is manufactured from the leaves of the tobacco plant. Medicines obtained from plants include quinine, camphor, belladonna, digitalis, and senna.

USDA

A plant-quarantine inspector examines a plant that is being brought into the United States from Mexico. If pests or diseases are detected, the plant may be confiscated.

portant commercial products by subjecting it to various complex chemical processes. Cellulose products include rayon, cellophane, Celluloid, photographic film, lacquers, enamels, nitrocellulose (used in gunpowder and other high explosives), phonograph records, and many plastics.

PLANT QUARANTINE. Plants and most plant materials brought into the United States from foreign countries must be inspected for the presence of harmful insects, diseases, snails, nematodes, mites, and other pests. The purpose of such inspection, conducted by the Plant Quarantine Division of the Agricultural Research Service, United States Department of Agriculture, is to protect American crops, forests, and ornamental plants from the introduction of foreign pests that could cause serious losses.

During the past centuries at least a hundred important species of insects have been introduced to the United States from abroad. Many of them entered this country with plant materials before the passage of the plant-quarantine act in 1912. These pests rapidly spread to various regions of the United States and have caused widespread damage to agriculture. Some of the most notorious of these foreign pests are the European corn borer, the cotton-

boll weevil, wheat stem rust, Mexican bean beetle, oriental peach moth, Japanese beetle, gypsy moth, chestnut blight, and the fungus that causes white-pine blister rust.

To prevent the introduction of new pests from abroad the U.S. Plant Quarantine Division maintains inspectors at all major seaports, international airports, and border crossings. Arriving vessels, vehicles, and aircraft and their stores, cargo, and mail are inspected for regulated plants and plant materials. Plant-quarantine inspectors also participate with customs officials in examining the baggage of persons entering the United States. If the inspectors find any plant pests with the foreign materials, they are empowered by federal law to take appropriate action. This action includes refusing entry of the material into the United States, confiscating the material, or supervising proper treatment (such as fumigation) to destroy the pest before admitting the plant material.

The Plant Quarantine Division inspectors detect the presence of a damaging foreign plant pest at the rate of one every 17 minutes. Many of these pests have never been in the United States, so plant-quarantine inspectors prevent millions of dollars' worth of damage annually to U.S. fields, forests, crops, and ornamental plants.

PLASTICS are synthetic or natural materials that contain organic substances made up of large and complex molecules. A plastic material becomes hardened in its finished state, but at some stage during its manufacture it is soft enough to be easily shaped by the application of heat or pressure. Natural plastic resins, such as rosin and shellac, are naturally occurring organic materials that have large molecules. Synthetic plastic resins are either chemically modified natural complex organic materials or are complex materials synthesized from simple organic and inorganic compounds. The commonest methods of synthesizing resins from simpler substances are condensation and polymerization. See POLYMERIZATION.

A resin consists only of complex organic substances. If a resin, without being mixed with other materials, is capable of being shaped and hardened into a permanent form, it is a plastic. Most resins must be mixed with various substances before a plastic is compounded.

Although such materials as rubber and certain fibers are not excluded from the field of plastics by definition, they are not thought of as plastics.

In general, two types of plastic materials exist: thermoplastic materials and thermosetting plastic materials. Thermoplastic materials contain long-chain, or linear, organic molecules. Each time such a material is heated, it will soften; each time it is cooled, it will harden. A thermoplastic material can be heated and cooled any number of times. Once a thermosetting material has been heated and cooled, it is permanently hard. It cannot be softened by reheating. During the first heating process molecules in a thermosetting material link onto each other and form a three-dimensional network.

In making commercial plastic products resins are commonly modified by adding plasticizers, fillers, dyes, and pigments to give the properties desired in the finished article. A plasticizer is a material added to a resin to increase the flexibility and plasticity of the resin. Fillers are materials added to a resin to make the plastic product bulkier, stronger, harder, or more resistant to chemicals, heat, or water. Stabilizers are sometimes added to plastic compounds to increase their resistance to heat, sunlight, and other forms of energy that tend to break down the molecular structure of the plastic.

Reinforced plastics are plastics that contain foreign agents as reinforcements, such as threads, fibers, and wires. Some of the fibers include glass, asbestos, cotton, paper, and wood. Laminated plastics contain sheets of paper, fabric, or wood that have been coated with, or soaked in, resin and then bonded by heat and pressure.

The first synthetic plastic was cellulose nitrate, or Celluloid. It was made by combining cellulose nitrate and camphor. Celluloid is a thermoplastic material. It has many disadvantages: It is decomposed by heat, is hazardous to handle in large quantities because of its flammability, and is unstable in sunlight. Celluloid was discovered and manufactured during the 19th century. It is not widely used today.

The first commercial synthetic resin was phenol formaldehyde, a thermosetting plastic resin patented in 1909 and given the trade name Bakelite. It is still one of the most important resins. Telephone handsets, bottle caps, washing machine agitators and parts for electrical appliances are some of the products made from phenol formaldehyde plastics. These plastics are resistant to most acids, to weak solutions of alkalies, and to organic solvents. They will not support combustion. Various other phenolic resins, such as phenol furfural, also are now used to make plastic products.

Cellulose acetate is a thermoplastic material that has been in use since 1927. It is either nonflammable or will burn rather slowly. Cellulose acetate is used as a safety photographic film. It is also used in the manufacture of buttons, steering wheels, flashlight cases, and so forth. It is used in films and sheets as a packaging material. Cellulose acetate is a tough, strong material. Several cellulosic thermoplastic materials are now in use.

A thermosetting resin in wide use is urea formaldehyde. Its properties are similar to those of phenol formaldehyde plastics, except that urea formaldehyde plastics may be colorless. Urea formaldehyde plastics may be given any color by pigments and dyes. Urea formaldehyde resins are used as plywood glues and in the manufacture of paper that is strong when wet. Urea formaldehyde plastics are used in lighting fixtures, bottle caps, lightweight tableware, and other objects.

Melamine formaldehyde is an important thermosetting resin that has properties similar to urea formaldehyde but is more resistant to heat,

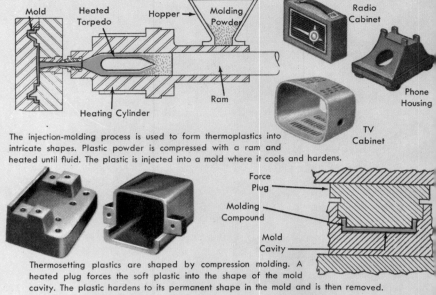

The injection-molding process is used to form thermoplastics into intricate shapes. Plastic powder is compressed with a ram and heated until fluid. The plastic is injected into a mold where it cools and hardens.

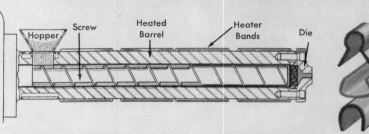

Thermosetting plastics are shaped by compression molding. A heated plug forces the soft plastic into the shape of the mold cavity. The plastic hardens to its permanent shape in the mold and is then removed.

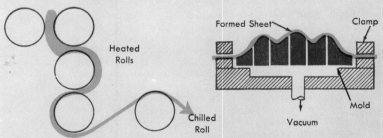

When plastic is to be shaped to a continuous profile, such as a channel shape, it is extruded. Plastic powder is forced through a heated cylinder by a screw. The plastic is melted, mixed, and forced through a die into a cold water bath where it hardens.

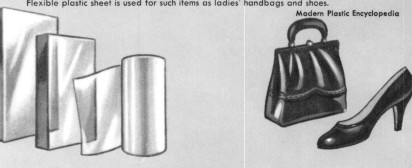

Plastic sheet is made by calendering (above, left). A mass of soft plastic is squeezed through heated rollers until a sheet of the desired thickness is obtained; the plastic sheet is then hardened by passing it over a chilled roller. A material to be coated with plastic, such as cardboard, may be fed through the rollers with the plastic. Plastic sheet can be shaped by softening it against a mold (above, right) and drawing it down on the mold by vacuum. Flexible plastic sheet is used for such items as ladies' handbags and shoes.

Modern Plastic Encyclopedia

water, and alkaline solutions. Melamine formaldehyde is used in the manufacture of dinnerware, instrument housings, map paper, tabletops, and ignition parts of engines.

The polyamide plastics include nylon, which is also used as a fiber. Nylon plastics are increasing in use and have some important properties. They can be boiled and sterilized and are exceedingly tough, resistant to abrasion, and flexible in some forms.

The low-pressure resins are a special group of thermosetting resins. Low-pressure resins are usually liquids that can be used in manufacturing plastics by casting or laminating. They need only the application of heat, with no extra pressure, to make them harden. Polyester and epoxy resins are low-pressure resins. Low-pressure resins often are used to make large lightweight pieces, such as radar domes, parts of trailer bodies, and small-boat hulls. Reinforcing materials, such as glass fabric, are often used with the resins.

Among the thermoplastic materials the most important are the polyvinyl resins. Several different types of polyvinyl resins exist, but they all have some properties in common. All vinyl resins are hard and tough. To make most useful objects, a plasticizer, or softener, must be mixed with the vinyl resin. Vinyl plastics (flexible or rigid) are used in film and sheeting form for upholstery and luggage, wire and cable coatings, shower curtains, phonograph records, printing plates, floor tile, rain wear, films for packaging, garden hose, plastic pipe, and other objects. A sheet of polyvinyl butyral is used as the interlayer material in safety glass.

Another important and inexpensive thermoplastic resin is polystyrene. Polystyrene is extensively used as an insulating material in radio, radar, and television apparatus. Because of its light-transmitting properties, it is used in lenses and parts of optical equipment. It is also used in the manufacture of adhesives, coatings, containers, and refrigerator parts.

Such thermoplastic acrylic resins as Plexiglas or Lucite are well known. Acrylic resins are colorless, transparent, and resistant to most chemicals, have adhesive qualities, and do not break easily. Acrylic plastics are used as airplane cockpit enclosures, optical parts, artificial dentures and limbs, lighting reflectors, adhesives, and protective coatings.

Polyethylene resins are thermoplastic resins that are colorless, translucent, and rubbery. They are resistant to chemicals and solvents and to moisture. They are electrical insulators. Polyethylene is used as coaxial-cable insulation, film for food packaging, linings for chemical equipment, gaskets, and packings for valves. Related to polyethylene is polypropylene, a clear, tough plastic, stronger and harder than polyethylene.

Some other important thermosetting resins are casein, diallyl phthalate, furan, polyacrylic, and silicone molding compounds. Allyl, glyceryl phthalate, and phenolic compounds are thermosetting cast resins.

Some plastics, such as Teflon, are produced by combining hydrocarbons with fluorine. Such fluorocarbons are very durable, electrically resistant, and chemically inert.

Before most plastic resins are processed, they are compounded with fillers, plasticizers, stabilizers, and so on. After they are compounded, the plastic materials are put in a convenient form for processing, such as liquid, powder, or granules.

Plastics in liquid form may be made into coatings by being sprayed, brushed, or dipped onto the material to be coated. Liquid plastics may be used as ingredients in lacquers, paints, and adhesives. Liquid plastics are also cast into sheets.

Plastics in powdered or granular form are made into articles by compression molding, injection molding, transfer molding, extrusion molding, calendering, blowing, and casting.

Injection molding is the commonest method of forming articles from thermoplastic materials. Powder or granules are fed into a heating cylinder and forced through a nozzle into a cold mold, which has the shape of the finished product. When the plastic has cooled and solidified, the mold is opened and the product removed.

Thermosetting plastics are commonly formed into products by compression molding. The plastic molding compound is heated and placed in an open mold cavity. The mold is closed, and the two parts of the mold are forced together. The plastic hardens permanently into the shape of the mold.

Transfer molding is also applied to thermosetting plastics. Powdered or granulated molding compound is heated in a chamber until it becomes fluid. The fluid is forced into a mold, where heat and pressure are applied until the plastic hardens.

Extrusion molding is used in the production of continuous film, sheeting, rods, tubes, and threads from thermoplastic materials. Powdered or granular material is fed into a cylinder, where it is melted by heat and friction. The melted plastic is forced through a die at the end of the cylinder, and the die gives the plastic a final shape.

Blow molding is used to shape such objects as plastic bottles. Warm tube-shaped material from an extrusion molding machine is placed in a closed mold in one type of blow molding. The material is forced to spread out against the walls of the mold by air or by steam that is blown into the mold.

Casting is a forming technique used on either thermosetting or thermoplastic materials. The plastic, in liquid form, is poured into a mold. Thermoplastic materials may be allowed to solidify at room temperature. Thermosetting materials may be solidified by heating or by the addition of a catalyst.

Slush casting is used for making hollow, flexible shapes, such as overshoes. A slush of thermoplastic material is poured into a warm mold, where a thin layer of plastic adheres to the walls of the mold. The remaining slush is poured out of the mold. The layer in the mold is hardened by heating or by air drying. In its final form the flexible layer is stripped out of the mold.

Calendering is used to produce films and sheets of plastic. A warm, doughy mass of plastic compound is passed between a series of heated rollers. The rollers squeeze the material into flat film or sheet.

PLATEAU, a fairly level and smooth land area, similar to a plain but of greater elevation, often connected with a system of mountains and situated either as foothill highlands or between ranges in the higher altitudes. The Tibet and Pamir plateaus in Asia are the most prominent in the world in area and height. The plateau of the Andes in South America and that of the Rocky Mountains in North America are next in importance. The altitude of those in Central Asia ranges from 10,000 to 14,000 feet. Between the Sierra Nevada and the Rocky Mountains is located the Colorado Plateau, which ranges between 5,000 and 11,000 feet in height. East of the Rocky Mountains and between them and the central plains in the Mississippi Valley lie the Great Plains, ranging in height from 2,000 to 6,000 feet above sea level.

PLATINUM, symbol Pt, a grayish-white metal, is one of the world's most permanent substances, It is noted for its hardness, its high specific gravity (21.45), and its chemical nonactivity. It is one of the noble metals, a division that includes gold, silver, platinum, and metals of the platinum group (palladium, iridium, rhodium, osmium, and ruthenium).

Platinum—unaffected by exposure to air, water, and common acids, even at high temperatures—reacts chemically, or combines with nonmetallic elements, only under extreme and unusual conditions. When platinum does combine with other elements, it does so in one of two ways. It may form compounds in which platinum has a valence of two, such as PtO, or it may form compounds in which platinum has a valence of four, such as PtO_2.

Because of its chemical nonactivity platinum is usually found in its pure state or alloyed with iron, nickel, gold, copper, and metals of the platinum group. Much of the world's supply of platinum comes from mines near Sudbury, Ontario. Another important source is the Ural Mountains of the Soviet Union. Platinum is also found in Colombia, Alaska, and South Africa.

Platinum has many uses because of its unusual properties. Its commonest use is in jewelry. It is valued for its bright luster and unusual hardness for a metal. A very hard alloy of platinum and iridium is used in penpoints. Because of its lack of chemical activity it is used in electrical apparatus and in laboratory crucibles that must be in contact with chemicals at high temperatures without contaminating them. Because of its permanence platinum is used for standard weights and measures. One of the most important uses of platinum is as a catalyst, a substance that aids a chemical reaction without becoming chemically changed itself. Large quantities of platinum are used as a catalyst in the production of high-octane gasoline, in the manufacture of sulfuric and nitric acids, and in the manufacture of synthetic organic compounds.

Platinum (at. no. 78, at. wt. most abundant isotope 195) has 78 electrons (−) around a nucleus of 78 protons (+) and 117 neutrons.

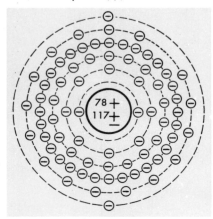

PLATO (427?-347? B.C.), an Athenian philosopher. Plato has been one of the most influential philosophers of all time. Benjamin Jowett, a translator of Plato's works, once remarked that "the germs of all ideas are to be found in Plato."

Plato's father was Ariston. His mother's family included Critias, one of the Thirty Tyrants who seized power in Athens following the Great Peloponnesian War. As a young man Plato was a devoted friend of Socrates'. Later, he taught in a grove called Academus and created the philosophical school known as the Academy, which produced such thinkers as Aristotle. Other facts about Plato are less certain. He was said by Diogenes Laërtius to have been a good wrestler, a poet, and a soldier who fought in three great battles. Diogenes also related that Plato conversed with Egyptian priests. He was said to have traveled to Sicily, where he attempted unsuccessfully to educate Dionysius II in the principles of the philosopher-king.

Athens in Plato's day was a place of philosophical speculation. Athenians discussed problems that still engage the minds of men. Socrates began to seek what knowledge he could regarding the ideas of Athenians on right and wrong. Socrates' questioning was expressed and amplified by the *Dialogues* of Plato.

Plato's work is in the form of philosophical dialogues. These are conversations in which questions are discussed as they would have been among Athenian intellectuals. Through all these dialogues, in which Socrates is usually the principal speaker, runs the idea that the intellect has the power to work for human betterment and that truth is good. The subjects treated are generally psychology, education, and political reform. Some of the dialogues are clear and logical, like the "Theaetetus," while others are mystical, like the "Timaeus." In *The Republic* Plato explores the question of justice, and in so doing he develops an idea of the perfect state. See SOCRATES.

Brown Brothers

Plato has been one of the world's most influential thinkers. The prose style of his dialogues is both beautiful and powerful.

PLATT AMENDMENT, legislation passed by the U.S. Congress, Mar. 2, 1901, and incorporated in the Cuban constitution of June, 1901, which governed relations between the United States and Cuba until 1934. Following the victory over Spain in the Spanish-American War (1898) the U.S. government was faced with the problem of how to treat Cuba since there was no intention of annexing the country. The Platt Amendment, attached to an army appropriation bill, was the answer of the Senate Committee on Cuban Relations headed by Senator Orville Platt of Connecticut.

The principal provisions provided for U.S. naval bases in Cuba and allowed the United States to intervene to protect Cuban independence and to maintain a stable Cuban government. There was strong opposition in Cuba to these provisions, and they were accepted only under great pressure from the United States. The United States actually intervened in Cuba on only three occasions after the passage of the amendment—from 1906 to 1909, in 1911, and during World War I. The primary reason for intervention was the protection of the constitutional government from revolts led by opposition parties. Cuban opinion continued to oppose the policy. However, on May 29, 1934, the U.S. government acceded to demands and repealed the Platt Amendment. Rules of international law have since been the basis of the United States right of intervention.

PLATT NATIONAL PARK, established in 1906, is situated in southern Oklahoma at the northeastern base of the Arbuckle Mountains. It is adjacent to Sulphur, Okla. The park includes more than 900 acres. The region is forested and hilly. There are a number of sulfur springs as well as some bromide and freshwater springs in the park.

PLATYPUS, one of the strangest of all mammals, also called duckbill and duckbilled platypus. It is found only in Australia and Tasmania. Like all mammals, it is fur covered; the animal is 18 to 20 inches long and lives in and near the water. It has a broad, ducklike bill and feet that are webbed and clawed. The mother platypus lays eggs yet provides milk for the young to feed on when they hatch, blind and naked. The platypus is thus a queer combination of mammal, bird, and reptile. The animals live in ponds and slow-moving streams and dig long burrows into the bank. These end in grass-lined chambers, in which the platypuses usually spend the day; they come out at dusk to search

Because it has mammary glands and fur, the platypus, which lays eggs, is a mammal.

for the water insects and small shellfish on which they feed. The eggs, generally two in number, are about ¾ inch long, with thin, white, membranous shells. The flesh, which is strong smelling, once was eaten by some of the native Australians, who dug the animal out of its burrows.

PLAY, a story acted on a stage or the script of such an action. The play has evolved in many separate societies. The most important element of drama, the play is a combination of essential elements and of conventions established in particular times and societies.

Wherever it has evolved as an art form—India, China, Japan, ancient Greece, medieval Europe—the play has originated in religious ritual. Today plays may be performed for religious purposes, but they are more often given for recreational or educational purposes. They may be performed by almost any group—from primitive people to amateur or professional theater groups. The play is truly an almost universal form of artistic expression.

The play (script) is the first and most important element of drama. Actors are essential, for they translate the play from written form into the live form envisaged by the playwright. An audience is also of primary importance. But the play is the master blueprint that guides actors, director, and technicians in helping to create the performance.

Some characteristics seem to be essential to the play in any society; others are conventions that may change from time to time and place to place. Among the apparently essential elements of the play are action, conflict, unity of purpose, and resolution. Commonly used dramatic conventions include masks, conventional gestures, choruses, and asides. Division into acts and scenes and methods of changing scenery are also determined by convention. An ancient Greek play was continuous from beginning to end, with no curtains or wide shifts of scene; plays today are commonly divided into several acts and scenes. In Western plays scenery is usually changed between acts or scenes; in Chinese and Japanese plays there is little or no scenery, and a black-clad property man stands on the stage and supplies properties as they are needed.

In fact the whole effect of a play depends upon the spectator's acceptance of certain conventions. For example, when a person sees a performance of Shakespeare's *Julius Caesar,* he is called upon to believe

he is in Rome, the time is 44 B.C. and the men he is watching are Julius Caesar, Mark Antony, and so on. The Romans speak Elizabethan English. Rooms and houses have one side missing. But the spectator does accept all these things as quite natural in the play. These effects depend upon a kind of dramatic faith similar to the poetic faith defined by Coleridge: the "willing suspension of disbelief for the moment."

PLEDGE OF ALLEGIANCE. See FLAG OF THE UNITED STATES.

PLESIOSAUR. The plesiosaurs were once an important marine reptile group. They lived during the Jurassic and the Cretaceous in continental seas. Two distinct groups of plesiosaurs developed. One group had small, short heads and long necks. The other group had long heads and short necks. All plesiosaurs had thick, egg-shaped bodies and fin-shaped or paddle-shaped limbs. Some plesiosaurs were as long as 50 feet.

During the Jurassic, plesiosaurs were plentiful in European seas but were scarce elsewhere. During the Cretaceous, plesiosaurs were most numerous in western North America. Two well-known genera are *Kronosaurus,* a long-headed, short-necked plesiosaur that lived in Australia during the Cretaceous, and *Elasmosaurus,* a very long-necked genus that lived in North America during the Cretaceous. At the end of the Cretaceous all plesiosaurs became extinct.

Two Upper Cretaceous plesiosaurs are, above, *Elasmosaurus;* right, *Trinacromerum.*

PLOVERS AND TURNSTONES, small to medium-sized wading birds found worldwide on shores and uplands. On the shore they are often with sandpipers but differ from them in having more compact bodies, thicker necks, bolder patterns, and shorter, stouter bills. Their call notes are important aids in identification. Most are gregarious and migratory. They feed on insects, crustaceans, small mollusks, and worms. Usually they run in quick starts and stops.

Best known plover is probably the killdeer, distinguished by two black breast rings and bright-chestnut lower rump and tail coverts. It breeds in meadows and pastures, where its noisy "kill dee" serves as an alarm at the slightest sign of danger. Four eggs are laid in a scrape on dry ground or gravel shore. When an intruder nears the nest, the killdeer does an excellent distraction act by simulating the dragging of a broken wing until the intruder has been drawn from the area. Then the bird "recovers" and flies off.

Other North American plovers include the semipalmated, with one black breast ring; the piping, with one ring and a color like wet sand; the snowy, very pale in color; Wilson's, with a thick black bill; and the mountain, a western species of the dry prairie. A plover famous for a long migration is the golden plover, easily recognized in its breeding garb by its black under parts and golden-brown upper parts. The black-bellied plover is similar except that its upper parts are grayish.

The plover family also includes the surfbird of the American western coast, which nests on crags in the Alaskan mountains; the ruddy

Courtesy of Ford Motor Company
A farmer is working his fields with a three-bottom plow, above. With it he can plow an acre in 45 minutes.

turnstone, so named from the russet in its bold pattern and its habit of turning over stones and other objects in search of food; and the black turnstone, which feeds on small aquatic animals found among the wave-washed rockweed and barnacles. The upland plover, in spite of its name, belongs to the sandpiper family. See Sandpiper.

PLOW, an agricultural implement used for breaking up and turning over a layer of topsoil in preparation for planting. One of man's fundamental inventions, it made possible the development of agriculture. The most ancient type, which is still used in many parts of Asia and in some parts of Europe, is simply a sharpened stick attached to a frame. It is pulled by an animal and does little more than break up the soil surface.

The simplest type of modern plow includes a steel cutting blade, called the share, fastened to a curved part,

The blacksmith plover, **1,** from Africa, uses the sharp spur on its wing in fighting. The black-bellied plover, **2,** and the golden plover, **3,** migrate through North America. The red-wattled lapwing, **4,** is an Asian species. Common American plovers are the killdeer, **5,** and the semi-palmated plover, **6.** The ruddy turnstone, **7,** and the dunlin (a sandpiper), **8,** are colorful North American shore birds. The common lapwing, **9,** is a well-known bird in Europe and Asia.

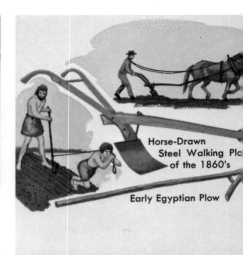

Horse-Drawn Steel Walking Plow of the 1860's

Early Egyptian Plow

called the moldboard. These combined components, called the bottom, are fastened to a framework that has two handles used by the operator in guiding the plow through the soil. This simple type, called the walking plow, is now little used. Nearly all plowing is now done by gang (multiple-bottomed) plows mounted on wheels or mounted directly on the rear of a tractor. A different type of plow used in some areas is called the diskplow. It consists of a series of revolving disks that travel through the topsoil at an oblique angle. The diskplow does not ordinarily plow so deep as the moldboard plow, but it creates a finer mulch. It is most commonly used in preparing land for the planting of wheat.

PLUM, a deciduous tree fruit that is closely related to the peach, apricot, cherry, and almond; all are drupes in one genus of the rose family. There are many species and varieties of plums, but the ones in which the world is chiefly interested are the European plums, native to western Asia.

The European plums of commercial importance are of three main types. The first group, the prunes, are fairly large, firm-fleshed, oval, and usually blue or purple. They have a high sugar content and free stones. Prunes are actually plums that, because of high sugar content, can be dried whole without fermentation at the pit. The United States leads the world in prune production, most of the crop being produced in California, Washington, Oregon, and Idaho. Yugoslavia, France, Argentina, Australia, and Chile are other important prune-growing countries.

Wild plums are small and very sour.

The second type of European plum is called the Reine Claude, or greengage group. These fruits are nearly round and, when mature, are green, yellow, or slightly red. The flesh is sweet, tender, and juicy and adheres to the pit. These plums are not suitable for drying but are important varieties for canning.

The third type is the yellow-egg group, which varies from the second mainly in size and shape. The fruits are very large; they are long oval in shape and vary from yellow to purple. They are desirable for canning only.

The damson plum is a botanical variety of the European species. The fruit is small, oval, purple to black, and quite tart. Damsons are highly esteemed for jam or plum butter but are seldom eaten fresh. They are produced mainly in home gardens and for local markets in the United States.

The Japanese plum, another species, is next in importance to the European species. Japanese plums were domesticated in Japan but originated in China. They were introduced into the United States about 1870 and are now grown extensively in California. Japanese plums are round or heart-shaped, large, and bright yellow or red, never blue. They are clingstones and are suitable for eating fresh only.

PLUMBING, the furnishing, installing, and repairing of water and waste-disposal systems. The word *plumbing* may also refer to the piping and fixtures that make up such systems. Although minor plumbing repairs may be made by an amateur, major ones should be left to an experienced plumber.

A building's plumbing system is made up of two parts—piping and fixtures. The piping, which repre-

sents the basis of all plumbing, is usually hidden, for the most part, behind walls and beneath floors. The plumbing system in an average home includes about 300 feet of piping. The piping includes two separate systems—the supply piping, which brings pure water to the fixtures, and the waste piping, which carries waterborne wastes away from the fixtures. To be adequate the piping should be durable, leakproof, and large enough in diameter to meet the demands put upon the plumbing system.

The supply piping may include piping for both hot and cold water. Hot-water piping originates at a hot-water heater. Circulation of the hot water is maintained by pressure from pumps or from a city water system and by the relative difference in weight of cold water and hot water. Cold water is circulated by pressure from a city water system or by pumps, which may pump the water into a tank from which it feeds by pressure or gravity.

The waste piping connects to drains and toilets through traps, devices that form a water seal against sewer gases. Sewer gases, formed by action of bacteria on waste materials, are both offensive and deadly if they escape into a house. Waste pipes from each floor of a building connect with a soil stack, which connects in turn with a drainage or sewage system. The soil stack extends upward to form a vent, through which sewer gases are released above roof level.

Fixtures include lavatories, bathtubs, showers, toilets, sinks, and washing machines. The fixtures connect with the pipings through fittings of various kinds.

With a minimum of instruction the amateur may make minor repairs on a plumbing system, such as cleaning clogged drains and fixing leaky faucets. It is particularly important that all members of a household be able to find and to turn off in case of emergency the main shutoff valve for the house's plumbing system. The amateur should never undertake major plumbing repairs but should call an experienced plumber. Most communities have plumbing and building codes that regulate such repairs.

In addition to installing water and waste-disposal systems, plumbers sometimes install and service gas and heating systems. Plumbers are trained through apprenticeship, including classroom instruction and five years of on-the-job training. See CONSTRUCTION INDUSTRY.

PLUTARCH'S LIVES, more properly *Parallel Lives*, the title of the famous work of the Greek historian and moralist Plutarch (A.D. 46?-120?). The work consists of 50 biographical studies—23 pairs and 4 single—of eminent Greek and Roman soldiers and statesmen, ranging chronologically from the age of the semilegendary Theseus and Romulus down to the time of Plutarch himself. Included in the collection are biographies of such interesting persons as Solon, Themistocles, Alcibiades, Demosthenes, Mark Antony, Julius Caesar, Pompey the Great, Alexander the Great, and Cicero. Plutarch's emphasis was not on the political events that surrounded these figures but rather on moral character as it was revealed through certain episodes in each man's life. Despite prejudices, occasional historical inaccuracies, and a stress on moralizing, *Plutarch's Lives* stands as an extremely valuable sourcebook of Greek and Roman history. Few books, ancient or modern, have been more widely read or admired.

Most famous translation of the work was Sir Thomas North's, which was published in 1579. It was not based on the original Greek but rather on the French version according to Jacques Amyot. Shakespeare drew material from the North translation for his plays *Julius Caesar*, *Anthony and Cleopatra*, and *Coriolanus*. Another notable translation, which was published in 1770, was made by the brothers William and John Langhorne.

PLUTO, in classical mythology, the son of Saturn, the brother of Jupiter and Neptune, and the god of the realms of the dead, lying far down in the earth. He rarely left his dark kingdom to visit Olympus or the sunlit earth and remained a dim figure in the mythological literature of Greece and Rome. He was also called Hades by the Greeks and Dis by the Romans. As Dis he was worshipped as the god of the riches of the earth—gold, silver, and other precious minerals.

The only notable story about him is a very early poem, which tells how he carries off Proserpina, daughter of Ceres, goddess of the corn and patroness of farmers. Proserpina is playing in the fields when Pluto comes out of a chasm in the earth, riding in his black chariot drawn by black horses. Falling in love with the beautiful young girl, he snatches her into his chariot and carries her back with him to rule as queen of the underworld.

PLUTO, the remotest of the known principal planets of the solar system. It was discovered in 1930 by U.S. astronomer Clyde Tombaugh, who was aided by the earlier calculations of Percival Lowell. Primarily because of Pluto's great distance from the sun, less is known about it than about any other planet.

Pluto orbits the sun at a mean distance of almost four billion miles, nearly 40 times the earth's distance from the sun. It revolves once around the sun in 248 years. The exact nature of Pluto's surface is not known, but its atmospheric temperature is probably even colder than that of its nearest neighbor, Neptune.

Considerable question surrounds the matter of Pluto's size and mass, and hence of its density. According to an estimate based upon the behavior of Neptune, Pluto's mass was set at 80 percent of the earth's mass. Pluto's diameter was set at about 4,000 miles. However, when these figures are used to compute Pluto's density, a figure is obtained that is very much higher than the density of any other planet. Therefore it is suspected that either Pluto's mass or its diameter has been incorrectly measured. The problem has yet to be resolved.

Pluto is unique among the larger planets in at least two respects. Its orbit is inclined 17 degrees to the ecliptic, which means that at times it passes outside the path of the zodiac. Also, its orbit is more eccentric than are the other planetary orbits. At its greatest distance from the sun Pluto is nearly two billion miles beyond the orbit of Neptune, its nearest neighbor. However, at its closest distance to the sun Pluto is nearer the sun than is Neptune. Because of these characteristics the theory has been advanced that Pluto may be a former moon of Neptune that broke away from the planet. It is perhaps significant in this respect that Pluto has no known moons of its own.

PLYMOUTH COLONY, established in 1620 by the Plymouth Company on the coast of what was to become Massachusetts. In April, 1606, James I chartered the London Company and the Plymouth Company to found colonies in America within a certain limited region. First attempts of the latter group (1606-1608) at colonization were failures. However, after John Smith explored and mapped the northern coast in 1614, the dangers of settling in the new land did not appear so great.

On Nov. 11, 1620, the Pilgrims, who had sailed from England on the *Mayflower*, anchored off Cape Cod. On Dec. 21, 1620, after several weeks spent in exploring the coast, the group of colonists settled where the town of Plymouth, Mass., now stands. Scarcely 50 of the Pilgrims survived the first winter. On Nov. 11, 1620, the passengers on the *Mayflower* had drawn up the Mayflower Compact, and it served as the constitution of the colony until 1691, when the settlement was incorporated into Massachusetts. A treaty made in 1621 with Massasoit, chief of the Wampanoag Indians, insured friendly relations with the Indians to the south and east for 50 years. The Narragansetts to the west were hostile, but Governor William Bradford courageously kept them in check. Thanksgiving Day was first observed by the Pilgrims in the autumn of 1621.

PLYMOUTH ROCK is the rock on which the Pilgrims supposedly first stepped as they disembarked from the *Mayflower* at what is now Plymouth, Mass. Although the story has never been proved, Plymouth Rock has become a famous shrine. It is now sheltered by a marble-columned building. Most of the rock is buried in the earth, and a fence surrounds the part above ground to prevent souvenir hunters from chipping away at the rock.

PLYWOOD, a lumber product consisting of an uneven number of thin layers of wood glued together, with the grain of each layer lying at a right angle to the grain of the adjoining layer. The layers are glued together so strongly that the fibers of the wood will break before the glued bond will fail. You can smash plywood, but you cannot split it. The peculiar strength of plywood depends on the use of waterproof glues and on the fact that wood is 40 times as strong when bent across the grain as when bent with the grain. A three-ply piece of plywood is almost 20 times as strong as a piece of lumber of similar thickness when the ordinary piece of wood is flexed with the grain. Five-ply plywood is stronger still, and the heaviest plywood is built up with seven layers.

While almost all kinds of lumber can be peeled into veneers for the making of plywood, most plywood in the United States is made from Douglas fir. Good plywood can be made from mixed woods, and the plies need not be of the same thickness. It is significant that one of the goals of the plywood manufacturers is to use all of the hitherto waste products of lumbering: The bark can be used for tanning; there is no waste as in the sawing of boards; the small limbs are chipped into pulpwood; and the centers of the great logs from which plywood veneers are peeled are shaped down to 2 by 4's.

Plywood is more stable and more uniform in strength as the number of plies, or layers of veneer, is increased (left).

Selected for manufacture into plywood, logs are sawed into peeler blocks (below) to be converted into rotary-cut veneer.

Amer. Forest Industries Products, Inc.

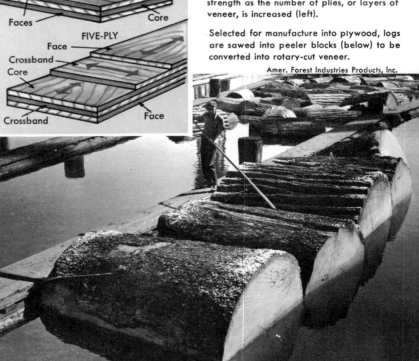

THREE-PLY

Faces

Core

FIVE-PLY

Face

Crossband

Core

Crossband

Face

Douglas Fir Plywood Assoc.

A long sheet of veneer for manufacture into plywood is turned out by a giant lathe (above). A log, its bark removed, is rotated against a long, heavy blade, and the veneer unwinds somewhat like paper from a roll.

Douglas Fir Plywood Assoc.

Finished plywood panels are given a final sanding and inspection before shipment.

Plywood is produced in two grades, exterior and interior. Exterior plywood is used for the outside walls of houses and for the hulls of boats. Its quality is determined by testing laboratories that boil and bake a half-million samples a year.

Interior plywood, used as sheathing and in furniture, is frequently beautifully polished and is glued to withstand only the ordinary exposure to moisture involved in the construction and maintenance of a building. Production of plywood has trebled since 1950.

PNEUMATIC TOOL, a tool whose action is derived from the action of compressed air. Pneumatic tools perform both heavy and light tasks and can be used in many operations. Pneumatic grinders, riveting hammers, caulking and chipping hammers, scaling tools, metal drills, rock drills, wood borers, wrenches, saws, picks, and road rippers are in common use.

Douglas Fir Plywood Assoc.

Sheets of veneer coated with glue by rollers are alternated with dry sheets of veneer in the assembly of plywood panels.

Compressed air, at some pressure from 60 to 120 pounds per square inch, is supplied to a pneumatic tool through tough, flexible hosing. The compressed air enters a cylinder with a piston. The compressed air expands and pushes the piston to one end of the cylinder. The expanded air is discharged from the cylinder, and the piston returns to its original position. The flow of air into and out of the cylinder is controlled by valves. As this process repeats, a rapid back-and-forth motion of the piston is produced. The motion of the piston is used to give the necessary motion to the bit, pick, or other tool piece of the pneumatic tool. Many pneumatic tools have more than one cylinder and piston. Two or four cylinders and pistons provide more power and smoother operation than one cylinder and piston.

The earliest pneumatic tools were used by miners as rock drills. Pneumatic tools are still much used in mining operations. Large hammer drills that weigh several hundred pounds and are mounted on frames are used in making tunnels. Smaller hammer drills that can be carried and held in position by a man are

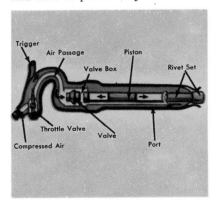

used for drilling out ore and for other purposes.

Pneumatic picks and road rippers are used to cut or break up concrete roads and sidewalks. Pneumatic spades are used for digging trenches and ditches. Pneumatic rammers are used to pack earth, sand, or gravel firmly in place.

Many pneumatic tools are used in factories and machine and repair shops. Riveting hammers, scaling hammers, chipping hammers, and portable metal drills are some commonly used tools. Riveting hammers that drive in rivets by direct pressure strike 1,000 to 2,000 blows per minute. Another type of riveting hammer, called a valveless hammer, gives very light, rapid blows. It strikes up to 20,000 blows per minute. Scaling hammers are also valveless and deliver very light blows very rapidly. Scaling hammers are used to remove paint or incrustations from surfaces.

PNEUMONIA is an inflammation of the lungs from an acute infection of the smallest divisions of the lungs, the air sacs. Both bacteria and other micro-organisms, such as viruses and fungi, may cause the infection. Often pneumonia follows an infection of the upper respiratory tract. A form called aspiration pneumonia is due to the lodging of foreign matter in the respiratory tract.

Pneumonia is an acute illness with chills, high fever, chest pain, and cough, with a typical rusty sputum in the beginning. The disease has a recognized course; after approximately a week a so-called crisis occurs, or a turn for the better unless there are complications.

Since the use of chemotherapy in the treatment of upper-respiratory-tract infections pneumonia has become less common. Also, with the use of the sulfonamides and penicillin and other antibiotics, the disease can be more successfully treated than formerly.

POCAHONTAS (1595?-1617), who was the favorite daughter of Powhatan, the chief of a group of Virginia Indian tribes, is almost a legend in U.S. history. The incident on which her fame rests—her saving Captain John Smith's life when the famous Jamestown leader was a prisoner of Powhatan in 1608—is believed to be true by some historians and is doubted by others.

In 1613 the English, by threats and arguments, persuaded Pocahontas' father to give her to them as a hostage because he had taken English prisoners. She was taken to Jamestown, where she was well treated, and became known for her gentleness and intelligence. There she was converted to Christianity, and there in 1614 she married the English gentleman John Rolfe. Their marriage resulted in an eight-year peace between the settlers and the Indians, a peace that was vital to the infant colony.

In 1616 Pocahontas traveled with her husband to England, where she attracted much favorable attention. She was treated as a princess and was presented to the queen. In 1617, while preparing to return to America, Pocahontas suddenly became ill and died.

POCKET BILLIARDS. See BILLIARDS.

POE, EDGAR ALLAN (1809-1849), American poet, short-story writer, and critic, born in Boston. Orphaned at an early age, Poe was taken into the family of John Allan, of Richmond, Va. Following private schooling in Richmond and a trip to Scotland and England, Poe entered the University of Virginia in 1826 but was soon dismissed because of gambling and excessive drinking. He then joined the U.S. Army, in which he served for two years. His foster father procured him an appointment to West Point. Poe was expelled from the academy after seven months. At odds with his foster father, Poe settled in Baltimore with an aunt, whose 13-year-old daughter, Virginia Clemm (his cousin), he married in 1836.

Meanwhile, Poe had commenced his literary career. His earliest published poems appeared in 1827 under the title *Tamerlane and Other Poems.* His short story "The Manuscript Found in a Bottle" won him a place on the editorial staff of the *Southern Literary Messenger* in 1835. Subsequently, he held editorial positions with a number of publications, including the *Gentleman's Magazine, Graham's Magazine,* the New York *Evening Mirror,* and the *Broadway Journal.* He held no position for longer than three years. Despite his unreliability and increasingly unstable temperament, Poe attained a position of influence in American letters, both as a creative writer and as a critic.

Today Poe is recognized as a master in, and a pioneer of, the short story, particularly the mystery story. His stories can be categorized as either tales of horror and the grotesque ("The Fall of the House of Usher," "The Tell-Tale

EDGAR ALLAN POE

Heart," "The Black Cat") or tales of adventure and mystery, the latter being forerunners of today's detective story (*The Narrative of Arthur Gordon Pym,* "The Gold-Bug," "The Murders in the Rue Morgue"). His poems, marked by a lyrical, melancholy beauty, include "Ulalume," "Annabel Lee," "The Raven," and "To Helen." Virtually all his creative work has a peculiarly morbid tone.

In addition to being recognized as a major force in American letters, Poe's creative writing exerted a great influence on European literature, particularly on Charles Baudelaire and the French symbolists.

POEM, a composition in which the language is compressed in a stricter rhythmical form than in everyday speech or in the most artificial prose. In this article the structure of poetry, different kinds of poems, and poetic language and practice will be examined.

Rhythm is the repetition of the same literary device at regular intervals. It occurs in prose, where it is much more varied than in the strict rhythm of poetry.

Various rhythmical patterns have been used to tie language into poems. Similarity in the sound of words is a common device. Rhyme is the repetition of final sounds: b*ook,* l*ook.* It occurs at the end of a line (final rhyme) or inside the line of verse (internal rhyme). Rhymes are called masculine or feminine, depending on whether the rhyme word ends in a stressed or an unstressed syllable. They are divided according to a rhyme scheme. The rhyme scheme of two quatrains (four-line stanzas) with alternating rhyme would be *a b a b   c d c d.*

Not every poem rhymes, for there are many other rhythmical devices that can be used in poetry. As-

sonance is the repetition of the vowel sound only: str*a*nd, b*a*ng. Alliteration is the repetition of the initial consonants: *c*rank, *c*rown. Old English poets preferred alliteration to rhyme.

In ancient poetry regularity of syllable length was used as a rhythmical device, somewhat as tone length still determines musical rhythm. Such a regular division of qualities was called meter. The individual rhythmical measure was called a foot of the meter. In modern languages the syllable length is not regular. Its place is taken by stress, but the same words are still used to name a pattern of stressed and unstressed syllables, as the Greeks used to indicate a pattern of long and short syllables.

In the line "To bé / or nót / to be / / that ís / the qués- / tion" the stress is on the second syllable of the measure, and the line is five feet long. The incomplete foot at the end is not counted. According to the number of feet per line, verse is said to be written in monometer (one foot per line), dimeter (two feet), trimeter (three feet), tetrameter (four feet), pentameter (five feet), hexameter (six feet), heptameter (seven feet), or octameter (eight feet). According to the various patterns of stressed syllables and unstressed syllables, or slacks, a foot may be called iambus (slack-stress, as in *forget*), trochee (stress-slack, as in *happy*), dactylus (stress-slack-slack, as in *centipede*), anapest (slack-slack-stress, as in *resurrect*), and spondee (stress-stress, as in *bright-eyed*). The division of verse into feet according to stresses is called scansion. The quote from *Hamlet* is in iambic pentameter. The double dividing line indicates a pause in the middle of the verse. This is called a caesura. Unrhymed iambic pentameter is blank verse.

Poems do not always have a strict meter. Old English poetry has an irregular number of syllables per line but always four stresses and a sharp caesura in the middle. Free verse employs a variety of rhythmical devices but avoids rhyme and rhythmical regularity. Whitman's poems are an example of this form.

Poems are often divided into stanzas. A two-line stanza is a couplet. Iambic pentameters rhymed in pairs are called heroic couplets. A three-line stanza is a tercet. Four lines form a quatrain; six, a sextet; eight, an octave. Chaucer often uses rhyme royal, a seven-line iambic pentameter stanza, rhyming *a b a b b c c.* In the *Faerie Queene* Spenser uses the

Spenserian stanza, consisting of eight iambic pentameters and a final alexandrine (iambic hexameter) with rhyme scheme *a b a b b c b c c*. Sometimes a stanza will contain one or more lines that are repeated in the other stanzas of the poem. This is called a refrain.

Poems may have almost any length or subject. Epigrams (short inscriptions, often with a witty twist) are sometimes only two lines. Epics are very long (See EPIC.) Philosophical treatises have been written in verse, and many plays use the poetic form. (See DRAMA; PLAY.) A narrative poem (one telling a story) is usually longer than a statement of personal emotions, but some ballads (narrative songs) are very short, whereas Wordsworth's intensely personal *Intimations of Immortality* is fairly long.

Poems that express feelings or emotions are called lyric after the lyre, with which the Greeks used to accompany their songs. These poems may treat of the beauty of nature and of love, death, wine, religion, and a variety of other subjects with emotional appeal. Different types of lyrical poems have names like elegy (a song of the dead), ode (a song of praise), or epithalamium (a bridal song). Often narrative poetry contains lyrical passages.

Poetry strives for great economy and effectiveness of language. This is poetical intensity. Coleridge and many other poets have contended that in very long poems there is necessarily a loss of poetical intensity. By this criterion mathematical treatises in verse and the like can seldom be called real poems. It has been argued that even Milton's *Paradise Lost* contains many unpoetical passages.

Poetic language should not be confused with poetic diction. Poetic diction is the use of pretty-sounding stereotypes and roundabout descriptions like "the finny tribe" for *fish*. Many amateur poets use poetic diction, but instead of making their poems more poetic it results in unoriginal, vague, pompous writing.

There are many amateur poets; and most people try their hand at a poem at some time or other. In many larger towns there are poetry clubs, where members compare and discuss poems and sometimes publish them in little magazines. Many schools award prizes in poetry competitions. Colleges and universities publish poems in quarterly literary magazines. A few national publications, like *Poetry Magazine*, specialize in poetry.

POGONOPHORE, or beard worm, a member of a wholly new phylum of animals discovered during the 20th century. This strange creature, which has no digestive system, no excretory organs, and no means of breathing, lives in a slender tube at the bottom of the ocean.

The first pogonophores known to science were dredged up off Indonesia during a Dutch expedition of 1899-1900. Zoologists could not classify the creatures. In 1949, after more specimens were found, the creation of a new phylum was proposed.

A pogonophore is up to 13 inches in length and $\frac{1}{10}$ inch in diameter. Two theories have been advanced to explain how it gains nourishment. One states that it traps with its tentacles the decomposition products of deep-sea bacteria. The other states that the pogonophore controls digestive processes in a space outside its body.

POISON GAS, any gas or vapor, particularly those used in chemical warfare, that can occur in the air in concentrations sufficient to endanger the life or health of individuals inhaling that air. The best precaution against the commonly encountered poisonous gases is ventilation, with large amounts of moving fresh air. When persons are where dangerous concentrations of toxic gases are known to exist, ventilation should be supplied at all costs, and the persons should be evacuated, kept warm, and kept quiet until a physician arrives. Artificial respiration should be applied to persons who have stopped breathing.

Many highly irritating poison gases, including some war gases that tend to remain on and damage the skin, may be removed by gently washing with soap and water. If necessary, the eyes may be rinsed with clean, cool water (no soap). Contaminated clothing should be immediately replaced. The same precautions apply to dangerously radioactive dust or other material.

War gases are usually classified in terms of their physiological effect. Choking gases affect the respiratory tract, causing the lungs to fill with liquid. Phosgene (U.S. Chemical Warfare designation, CG) is one of the more common and more dangerous of these. Other choking gases include diphosgene, DP; chlorine (no longer used); and chloropicrin, PS, which is rarely used. Blister gases, or vesicants, cause severe irritation, blistering, and general destruction of any portion of the body with which they come in contact.

Extremely dangerous on the skin, they are worst when inhaled. Vesicants include mustard gas (H, or HS), lewisite, nitrogen mustards, and organic arsines.

Vomiting gases, or sternutators, cause coughing, nausea, sneezing, and intense head pains. Gases of this type that are in wide use, such as adamsite, are all organic derivatives of arsine. Blood gases, like cyanide (hydrogen cyanide, hydrocyanic acid), cyanogen, and cyanogen chloride, are absorbed through the lungs and skin or are taken in with food or water and act through the blood to disturb the proper functioning of the body.

Nerve gases, particular types of organic phosphorus compounds, may be absorbed in the same ways as blood gases. Nerve gases affect the enzyme action necessary to the operation of the nervous system and cause paralysis and death, frequently within minutes. Without odor or taste, nerve gases are difficult to detect before a disabling or deadly dose has been absorbed.

Gas masks, protective clothing, and special ointments to protect the skin are combined in war-gas defense with adequate dispersal of persons in order to avoid presenting a concentrated target. Instructions to remain out of hollows or depressions in the land, where the gas tends to accumulate, are also given.

POISONING is the absorption into the organism of a substance tending to produce death or ill health. In an average household many products containing poison may be found. These include cleaning compounds, insecticides, medicines, bleaches, rat poisons, and some cosmetics. All such materials should be stored where they are safe from children and where they cannot be accidentally mistaken for a food or other harmless material. The instructions for the use of any material containing poison should be carefully followed. The hands should be washed after the preparation is used. Dry-cleaning solvents and other solvents, kerosene lamps, and gasoline engines should be used only in well-ventilated locations. Extended skin contact with poisonous materials should be avoided, because many of them may be absorbed through the skin in toxic amounts.

Inside the body, poison may act in many ways. Caustic materials (acids and alkalies) burn and corrode through the tissues. Treatment for these poisons is quite different from treatment for other poisons.

Some poisons, such as carbon monoxide and cyanide, interfere with the ability of the blood to carry oxygen and thus cause asphyxiation. Alcohol and sleeping tablets are depressants. Acute stimulation of the central nervous system is produced by strychnine and chlordane. Because of the many different modes of action of poisons, it is important, in the event of poisoning, to remember the symptoms and, if possible, the source of the poisoning so that the physician may begin effective treatment as soon as he arrives.

First-aid treatment for poisoning should be given while waiting for a physician to arrive. If breathing fails, artificial respiration should be applied.

To dilute a noncorrosive poison and remove it from the stomach, about 2 quarts of an emetic solution, such as soapy water, baking-soda solution, or mustard in water (1 teaspoon of prepared mustard per glass of water) should be given. The stomach contents should be saved for analysis if the cause of poisoning is not definitely known. After vomiting has ceased, a glass of water may be given containing two tablespoons of the following mixture, known as the universal antidote: two parts of activated carbon (powder) and one part each of magnesium oxide and tannic acid. After this has been in the stomach two or three minutes, it should be followed by an emetic, and the stomach should again be emptied. This should be repeated until the emetic alone shows no discoloration on being vomited. Substitutes for the universal antidote are large quantities of milk, possible containing raw egg whites beaten in; coffee; tea; or water. The process should be the same. If the stomach is too full to take an emetic, vomiting may be induced by tickling the back of the throat with the finger.

Corrosive poisons (acids and alkalies with the exception of carbolic acid) should be neutralized; otherwise they will further corrode the sensitive throat and mouth. A corrosive acid may be treated with universal antidote, milk of magnesia, baking soda in water, or chalk mixed in water. As much of this should be taken as possible, and vomiting should not be induced. Corrosive alkalies should be treated with orange juice, lemonade, or slightly diluted vinegar or lemon juice. Milk, cream, butter, cooking oil, or cooked cereal may then be given to give the tissues a soothing and protective coating.

The leaves of poison ivy

POISON IVY, the common name of widely distributed plants that, upon contact, are irritating to the skin of many people. The plants are similar in appearance to the Virginia creeper but are distinguished from it by having three instead of five leaflets. The three leaflets are broad, oval shaped, and coarsely toothed. Generally, the middle leaflet is larger than the other two. In the fall poison ivy leaves turn brilliant red. The inconspicuous, greenish-white flowers are borne in loose clusters and bloom during late spring. They are followed by small, round, hard berries that may be white, cream colored, or pale green.

The skin eruption caused by poison ivy and related species—poison oak and poison sumac—is due to an oil secreted on the leaves. Irritation can often be prevented if the skin is immediately washed with a strong soap. In serious cases a physician should be consulted. These plants represent practically the only native American species that is poisonous upon contact, although other species such as nettle may be very irritating.

POISONOUS PLANT. See PLANT, POISONOUS.

POLAND, a republic in north-central Europe, between the U.S.S.R. and Germany, is bounded on the north by the Baltic Sea. The area is 120,000 square miles, and the population is about 30,000,000. The capital is Warsaw; other chief cities are Lodz, Krakow, Poznan, Worclaw, Gdansk, Szczecin, Bydgoszcz, and Katowice.

The country lies mostly in a low rolling plain partly forested and dotted with many small lakes. The surface slopes gradually up to the Beskid, Sudetes, and Carpathian mountains in the south. The chief rivers are the Vistula, Oder, Western Bug, Narew, and San. A system of canals links the various rivers and provides economical transportation routes throughout the country. The southern part has mineral deposits, the most important being coal, iron, lead, and zinc.

Poland, before World War II, was mainly an agricultural country with 70 percent of the people engaged in farming. Following the terrible destruction of the war, great changes took place in the economy, and an industrialization process was begun. Today less than half of the population is connected with agriculture. The principal crops raised are rye, potatoes, oats, barley, wheat, flax, sugar beets, rapeseed, and hemp. Lumbering and stockraising are also important. Industrial production has increased since World War II and now plays a large role in the Polish economy. Principal manufactures are tractors, locomotives, steel, machine tools, railroad freight cars, chemicals, radios, and textiles. The leading exports are coal, steel, cement, lumber, locomotives, railroad cars, and textiles.

Formerly the free city of Danzig, Gdansk is now a major Polish port on the Baltic Sea.
Eastfoto

John Strohm

These peasant women are planting potatoes. In spite of collectivization Poland still has many small farms.

Eastfoto

Paul Hufner—Shostal

1985

Above is a new Polish steel mill located at Nowa Huta, a recently built industrial city near Krakow.

These Polish young people are dressed in colorful national costume, which is worn on festive occasions.

Most of the people of Poland are Roman Catholics. There are also a few members of the Orthodox Church and of the Lutheran, Reformed, and Baptist churches. Jews, who made up 10 percent of the population before World War II, are now estimated at under 50,000. Education is free and compulsory to the age of 14. In 1959 Poland had 57 institutions of higher learning. The largest universities are the Catholic University of Lublin, the Worclaw University, the University of Warsaw, and the Jagiellonian University (founded in 1364).

Polish history began in the 9th century, when the *Polians* (dwellers in the fields) established their authority over the other Slavic tribes in the country. The rulers accepted Christianity in 966. Gradually expanded by conquest and marriage over the next five centuries, the state reached its peak in 1569, when Poland absorbed Lithuania. The territory of the Poles then extended from the Baltic Sea to the Black Sea. A series of wars with Sweden and

Russia in the late 17th and early 18th centuries began the downfall of Poland. Internal squabbles further weakened the nation and resulted in the three partitions of Poland in the late 18th century. After the last partition, in 1795, the nation ceased to exist until 1807, when Napoleon set up the short-lived Grand Duchy of Warsaw in part of the former Polish territories. This disappeared after Napoleon's defeat in 1815. Poland was not revived as an independent country until the peace treaties following World War I. The new republic of Poland lasted until World War II, when it was conquered in simultaneous invasions by the Soviets and the Germans. It was again revived in 1945 with altered boundaries. Large parts of the German regions of Pomerania, Silesia, and East Prussia were given to Poland in exchange for large areas in the east, which were taken by the Soviet Union. Under Soviet occupation a communist form of government was established in Poland following World War II.

POLAND

Area: 120,000 sq. mi.
Population: 30,000,000
Capital: Warsaw
Largest cities: Warsaw, Lodz, Krakow, Poznan, Worclaw, Gdansk
Highest mountain peak: Rysy Peak (8,212 feet)
Chief rivers: Vistula and tributaries, Oder and tributaries
Chief lakes: Sniardwy, Mamry
Climate: Temperate—warmer summers inland—colder winters in northeast—moderate rainfall
National flag: Upper half white, lower half red
National anthem: *Jeszcze Polska nie zginela* (Poland Is Not Yet Lost)
Form of government: Communist people's republic
Unit of currency: Zloty
Language: Polish
Chief religion: Roman Catholic
Chief economic activities: Agriculture (including livestock raising), manufacturing, mining
Chief crops: Rye, wheat, barley, oats, potatoes, sugar beets, tobacco
Chief manufactures: Textiles, iron and steel, chemicals, metal and wood products, machinery, automobiles, ships, aircraft
Chief minerals: Coal, lignite, iron ore, zinc, natural gas, petroleum
Chief exports: Coal and coke, locomotives and railroad cars, ships
Chief imports: Iron ore, petroleum, fertilizers, wheat, cotton, wool

Location map

The red and white Polish national flag was adopted after World War I, when an independent Poland was established. The colors are based on those in the coat of arms.

The coat of arms of Poland depicts an eagle. Colored reproductions of this bird date from 1241. These arms are of the precommunistic period.

The stamp (below) commemorates the famous Polish composer and pianist Chopin.

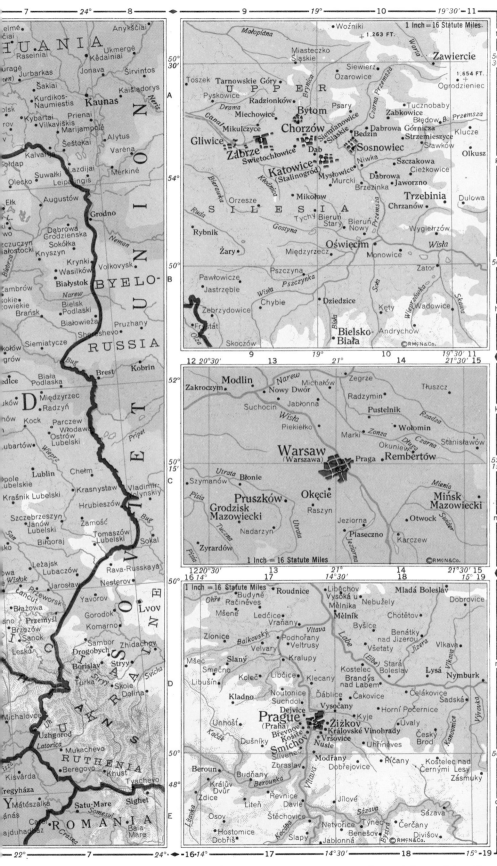

POLAR EXPLORATION, exploration carried on in the vicinity of the North Pole and the South Pole. The polar regions of the earth held out against attempts to explore them until the end of the 19th and the beginning of the 20th century. Nowhere else on earth are the elements so formidable. Yet, driven by the lure of the unknown, the thirst for adventure, and scientific curiosity, man has even conquered these regions. Indeed, as Ernest Shackleton once said, "... The stark polar lands grip the hearts of the men who have lived on them."

In the days of the first geographical conquest of Antarctica and the Arctic, explorers like Robert Peary, Ernest Shackleton, Douglas Mawson, Roald Amundsen, and Robert F. Scott used very different equipment than that in use today. In his 1907-1909 expedition Shackleton relied on his own money and that of friends. The sledges, made of ash and American hickory, were 12 feet and 7 feet long. The longest were to be drawn by horses, the others by men. Skis were provided for the men.

Shackleton's ship, the *Nimrod*, was a dilapidated sealer of only 700 tons burden. For transportation on the ice Shackleton used Siberian dogs and Manchurian ponies. One item on Shackleton's expedition heralded a new era of polar exploration. It was a 15-horsepower New Arrol-Johnson car.

Modern polar exploration is completely mechanized. Adventure is derived more from what man can learn than from what he can achieve physically. Huge areas were photographed and mapped by airplanes flown by Lincoln Ellsworth and that veteran of the North Pole and the South Pole, Admiral Richard E. Byrd. The crossing of Antarctica was done by Vivian Fuchs with a clanking caravan of tracked Sno-Cats, Weasels, and tractors. Airplanes were used to support the mechanized expedition. At the North Pole the atomic submarines *Nautilus* and *Skate* traveled beneath the ice over which Robert Peary had sledged 50 years earlier. Such expeditions, of course, cost millions of dollars and are financed by national governments. See AMUNDSEN, ROALD; BYRD, RICHARD EVELYN; FUCHS, SIR VIVIAN ERNEST; PEARY, ROBERT EDWIN; SCOTT, ROBERT FALCON; SHACKLETON, SIR ERNEST HENRY; STEFANSSON, VILHJALMUR.

POLE VAULT. See TRACK AND FIELD SPORTS.

Wide World Photo

The Navy icebreaker *Glacier*, steaming in antarctic ice floes during the 1958 Operation Deep Freeze, launches a balloon-supported rocket designed for high-altitude research.

POLICE DEPARTMENT, the agency of government designed to protect persons and property and to preserve order. The duties of the police department vary from country to country. In the United States, Great Britain, and Canada the police arrest criminals, protect the innocent, prevent crime, and perform certain welfare tasks. These welfare tasks include the major problem of traffic regulation and of handling crowds, parades, and riots. On the continent of Europe the duties of the police are sometimes more extensive. The national police force of the Republic of Ireland not only performs police duties throughout cities and rural areas but also enforces laws and regulations pertaining to school attendance, forestry and fisheries, the compilation of census and agricultural statistics, food and drugs, smuggling, pension and income-tax verification, and the maintenance of lists of voters and jurors. The specialized political police are covered elsewhere. See POLITICAL POLICE.

The lack of uniformity of police departments makes it difficult to develop a general picture of the police administration of a large city. The typical functions may be seen in the Metropolitan Police of London. The jurisdiction of the Metropolitan Police covers an area of some 800 square miles and a population of about 9,000,000. Order is maintained in this jurisdiction by about 15,500 men, who are aided in the City of London (an area of about 1 square mile) by some 700 men of the separate City police. The commissioner of police heads the Metro-

politan Police Department. A deputy commissioner is second in command. The department is divided into the uniformed branch, which handles patrol and traffic duties, and the Criminal Investigation Department (CID). Some 1,500 detectives belong to the CID, most of them assigned to ordinary detective work, while several hundred are members of the Special Branch, which protects prominent persons, handles subversion, and observes seaports and airports. Other branches of the CID include the Central Criminal Record Office, the Fingerprint Office, and the Fraud Squad. Scotland Yard is the central headquarters of the Metropolitan Police. Recruits are given some 10 to 17 weeks' training at Peel House; detectives receive further training at the Metropolitan Police Training School. In addition, there is the National Police School at Ryton. The ranks of the Metropolitan Police are those of constable (patrolman in the United States), sergeant (two ranks), inspector (two ranks), and superintendent (two ranks).

Sometimes persons may be apprehended in the act of crime. Often, however, much effort goes into locating a criminal. The pioneer in modern ideas of tracing and identifying criminals was Hugo von Jagemann, a judge of Baden, Germany. The patrolman or detective develops sources of information. These may be popular hangouts or the offices of criminal records maintained by police departments. Sometimes a suspect must be trailed, a task that demands patience and endurance.

Once located, the suspect must be identified as the criminal. Alphonse Bertillon, of the Paris police, developed a measurement system of identification based on the thesis that no two men are exactly alike. His method was immediately effective and was adopted in other countries, although in the early 1900's it was displaced by the science of identification by means of fingerprints, or dactyloscopy. The method of fingerprint classification used in Europe and the United States is the Henry-Galton system, introduced in Scotland Yard in 1901. Spain and much of Latin America use a system devised by the Argentinian Juan Vucetich. Dactyloscopy is also valuable in tracing missing persons and identifying corpses, a major contribution of police departments. Even the tiniest trace of a fingerprint can often be identified through the science of poroscopy—identification by means of sweat pores. (See FINGERPRINT.) Bertillon also developed the *portrait parlé*, a precise system of describing an individual, which is useful to policemen, most of whom are trained to be perceptive witnesses. Criminal photography, a useful identification device, was improved by Bertillon, and Paris had the first police photographic studio.

A modern development in police methods is the police laboratory. Police laboratories, which are of little use in some cases, have often resulted in solutions of difficult cases. Moreover, the laboratory is valuable in less dramatic crimes, such as forgery, burglary, and theft. The head of such a laboratory may be an experienced detective aided by a

In this Los Angeles police office radio contact is maintained with all units in the field.

chemist, physicist, or biologist. Under his authority are technicians and detectives trained for special field work. These laboratories may measure and compare clues gathered at the scene of a crime—fingerprints, for example. They also chemically examine narcotics, bloodstains, and explosives; physically examine tool impressions, broken locks, or broken windows; identify persons by means of footprints, teeth, and laundry marks; study documents for forgeries or secret inks; conduct ballistic tests to identify weapons; and photograph the scene of the crime (or of an automobile accident and the like). The use of forensic medicine has been of inestimable value in identifying the cause of death and in determining

whether a death is suicide, natural, or murder. As a result of police laboratory work it was possible in one case to identify a burglar from impressions left on a lock by a screwdriver in his possession. The study of broken windows, developed by the Russian criminologist Matwejeff, has been used to prove that windows were broken from inside a room in burglaries simulated in order to collect insurance. Nevertheless the work of the conscientious patrolman is still the backbone of the police department.

Once they are identified and apprehended, it is necessary to interrogate the suspect or the witnesses to a crime. The notorious third degree, extracting confessions by beating or prolonged questioning, has not disappeared, but evidence shown to have been obtained in this way will be ruled out as evidence in court. Progressive criminal investigators, however, utilize psychology. By shrewd questioning an experienced interrogator may be able to extract valuable information or even a confession from a suspect. After having observed that lying causes physiological disturbances, Cesare Lombroso in the 19th century suggested measuring the blood pressure and respiratory changes in suspects under questioning. The polygraph, which measured blood pressure and other physiological changes, was later devised. It has been replaced by more efficient lie detectors, such as the Pathometer and the Psycho-Detecto-Meter, which measure electrical changes in the body of the suspect. In the hands of an expert the lie detector may bring about a

Traffic policemen must often warn or fine motorists who have broken traffic regulations.

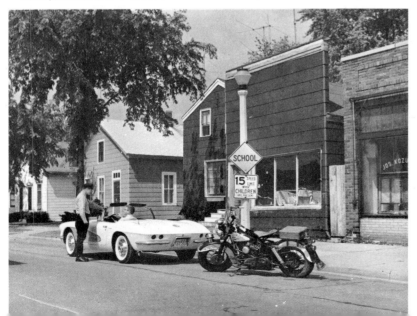

A police officer has practice in handling certain small arms as part of his training.

confession that is acceptable in court. Most courts still do not consider the lie detector adequate enough to be admitted as evidence over the objection of a defendant.

The police department in the modern sense was not recognized until the Parliament Act of 1787 in England and is often dated from the establishment of the Metropolitan Police of London in 1829. Thereafter, police systems developed in most nations. The police system of the United States is highly decentralized. The federal government, the states, and local communities operate independent police departments. In small communities the sheriff or constable, generally an elected officer, comprises the police department. Larger towns and cities have police departments headed by a chief of police, who is under the authority of the mayor and city council, commission, board, or city manager. The states operate police forces that are equipped to patrol highways and to work in rural communities. The federal police protect federal revenue (Intelligence Unit of the Bureau of Internal Revenue, the Alcohol Tax Unit, and the Division of Investigation and Patrol of the Bureau of Customs), investigate violations of federal laws and uncover espionage (Federal Bureau of Investigation), suppress the narcotics racket (Bureau of Narcotics under the Department of the Treasury), and investigate violations of laws concerning the mails (Bureau of the Chief Inspector of the Post Office Department). There are several other federal police forces, such as the U.S. Secret Service, whose functions are to prevent counter-feiting and forgery of government checks and to protect the president and the vice president of the United States.

The police system of Canada is also highly decentralized, consisting of independent municipal police in all the larger urban centers. Ontario and Quebec maintain provincial police departments. The Royal Canadian Mounted Police is a federal force with wide jurisdiction and numerous duties other than police work. See MOUNTED POLICE, ROYAL CANADIAN.

Great Britain's police system is only partially decentralized. Boroughs have a chief constable controlled by the Watch Committee of the local town council. The counties may have separate police departments headed by a chief constable (who is more powerful than the borough constable) under the direction of a joint committee comprised of justices of the courts and members appointed from among the county council. Many of the counties and boroughs have combined their police forces. These police departments (in England and Wales) are partially under the control of the national Home Office, which is the direct authority over the police of London. However, this control is exercised mainly through financial assistance from the national government.

The French police system is typical of a more centralized system. The minister of the interior controls the Sûreté Nationale, which has several branches, including the city police forces, which perform normal police functions; the Judicial Police Force, which specializes in investigating major crimes; the Republican Security Guards, a mobile emergency unit that normally assists city police forces and guards sensitive areas; the Area Surveillance Police Force, a counterintelligence unit; and the general intelligence, which controls the movements of travelers and informs the government on public-opinion trends. The Sûreté Nationale also includes the prefecture of police for Paris and its environs. The Paris chief of police has extensive duties, which include, besides ordinary police work, passport administration, sanitation control, and the implementation of labor legislation. The minister of armed forces directs, on behalf of all government ministries (and especially the ministries of interior, justice, and finance), the Gendarmerie Nationale. The two arms of the Gendarmerie Nationale provide public security in rural areas, highway traffic control, and general police service and military service, such as apprehension of deserters.

The secret-police organization of the Soviet Union is well known, but an ordinary police force, called the militia, also exists. The militia has a uniformed branch and a detective branch and operates excellent police laboratories.

The International Criminal Police Commission (ICPC), the telegraphic address of which is Interpol, was established in 1923 under the patronage of the police commissioner of Vienna. The ICPC facilitates the cooperation of police systems of member nations. Its headquarters are in Paris. It publishes in French and English the *International Criminal Police Review*. See CRIMINOLOGY; FEDERAL BUREAU OF INVESTIGATION; PENOLOGY.

Jonas Salk developed one of the first successful antipoliomyelitis vaccines.

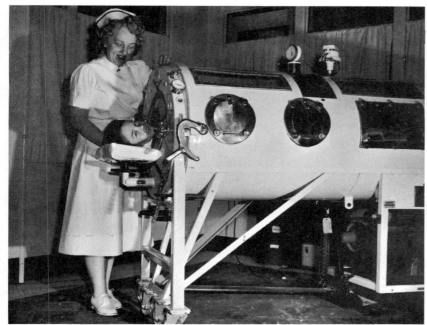

Natl. Foundation for Infantile Paralysis

An invaluable aid in the treatment of poliomyelitis is the iron lung for assisting breathing.

POLIOMYELITIS, or infantile paralysis, is an acute disease involving the central nervous system and producing weakness and paralysis of the voluntary muscles. The cause is a virus, of which there are several strains. The virus is found chiefly in the alimentary tract and the central nervous system. The disease may be mild, with symptoms limited to the gastrointestinal and the respiratory tracts. Early symptoms —malaise, headache, low-grade fever, sore throat, nausea, and vomiting—mimic those of many acute infections. These symptoms are followed by spasm and pain in the neck, back, and thighs. Treatment during the acute stage is aimed at saving life, relieving symptoms, and preventing deformities. Physical therapy is important in restoring muscle function. A vaccine against polio was introduced in 1955. Developed by Jonas Salk, it was made of the three strains of the virus killed with formaldehyde. Subsequently, a live poliovirus vaccine for oral administration was developed under the auspices of the U.S. Public Health Services.

POLITICAL PARTY, an independent organization of people who make nominations and compete in elections with the hope of gaining control of the machinery of government. The political party is the major social institution interested in public affairs as a whole. Democracy can-

not operate without competing political parties.

The concept of party suggests that it is a group that propounds a platform, or program of action, differing from the programs of other groups. The political party competes with other political parties in furthering its own program. Thus, for a political party to exist as such it is necessary that at least one other competitor exist. This may not be true of totalitarian parties that stamp out all organized opposition within a state, but these compete in effect against opposition from outside the state. All political parties seek to participate in the governmental policymaking process. They must have at least a chance to gain power. The Christian Democratic Union of the German Democratic Republic, which has no chance of influencing policy, serves only as a façade for the one-party rule of the Communist-controlled Socialist Unity Party. Vital to the successful operation of the political-party system of democracies is the loyalty of these parties to certain broad social concepts—constitutionalism, freedom of the individual, and so on. Thus, while political parties may differ bitterly on certain specific policies, they are in accord on enough points so that they may coexist in the same state.

The major task of the political party is to clarify, systematize, and propound as the party program cer-

tain facets of the public will. By propaganda and campaigning the party may educate the voter and point up the issues on which the voter must exercise a choice. In democracies political parties are the bridge that connects social interests and ideals to the policymaking apparatus of government. In this respect it is difficult to differentiate the political party from the pressure group or lobby. The political party, however, although it resembles in some ways the pressure group, is also aware of a responsiblity to the society as a whole. Finally, the political-party system offers a method of choosing governmental leaders. In the days of monarchies the leader of a state held his position on the basis of hereditary succession. This system sometimes resulted in effective heads of state but often brought weak, extravagant, and even insane rulers to the throne. The political-party system, while not perfect, offers a greater number of citizens a voice in the selection of leadership.

The most immediate method of classifying political parties is to distinguish between the party in power and the opposition. The party in power will defend things as they are, while the opposition party will advocate policy change or reform. In Great Britain the party out of power has a definite status as the loyal opposition and is expected not only to criticize but to present constructive alternative policies to the governing party. Parties may also be differentiated as parties of well-known persons (traditionally, the Radical Socialist party of France) or as parties of programs (the Communist party of France). Classification of parties may be made on the basis of class (the British Labor party represents in the main the working class), religion (the Lebanese Chamber of Deputies is composed of representatives of Maronite Christian, Sunni Moslem, Shia Moslem, and others), nationality (the Swedish People's party of Finland), and outlook on foreign policy.

Classification of parties may also be made on the basis of the type of party system they give rise to— one, two, or multiparty systems. The one-party system may be dictatorial or totalitarian. Examples are the National Socialist German Workers party of Nazi Germany, the Communist parties of Communist states, and the Fascist party of Mussolini's government. On the other hand, the one-party system may exist in newly liberated demo-

John F. Kennedy speaks in New Jersey in the presidential campaign of 1960. The candidates tried to appeal to voters through personality as well as approach to issues.

cratic nations. For example, the Indian National Congress party, popular for its role in the independence movement, has effectively controlled India, although opposition parties exist. The case is similar with the Party of Revolutionary Institutions in Mexico. The two-party system exists in the United States (Democratic and Republican parties), Great Britain (Conservative and Labour parties), New Zealand (National and Labour parties), Canada (Progressive Conservative and Liberal parties), and Australia (Liberal and Labour parties). Countries that have sharper divisions in the social structure—nationality, religious, class, or regional differences—may have a multiparty system. In such countries the government may be formed by a coalition among certain of the parties. Multiparty systems operate in Brazil, Panama, Iceland, Israel, Switzerland, France, Scandinavia, and Finland.

POLITICAL PARTY ORGANIZATION IN THE UNITED STATES.
The U.S. Constitution does not prescribe party organization, which grew, historically, through trial and error. The organization of the Democratic and Republican parties is in part voluntary, and in part it is controlled by state laws. Smaller parties are usually too insignificant to be affected by law and are allowed to create their own party organization.

Each of the two major parties is directed by a national convention, which replaced the caucus during the 1830's. Delegates to national conventions are chosen in party primaries, in which all party members may vote, or in state party conventions. The number of delegates is roughly equal to twice the electoral vote of the state. Because of the power of political machines in the 19th century, these primaries were regulated and the date for them was set by state laws. Some states went even further and defined the requirements for membership in a political party. In the first decade of the 20th century many states adopted the direct primary, in which the party members vote directly for party nominees rather than for convention delegates. The national convention did not give up its liberty of action, however. In the 1920's some states returned to the system of state conventions or repealed their presidential-primary laws.

The national convention elects members to a national committee, which consists of one man and one woman from each state and the District of Columbia. These committeemen assume office ten days after the adjournment of the national convention and hold office until the next national committee takes over. The members of the national committee are nominated by state delegations (which are bound by state laws when these exist) and are elected at the national convention.

The national committee in theory (but not in practice) directs the presidential campaign. A chairman is selected by the party's candidate for president. The chairman is responsible for all the duties of the committee, for issuing the call for the next national convention, and for examining the credentials of the delegates to the next convention.

Although the national convention is the supreme representative of the party (it adopts the party platform, for example), the work of the committee proceeds between meetings of the convention. In theory, a successful presidential candidate is the leader of his party and its policies, for he has chosen the chairman of the national committee. The de-

Richard M. Nixon greets the crowd outside his hotel in Chicago, where the Republicans nominated him as their presidential candidate in the 1960 campaign.

HOW A U.S. POLITICAL PARTY IS ORGANIZED

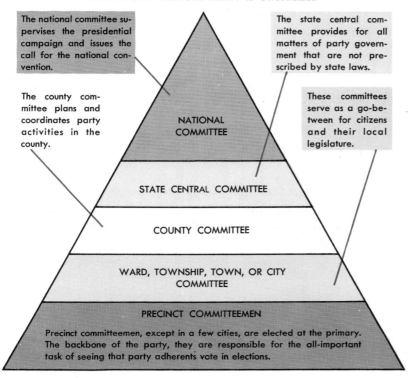

The national committee supervises the presidential campaign and issues the call for the national convention.

The state central committee provides for all matters of party government that are not prescribed by state laws.

The county committee plans and coordinates party activities in the county.

These committees serve as a go-between for citizens and their local legislature.

NATIONAL COMMITTEE

STATE CENTRAL COMMITTEE

COUNTY COMMITTEE

WARD, TOWNSHIP, TOWN, OR CITY COMMITTEE

PRECINCT COMMITTEEMEN

Precinct committeemen, except in a few cities, are elected at the primary. The backbone of the party, they are responsible for the all-important task of seeing that party adherents vote in elections.

feated candidate does not always retain this leadership, however, and may easily lose control of the party, for example, to influential senators, who are backed by state political machines.

Working in liaison with the national committee are the independent congressional and senatorial committees. The congressional committee consists of one member from each state that has a party representative in the House of Representatives. This member is chosen by the state delegation in Congress for a two-year term. The congressional committee, as well as the senatorial committee, maintains a small staff in Washington, D.C., and works to get party members elected. The senatorial committee of each party is picked by the chairman of the party's Senate caucus.

Within each state the parties have special delegation conventions for each territorial area from which officers are elected—the assembly district convention, the county convention, the judicial district convention, and so forth. Each of these conventions has a committee that carries on its work after the convention is over. These various committees maintain liaison with other committees in the hierarchy up to

the state committee. The composition, selection, and importance of the committees vary from state to state. In some states all the committeemen may be elected at the primaries. In other states members may be selected at the area conventions. In any case, while the national party committees are a purely party affair, the state and local organization is prescribed by state laws.

In a typical state the party organization consists of the precinct committee, the city committee, the county committee, the congressional-district committee, and the state central committee. The basis of this party structure is the precinct, within which area the primary is generally held. The precinct committeeman "gets out the party vote" and develops party contacts with the individual voter. To complicate matters, the chairman of the state committee, which is the highest party authority in the state and controls all party affairs not controlled by state law, is not always the real party leader. Power may be in the hands of a governor, a senator, or a man behind the scenes. The true hierarchy of power in a political party may depend more on the men and women who compose the party than on the party structure.

POLITICAL POLICE, a special police force whose function is to deal with illegal political opposition to an existing regime. Since earliest times rulers and governments have employed domestic spies and private bodyguards and have administered swift and arbitrary punishment for political offenses. But the formal combination of these elements into political police organizations is a relatively recent development.

Every modern government has its secret service, whose tasks include safeguarding the state against internal enemies. However, in a Western democracy, where political dissent is associated with free speech and a free press, the powers of such organizations are severely limited by law. For example, in the United States no separate body of national political police has ever existed. To be sure, the Federal Bureau of Investigation, as part of its job, investigates persons suspected of conspiracy or illegal acts against the security of the nation and arrests them if evidence warrants. The FBI must present this evidence to the courts, which will try the accused, establish their guilt or innocence, and levy any necessary punishment. In autocratic states the political police often possess these powers; they serve as investigator, prosecutor, judge, and jailer-executioner.

The common features of modern political police are all too familiar to people of today. Whether units of the civil police or of the army, they exhibit a highly disciplined, centralized, military type of organization. They may wear a special uniform, although much of their work is done under cover by plainclothesmen. The latter spy on suspects and often infiltrate their groups. Some techniques of the political police are calculated to inspire fear in the populace and thus to discourage resistance. Informers are planted everywhere. Arrests are made at night, and trials are held in secret. Torture is used freely in interrogating prisoners, and severe penalties—usually long imprisonment or death—are meted out. Because of their efficiency and discipline the political police are often assigned additional vital functions. Sometimes they become so powerful that they actually constitute a state within a state. When they acquire such powers, they are a danger to the very government they are supposed to protect.

The best examples of modern political police are to be found in the great dictatorships of the 20th century. Here there exists the constant threat of an uprising against the party or class in power, and political opposition must be controlled or suppressed. In Nazi Germany the Gestapo was set up in 1933 and under Reinhard Heydrich became part of the Main Security Office of the Reich. Ultimate control was exercised by Heinrich Himmler, leader of the dreaded SS (Schutzstaffel). At first the Gestapo concentrated on suspected opponents to Hitler's regime. Later it became the instrument for terrorizing the populations of the countries conquered by Germany. Finally, as the spearhead of the SS, it became deeply involved in the grisly work of the concentration camps and in the attempted extermination of the Jews.

The most elaborate system of political police is that of the U.S.S.R., which has its roots in the autocratic tradition of the czars. After the Decembrist Revolt of 1825, Nicholas I created a political police unit called the Third Section. It was responsible only to him and was charged with the elimination of all resistance to his despotic rule. Alexander II, a more liberal emperor, abolished it in 1880. However, when he himself was assassinated by a political terrorist in 1881, an even stronger police force was established by his successor, Alexander III. It in turn was abolished by the provisional government in 1917. In the period of terror that followed the revolution the Bolsheviks set up an extraordinary commission called the Cheka to combat counterrevolutionary elements. After the civil war this was replaced by a permanent system of political police—in 1922 by the GPU and in 1934 by the NKVD. The latter played a major part in the mass purges of the 1930's in the Soviet Union. After World War II the NKVD became the MVD, and under Stalin its vast authority was zealously maintained and exercised. But in 1953, after Stalin's death, the MVD's powers were somewhat reduced, and its chief, Lavrenti Beria, was executed. Nevertheless, the political police remain a major prop of the Soviet regime. Its agents are to be found everywhere—in apartment buildings, factories, schools, collective farms, and even in the army. Among its numerous extra functions is the administration of a vast network of forced labor camps and the hiring out of the inmates of the camps to Soviet industrial enterprises. See GESTAPO; MVD.

POLITICAL SCIENCE, a branch of study that is concerned with the theory, organization, and activities of the state. It treats of those relations among people that are regulated by the state, of relationships of individuals or groups to the state, of relationships between one branch of government and another, and of relations among states. The words *government* and *politics* are not synonymous with political science, although it treats of both government and politics.

The field of political science comprises a number of divisions. Political theory, or political philosophy, tries to generalize and to draw conclusions on the basis of facts and observations gathered in other branches of political science and in many other fields of knowledge. Some political scientists regard political theory as the heart of the subject that ties all the other branches together. Political dynamics is the study of the forces (psychological, moral, social, and economic) that affect politics and government. Public law deals with the constitutional and legal principles controlling relations between states, relations between the various branches or agencies of the government, and relations between the state and the citizen. Public law is comprised of constitutional law, administrative regulations, and international law. The study of public administration, a relatively new branch of political science, deals with management and bureaucracy in government affairs. It covers the handling of personnel, the management of funds, and the organization of administration. Before World War I international relations was not regarded as a distinct field of political science. Since then, however, there has been increasing interest in international relations, which includes international politics, international law, international organization, foreign policy, and diplomacy. Most universities require students to have a thorough knowledge of their own government. Comparative government consists of a historical, descriptive, and analytical study of types of governments. Such a branch notes the similarities and differences between the governments, for example, of Canada, Germany, France, the Soviet Union, and India. A final division of political science is the study of government-business relations.

In recent decades the emphasis in political-science teaching has been on the fundamental relationships underlying the development of gov-

OCCUPATION: Political Scientist

NATURE OF WORK: Study of government at every level

PERSONAL FACTORS—ABILITIES, SKILLS, APTITUDES: An aptitude for research and detail, accuracy, and the ability to lead and to deal with people effectively and to express oneself clearly and simply are needed.

EDUCATION AND SPECIAL TRAINING: A master's degree is generally required for most positions. The Ph.D. is necessary for most teaching jobs.

WORKING CONDITIONS:
1. INCOME:
   COMPARED WITH OTHER CAREERS WITH EQUAL TRAINING: Average
   COMPARED WITH MOST OTHER CAREERS: Average
2. ENVIRONMENT: Educational institutions, research work, private industry, or government agencies.
3. OTHER: Regular hours; usual benefits; occasional travel; moderate opportunities

RELATED CAREERS: Historian, sociologist, politician, lawyer, diplomat, public administrator

WHERE TO FIND MORE INFORMATION: American Political Science Association, 1726 Massachusetts Avenue NW, Washington 6, D.C.

ernment. The descriptive treatment of the structure of government has given way to an extent to the study of the psychological and sociological bases of public opinion, political parties, pressure groups, policy formation, propaganda, and revolution and political reform. Political science has tended to revert to the broad concept of the subject held by Plato and Aristotle. As a result, political science draws upon economics, philosophy, sociology, anthropology, statistics, history, geography, and psychology.

Political science is not a precise science in the sense that chemistry and mechanics are. Its conclusions cannot be expressed in formulas. It cannot predict with the accuracy of the physical sciences. Yet, it operates in accordance with the scientific method. It is a body of knowledge about a definite subject, and this knowledge is gathered by systematic experience and observation and is studied, analyzed, and classified. Moreover, generalizations may be made on the basis of this knowledge, and conclusions of a practical nature may be derived.

A number of methods are used in the conduct of studies in political science. The investigator observes by interviews and statistical studies. He remains critical of his sources of information. While political scientists do not experiment in the sense that chemists do, they consider each new law or policy an experiment and observe its effect in followup studies. The statistical method is used where data can be measured or counted. Such a method is valuable in assessing population growth and in evaluating public opinion and voting trends. The biological method, made popular by Herbert Spencer, studies states by analogy with evolution or living organisms. This method, sometimes fruitful but always treacherous, has fallen from favor in the 20th century. The psychological method has been used by political scientists since Machiavelli and Thomas Hobbes. It seeks to explain political phenomena by studying human motivations. The legalistic method, popular for a time in Germany, studies the political society from the point of view of legal rights and obligations. The historical method seeks through historical facts to describe and explain the development of political institutions. The comparative method— the chief approach of U.S. political scientists in the last half of the 19th century and of Aristotle, Montesquieu, De Tocqueville, and James Bryce—develops general laws by comparing governmental systems. The philosophical or theoretical method draws conclusions from abstractions of the nature and purpose of the state. Theories derived in this fashion must then be tested on the basis of historical and contemporary facts. The geography-oriented approach, utilized in geopolitics, considers the development of political institutions from the standpoint of geographical studies of waterways, mountain ranges, and seacoasts. Most political scientists utilize all these methods to an extent.

The objectives of the subject are to produce good citizens, to train students for careers in public affairs, and to impart important aspects of the cultural heritage. The contemporary issues studied by political scientists include peace, the future of democracy, and the reform of imperfect political institutions.

POLITICS, the efforts concerned with obtaining or adjusting power among states, groups, or individuals. Those who engage in politics do so in order that they may further aims or ideals or obtain power for its own sake. Politics is the very life of a democracy. But there are no nations or organizations in which politics plays no role. To speak of eliminating politics from government is to speak of the impossible. Politics is the art of government.

The word *politics* derives from the Greek word *polis*, which means "city." In ancient Greece the city was the most important political unit, just as the state is at present. Long before the word was invented, however, politics existed. Politics is as old as human society. In the Bible, for example, one learns of the great ability of Absalom as a politician (2 Sam. 15:1-6). However, *politics* and *politician* became words with a slightly unsavory meaning. Shakespeare in his plays makes five references to politicians, all of them bad. Since then many a professional or military man has entered the political arena with the announcement that he is "not a politician." This is scarcely possible. To "throw the rascal politicians out" can only be accomplished by placing good politicians in their place. Everyone who votes or applauds (or protests) a political speech is engaging in political activity. And a great statesman is, of necessity, a great politician.

In a democracy politics should be everyone's avocation, because political decisions will ultimately affect everyone's life. Some people adopt it as a vocation. These people are those who like controversy. To be a politician a person must frequently "take a stand." This is one reason, perhaps, why so many politicians are lawyers. During the French Revolution the National Assembly consisted almost totally of lawyers. Many U.S. senators and representatives also have a background in law. A good politician should also have devotion to a cause. This cause may be humanitarian, national, social, religious, or cul-

OCCUPATION: Politician
NATURE OF WORK: Upholding the principles of the country while conducting the business of government
PERSONAL FACTORS—ABILITIES, SKILLS, APTITUDES: A politician should have some administrative ability, foresight, an unselfish devotion to the interests of the country, a liking for people, an interest in government, the ability to speak and write well, and high ethical standards.
EDUCATION AND SPECIAL TRAINING: No formal education is required. Education in law or business is helpful. On-the-job training is essential.
WORKING CONDITIONS:
1. **INCOME:** **COMPARED WITH OTHER CAREERS WITH EQUAL TRAINING:** Variable **COMPARED WITH MOST OTHER CAREERS:** Variable
2. **ENVIRONMENT:** Variable—from large, open gatherings to governmental offices and caucus rooms
3. **OTHER:** Irregular hours; physical and mental strain; few benefits; excellent opportunities for everyone
RELATED CAREERS: Lawyer, statesman, political scientist, economist, psychologist
WHERE TO FIND MORE INFORMATION: Democratic National Committee, Ring Building, Washington 6, D.C.; Republican National Committee, 923 15 Street NW, Washington 5, D.C.

tural. He should have the ability to look at realities calmly and with concentration. Since politics is the "art of the possible," the politician must always decide what is possible and what is not. A good politician in a democracy should also have a sense of responsibility. He should not hold power for his own sake but for the good of the community. See GOVERNMENT; POLITICAL SCIENCE.

National nominating conventions are a dramatic and colorful part of the U.S. political scene.
Wide World Photo

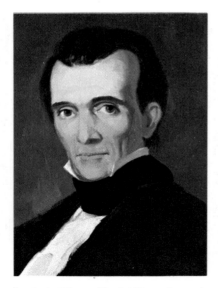

Rarely in U.S. presidential history has such an extensive and varied program as that proposed by James K. Polk been carried into action during the course of a single term.

POLK, JAMES KNOX (1795-1849), 11th president of the United States, born in Mecklenberg Co., North Carolina, on Nov. 2, 1795. He was of Irish descent, and his father was a farmer. In 1825 he was elected to Congress, where he served for 14 years. He then became governor of Tennessee. He was nominated for the presidency by the Democratic party in 1844 and was elected on a platform favoring the annexation of Texas and Oregon. The question of the annexation of Texas, touchy because it involved the slavery issue, had been settled at the end of Tyler's administration, but the problem of carrying it out was left to Polk. Disputes over the boundary line led to war with Mexico, which ended in the annexation not only of disputed territory but of California, New Mexico, and parts of Utah, Nevada, Arizona, and Colorado in exchange for a payment to Mexico of $15,000,000. The Oregon question was settled by the division of the territory, which extended to the border of Alaska, along the 49th parallel, England taking the part to the north and the United States the part to the south of this line. Polk was consistent and determined in all his policies. He supported a tariff large enough for revenue only and did not believe in a bank of the United States, although he supported the idea of a national treasury. He refused to be a candidate for reelection. He died in Nashville on June 15, 1849.

POLKA is a lively round dance, of Bohemian origin, that is performed by two people. The dance attained great popularity during the mid-19th century. The accompanying dance tune, to which the term is also applied, is written in two-four time, with steps occurring on the first three half beats of each measure.

POLLEN AND POLLINATION. The pollen of most plants appears to the naked eye to be a fine yellow dust. Pollen is produced only by angiosperms and gymnosperms, the highest plants in the evolutionary scale. The dust consists of individual grains of minute size. Pollen grains effect the formation of male reproductive cells, or sperms, which later fertilize the female reproductive cells, or eggs, of plants. The pollen grains of angiosperms are developed within anthers, which are the enlarged, often cylindrical, topmost portions of the stamens of flowers. The pollen grains of gymnospermous coniferous trees, such as the pine and spruce, are produced by their small pollen cones.

Pollination occurs differently in angiosperms than in gymnosperms. In angiosperms it is the transfer of pollen grains from an anther to a stigma, the enlarged upper portion of the pistil of a flower. Cross-pollination is the transfer of pollen from an anther of a flower of one plant to the stigma of a flower of another plant. Self-pollination is the transfer of pollen from an anther of a flower to the stigma of the same flower or of another flower on the same plant. The flowers of apples, pears, and grapes are usually cross-pollinated, whereas those of wheat, oats, and peas are usually self-pollinated. In most angiosperms—including roses, apples, willows, and sunflowers—pollen is transferred by insects, chiefly bees. In some angiosperms, including oaks, corn, and most grasses, it is transferred by wind.

Pollen grains, upon maturing, lie exposed on the anthers. The pollen of most insect-pollinated plants is sticky and adheres readily to the body of a bee visiting the flower in search of nectar. When the bee flies to another flower, the pollen grains adhering to its body sometimes rub onto the stigma of the other flower, and pollination occurs.

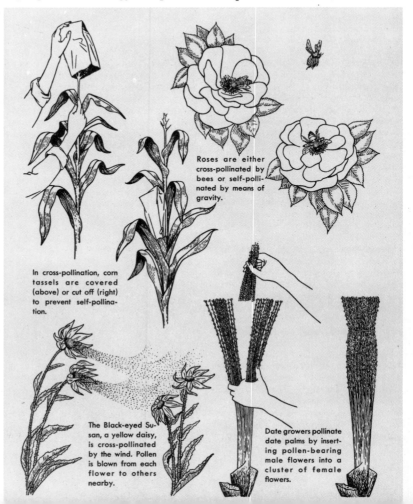

In cross-pollination, corn tassels are covered (above) or cut off (right) to prevent self-pollination.

Roses are either cross-pollinated by bees or self-pollinated by means of gravity.

The Black-eyed Susan, a yellow daisy, is cross-pollinated by the wind. Pollen is blown from each flower to others nearby.

Date growers pollinate date palms by inserting pollen-bearing male flowers into a cluster of female flowers.

While adhering to the stigma a pollen grain develops a pollen tube, which grows downward through the style of the pistil and into the ovary at its base. While the pollen tube is growing downward, two sperms are formed within it. The pollen tube then penetrates an ovule within the ovary and finally penetrates the embryo sac, which is inside the ovule. One of the sperms from the pollen tube then unites with, or fertilizes, the egg, which lies within the embryo sac. The fertilized egg then develops into a plant embryo.

In gymnospermous (coniferous) trees the mature pollen grains are shed from the pollen cones and are borne by the wind to the seed cones, which in most species grow on the same tree. Some pollen grains alight near the ovules, which lie exposed on the upper surfaces of the scales of the seed cones. After several months to a year or more a sperm, which develops from a pollen grain, fertilizes an egg, which is located within an ovule. The fertilized egg then develops into a plant embryo.

POLL TAX, a tax levied on the person of a citizen rather than on his income or property. It is often called a head tax, for each individual must pay the same amount. Since it is not a graduated tax, the poll tax weighs most heavily on those least able to pay it.

The poll tax was popular in all the American colonies. It constituted Maryland's only direct tax prior to the Revolutionary War. Provisions in the state constitutions of Maryland, Ohio, and California forbid the levying of the poll tax. A majority of the states, however, allow the collection of the poll tax. The amount may range from $1 to $5 a year. In some states the tax is used for schools. Some southern states use it as a requirement for the exercise of the right to vote.

POLLUX is the brighter of the famous twin stars Pollux and Castor in the constellation the Twins (Gemini). It is about 35 light-years from us. A few centuries ago Castor was brighter than Pollux. Astronomers have not yet learned which star is causing the change.

The brightest star in a constellation is usually named alpha, the next brightest, beta, and so on, using the letters of the Greek alphabet. The twin stars were given their Greek names when Castor was still brightest, so Pollux is named Beta Geminorum even though it is now the brightest.

Geschichte des Zeitalters, Ruge, 1881,
NYPL and AMERICAN HERITAGE
Marco Polo told Europeans of China's riches.

POLO, MARCO (1254?-1324?), a Venetian traveler, the most famous of the medieval adventurers, whose records of his observations and travels in the Middle East and Far East have had a great and lasting effect on the world. At a young age Marco accompanied his father and uncle, who were merchants, on their second trip to China and the court of the Mongol ruler Kublai Khan. The Polos had been sent by the khan as envoys to the pope to request 100 educated men to serve as teachers. They were unsuccessful in bringing these missionaries with them.

Traveling overland from Venice, in Italy, across Persia and the Pamirs and the desert of Gobi of central China, they reached Peking in northern China in 1275 after a four-year journey. They were warmly received by the Mongol leader, and Marco (then about 21 years old) soon came into high favor with the khan. The young lad traveled over much of China and neighboring regions in the service of Kublai.

The Polos, wishing to return home, found the khan reluctant to have them leave. However, in 1292 they were members of a party on a sea voyage, escorting a princess to Persia. The Polos continued to Venice, where they arrived in 1295. As a result of his many tales Marco received the nickname of "Marco Millioni" from his incredulous friends.

Marco's book of his adventures was dictated in 1298, while he was a prisoner of war in Genoa, in Italy, to a fellow captive. The book, which was to have worldwide appeal, was the first to tell of the magnificence of the Eastern world, of the various kingdoms and remote regions Marco visited, the brilliant court of Peking, and the wealth and vastness of China. It became a source of information, then as it is now, about China under the Mongols.

POLO, which originated in the East, was known in ancient Persia by the name *Changan* (mallet) and in Tibet as *Pulu* (willow), a word that became *polo*. The modern game was first played in India. In 1850 British planters of Assam joined in the local games and in 1859 founded the Cachar Polo Club—the oldest in the world. Three years later polo was played in Calcutta, where the army and the reigning princes adopted the game enthusiastically. The game was taken to England by army officers and soon spread to America, where the first international match for the Westchester Cup took place in Newport, R.I., in 1886. Today the Argentines stand as undisputed leaders of the polo world, yet the game is played the world over by men as well as by women—as in former times.

The official dimensions of a polo ground are 300 yards overall length and 200 yards width (160 yards for a boarded ground). Penalty lines are at 30 yards and 60 yards. A "spot" is placed centrally at 40 yards from each goalpost. The halfway line is short; the safety zone is 10 yards beyond the side boundaries and 20 yards beyond the back lines. Goalposts are 8 yards apart. It is interesting to note that at Isfahan, Iran, there are ancient goalposts 8 yards wide and 300 yards apart, exactly the measurements in use today.

The game is conducted by two umpires, with a referee on the sideline to whom appeal is made when necessary. Each side has four players—two forwards, one halfback, and one back. Each player is handicapped according to his ability, and all players must play right-handed. The game is usually divided into eight periods of $7\frac{1}{2}$ minutes each, but since 1945 big tournaments are played in six periods (chukkers) and smaller contests in four or five periods.

Play is started by throwing the ball ($3\frac{1}{4}$ inches in diameter, $4\frac{1}{2}$ ounces in weight) into the middle of the ground, the object being to hit the ball through the opponents' goal. The polo stick, which averages 52 inches long and over 1 pound in weight (the head weighing about half of the total), is attached to the wrist by a strap. Much practice is required to use it properly. The game is played on ponies. An unmounted rider cannot score a goal. The team that scores the greater number of goals at the conclusion of the 60 minutes of play is declared the winner.

POLONAISE, a slow, stately march in three-four time. As a dance it was performed at official court functions in Poland at least as early as the 16th century. Some believe the dance originated as a march of triumph among warriors, with women partners being added later. Some believe that it originated from a processional folk dance of the Polish peasantry; it was probably taken over by members of the court circle and made ceremonial. In any case, when Henry of Anjou acceded to the throne of Poland in 1573, the French word *polonaise* was given to the grand promenade performed in his honor by ladies of the Polish court.

Among 18th-century composers the polonaise was understood to mean a general type of folk music of eastern Europe rather than a specifically Polish song or dance. Like the stately march, the music was grave and ceremonious. It was written in three-four time, and characteristically the first beat of the measure was syncopated. Bach sometimes included the polonaise in his suites, and several of his contemporaries wrote polonaises as separate pieces. Handel, Mozart, Schubert, and Beethoven all made use of the form. But Chopin is undoubtedly the best known composer of polonaises. In his hands this piece became a personal expression of the patriotism, ardor, and nostalgia of the exile for his country.

POLONIUM. See SELENIUM, TELLURIUM, POLONIUM.

POLYMERIZATION is the formation of one large molecule from many smaller molecules by chemical reactions. The initial molecules that are combined are called monomers. The resulting large molecule is called a polymer, high polymer, or a macromolecule. One polymer molecule may contain several thousand monomer units. Many polymerization reactions involve organic substances. Polymerization products are used in fibers, plastics, films, and protective coatings. Some well-known synthetic-fiber polymers are Nylon, Dacron, and Orlon. Synthetic rubbers are manmade polymers. Natural rubber is a natural polymer.

An example of polymerization is the combination of ethylene molecules in the presence of a catalyst to form a polymer called polyethylene. This is a generalized equation representing the polymerization of ethylene.

Wilson & Macpherson Hole

The polymerized protein molecule found in silk is shown in a three-dimensional model.

$$\left[\begin{array}{cccc} H & H & H & H \\ | & | & | & | \\ C = C & + & C = C \\ | & | & | & | \\ H & H & H & H \end{array}\right]_n \longrightarrow$$

$$\left[\begin{array}{cccc} H & H & H & H \\ | & | & | & | \\ -C & -C & -C & -C- \\ | & | & | & | \\ H & H & H & H \end{array}\right]_n$$

The subscript n represents some very large number. A polyethylene molecule has n C_4H_8 units. There are $2n$ monomers of ethylene in the a molecule of polyethylene. Polyethylene is a well-known substance. It is a tough, solid material used in unbreakable dishes, bowls, and other articles.

Two general methods of polymerization are used. One is called addition polymerization, and the other is called condensation polymerization. The formation of polyethylene as shown in the equation above is an addition polymerization.

One type of addition polymerization involves the use of free radicals, molecular fragments with free valence electrons, and monomers that have a double bond, two pairs of shared electrons, between carbon atoms. A free radical may be represented by the symbol R·. The dot represents a free electron. A generalized example of such an addition reaction, called a propagation reaction, is

$$\text{R}\cdot + \begin{array}{cc} H & H \\ | & | \\ C = C \\ | & | \\ H & X \end{array} \longrightarrow \begin{array}{cc} & H & H \\ & | & | \\ R- & C - C \\ & | & | \\ & H & X \end{array}$$

The letter X is some group of atoms that is not directly involved in the

reaction. The $\begin{array}{cc} H & H \\ | & | \\ R-C-C\cdot \\ | & | \\ H & X \end{array}$ group acts

as a free radical, because it has a free electron, and combines with another monomer.

$$\begin{array}{cccc} H & H & & H & H \\ | & | & & | & | \\ R-C-C\cdot & + & C = C & \longrightarrow \\ | & | & & | & | \\ H & X & & H & X \end{array}$$

$$\begin{array}{cccc} H & H & H & H \\ | & | & | & | \\ R-C-C-C-C\cdot \\ | & | & | & | \\ H & X & H & X \end{array}$$

More and more monomers can be added to the growing chain. One end of the chain continues to act as a free radical. The reaction proceeds until the free-radical chain ends of two growing polymers collide with each other. The free-radical chain ends react with each other to form one large stable molecule out of the two chains. Butyl and Buna synthetic rubbers are made by this addition-polymerization method.

Many other addition mechanisms are used in polymerization.

When two monomers combine in condensation polymerization, a small group of atoms is set free and is not included in the combination product. Monomers are chosen so that the removal of atom groups as the monomers combine can be repeated many times. Condensation polymerizations are classified by the type of group that is eliminated during monomer combination.

This is an example of a condensation polymerization in which water is eliminated.

$$H-O-\left[\begin{array}{c}H\\|\\C\\|\\H\end{array}\right]_x-O-H+$$

$$H-O-C\begin{array}{c}O\\||\end{array}-\left[\begin{array}{c}H\\|\\C\\|\\H\end{array}\right]_y-C\begin{array}{c}O\\||\end{array}-O-H$$

$$H-O-\left[\begin{array}{c}H\\|\\C\\|\\H\end{array}\right]_x-O-C\begin{array}{c}O\\||\end{array}-\left[\begin{array}{c}H\\|\\C\\|\\H\end{array}\right]_y$$

$$\begin{array}{c}O\\||\end{array}C-O-H+\begin{array}{c}H\\||\end{array}O-H$$

The subscripts x and y stand for large numbers. The product of the reaction can combine again with a molecule of the original ingredients. The process continues until a very large molecule is built up.

In the examples of polymerization given, monomers combine by joining together at their ends. The resulting polymers are long chains of atoms. In other types of polymerization it is possible for monomers to join to form rambling three-dimensional networks. The networks consist of cross-linked chains. Network polymers can be made into hard and brittle substances, such as bakelite.

Polymerization does not result in the formation of a group of identical molecules. Some of the polymer molecules are larger, contain more monomer units, than others. The monomer units may be arranged in different orders or in different orientations in different molecules. A polymeric substance, such as a plastic, is made up of molecules of many sizes and shapes. The majority of the molecules are about the same size.

POMEGRANATE, a deciduous small tree or shrub of the myrtle family, native to Persia and neighboring countries. In the United States it is grown with especial success in California and Arizona. In addition to its commercial value, the tree is ornamental. Its branches bear rich red flowers and a hard-rinded fruit the size of an orange, which ranges in color from yellow to purple. From the fruit pulp a liquid is derived, which, when cooled, is served as a drink in warm countries. Wine is made from it in Persia, and sherbets are made in other countries of the East. Forms of the pomegranate are also cultivated as hedge plants. The plant, the floral emblem of Spain, symbolizes hope in Christian art.

POMPEII, an ancient city in southern Italy, near the foot of Mt. Vesuvius and the Bay of Naples, site of uncovered, well-preserved ruins that provide one of the most complete sources of information on ancient civilization.

Pompeii, a flourishing provincial city with a population exceeding 20,000, was completely buried A.D. 79 as a result of the eruption of Mt. Vesuvius. (Sixteen years earlier it had been severely damaged by an earthquake.) The rain of pumice stone, ashes, and volcanic mud and the suffocating vapors caused the death of about 2,000 persons.

Pompeii was forgotten until 1748, when by chance some art relics were found. Further searches were then made by the rulers of Naples. Excavations were carried on at later dates, and a large portion of the city was unearthed. However, it was only in the 20th century that the city was restored, and the relics were left at the site. The ruins, still not completely uncovered, provide almost the only source of information concerning the domestic life of the ancients.

Pompeii, an ancient Italian city, was buried by an eruption of Vesuvius A.D. 79. Research and excavation began in 1748.

Black Star

At the time of its destruction, the city was at the height of material prosperity. Many well-to-do landowners lived in this city, then ruled by Rome. Pompeii, built in the form of an irregular oval, was surrounded by walls, broken by eight gates. The city was not congested, as was Rome. Numerous lava blocks served as paving for the streets, which were lined with shops, taverns, inns, stables, and lavish mansions, some three storied. Inside these homes were beautiful mosaics, murals, and sculptures.

This well-ordered city contained temples, two theaters, an amphitheater seating 20,000, two sports parks or (palaestras), and three public baths. Its magnificent forum is the most perfect example of a Roman central square, more so than the Forum of Trajan in Rome.

POMPEY THE GREAT (106-48 B.C.), Roman general and political leader. At the age of 17, Pompey fought with Sulla against the forces of Gaius Marius, a general and a political leader. On Sulla's return from victories over Mithradates VI in Asia Pompey joined him and defeated the Marian forces in Sicily and Africa. For these victories Sulla allowed him to enter Rome in triumph in 81. He received the title *Magnus* (the Great) from Sulla.

In 77 Pompey drove the followers of Marcus Lepidus from Italy. From 76 to 71 Pompey fought the Marian contingents of the able Quintus Sertorius in Spain. On his return to Italy he helped Marcus Crassus defeat the formidable slave uprising under the gladiator Spartacus. He and Crassus were elected consuls in 70 B.C. Pompey was given extraordinary power in 67 to defeat the pirates, who plundered grain shipments from Africa and Sicily to Rome. Within three months the pirates were defeated, granted their lives, and allowed to colonize Mediterranean towns. Pompey's power was again extended to include Asia, and he defeated the reviving forces under the crafty Mithradates VI. In 64-63 he annexed Syria and Judaea. In 61 Pompey, hero of Spain, Africa, and Asia, was given the most magnificent triumphal reception ever held in Rome.

Pompey was a good soldier but a mediocre politician. In 60 Crassus, Julius Caesar, and he formed the First Triumvirate, which was renewed in 56. In 54 Julia, Pompey's wife and Caesar's daughter, died. Crassus died in 53. Pompey held great power, for he ruled most of the Empire, while Caesar controlled only two Gaulish provinces. Pompey quarreled with Caesar and demanded the latter's recall. Caesar acted with decision and advanced into Italy, while Pompey retired to mobilize an army in Macedonia. In 48 Pompey defeated Caesar at Dyrrachium (now Durazzo, Albania) but shortly thereafter was himself decisively defeated at Pharsala in Thessaly. He fled to Egypt, where he was assassinated. See JULIUS CAESAR.

PONCE DE LEÓN, JUAN (1460?-1521), an explorer and discoverer of Florida, was born in Spain of a noble family. He fought in the Spanish army and sailed, it is thought, with Columbus on the second voyage to America.

Hearing that there was gold in Puerto Rico, he conquered that island and in 1509 was made its governor. It was here that Indians told him tales of an island called Bimini, in which gold and a fountain that made men eternally youthful could be found. In 1512 he was commissioned by the Spanish king to discover this island, and in 1513 he set out from Puerto Rico with three vessels. It was on this voyage that he discovered Florida.

In 1514 he was commissioned by the King to settle Florida, but governmental duties in Puerto Rico kept him there until the year 1521. In this year he undertook a second voyage. Upon landing, he and his party were met by Indians, and Ponce de León was hit by an arrow. He was taken back to Cuba and died within a few days.

Ponce de León discovered Florida in 1513.

Historia General, Herrera, 1728, Rare Book Division, NYPL and AMERICAN HERITAGE

PONCHIELLI, AMILCARE (1834-1886), Italian composer, born near Cremona. He acquired his musical education at the Milan Conservatory, which he attended from 1843 to 1854. His first opera, *I Promessi Sposi*, was produced in Cremona in 1856. Within the next 11 years Ponchielli composed four more operas, three of which were produced. With the performance of *I Promessi Sposi* at the Teatro Dal Verme in Milan in 1872 the composer acquired a national audience. As a result of that opera's popularity Ponchielli was commissioned by the managers of Milan's La Scala to compose a ballet. The resulting work, *Le Due Gemelle*, was received with enthusiasm. Subsequent works included a ballet, a musical comedy, a cantata, and several operas. Ponchielli achieved international recognition when his opera *La Gioconda* was produced at London's Covent Garden in 1883. That opera and *I Promessi Sposi* have proved to be his most enduring works.

PONTIAC'S CONSPIRACY, an Indian war that took place in May, 1763, between the settlers of the western frontier and the Indian tribes on the west and south, especially the Delawares, Shawnees, and Chippewas.

Pontiac was the leader of the Indians; his plan was to prevent the English from settling the country toward the west. The Indians had much to complain of. Fur traders and land speculators cheated them. The attitude of Lord Jeffrey Amherst, who was in charge of Indian affairs, was that the best solution to the Indian problem was to kill off the Indians by spreading smallpox among them. Pontiac spent the winter prior to the attack consolidating the tribes of the region under himself, then struck suddenly along the whole western frontier. All the important advance posts fell into the hands of the Indians except Detroit and Pittsburgh, where the garrisons beat them off after desperate fighting. It took about nine months to subdue the Indians. Pontiac made a peace treaty with the English in 1766 but was killed by another Indian some years later.

Pontiac's Conspiracy hastened the announcement of the Proclamation of 1763, limiting colonists' settlement of new territories, although the proclamation's provisions had long been under consideration.

PONTOON BRIDGE. See BRIDGE.

The pony express extended to California.

PONY EXPRESS, a private mailing service undertaken to prove the possibility of an overland mail route from the central United States to California as opposed to the southern route then in operation. The system was conceived by William Gwin, a U.S. senator from California, and was undertaken by the freighting firm of Russell, Majors, and Waddell. The company hoped to obtain a contract from the federal government to serve as a regular government mail carrier. The pony-express mail service went into effect Apr. 3, 1860, over a route from St. Joseph, Mo., to Sacramento, Calif. This route covered an approximate distance of 2,000 miles, much of it lying in hostile Indian territory. The route was broken down into units of about 10 miles each, at which point the rider quickly

The leaves, catkins of flowers, and twigs of the large-toothed aspen—a member of the popular genus—are shown below.

changed horses. After about 75 miles a new rider would take over. The first trip took 10½ days, about half the time taken by the fastest stagecoach. The pony express lasted only 18 months. It was discontinued after coast-to-coast telegraph connections were established in 1861.

POOL (game). See BILLIARDS.

POPE, ALEXANDER (1688-1744), English poet, was born in London, the son of a linen draper. At the age of 12 a severe illness overtook Pope and, in varying degrees, remained with him for the rest of his life. Pope's *Pastorals*, a work written, according to the poet, when he was only 16 years old, was published in 1709. In succeeding years he published the works that have made his name an enduring one in English literature. Written in heroic couplets, these works include "Windsor Forest," *Essay on Criticism*, and *The Rape of the Lock*. Heroic couplets were also used for Pope's translation of Homer's *Iliad*, the first volume of which appeared in 1715. The work was completed in 1720, and Pope, with two assistants, then did a translation of the *Odyssey*. The *Iliad*, despite its remoteness from the Homeric spirit, is one of the great works of 18th-century literature.

Pope is noted for invective as telling as that of Dryden, his fellow master of the heroic couplet. In his *Dunciad* he brutishly attacks a former friend, Lady Mary Wortley Montagu, one of the great letter writers of the 18th century. In his "Epistle to Dr. Arbuthnot," a preface to his imitations of Horace's *Satires*, he attacks various critics. In addition to the foregoing work Pope published a long poem *Eloisa to Abelard*, an elegy "Verses to the Memory of an Unfortunate Lady," and a series of moral poems collected as *An Essay on Man*.

POPE. See PAPACY.

POPLAR, a genus of trees of the willow family, found in the North Temperate Zone. There are about 30 species, including the aspen, cottonwood, and poplar.

All poplars are fast-growing trees, usually reaching a large size. Their leaves are more or less broadly oval —sometimes almost heart shaped— with pointed tips, long stalks, and usually toothed margins. As a rule the leaves turn yellow in the fall. The flowers appear very early in the spring, before the leaves, and are

borne in slender, mostly drooping tassels.

In the white poplar the leaves are dark green above and white and hairy beneath. The wood is light and not very valuable. It is used for carved woodenware and for the manufacture of paper pulp. The balsam poplar is a common species in the northern United States and in Canada. The black and the white poplars have both been introduced from Europe. Several of the aspens and poplars have quaking leaves. The stalk of the leaf is flattened or compressed so that the leaf flutters in the slightest movement of the air.

The large flowers of the oriental poppy are pinkish white, yellow, orange, or red

POPPY, one of the plants of the poppy family. They are chiefly herbaceous plants, annual, biennial, or perennial. Poppies have showy flowers, many of the cultivated varieties being double. The capsules fling out their seeds in an unusual manner when the plant is shaken by the wind. Each capsule is somewhat like a round or oval pepper box with holes, not in the top where rain might get in them, but under the projecting rim.

The opium poppy of Greece and Asia, the corn poppy, and the Oriental poppy are the best known varieties. The opium poppy is cultivated for the narcotic contained in the milky juice of the unripe pod. The poppy is well known as the Veterans Day emblem for veterans of World War I and World War II. The Oriental poppy is a garden variety cultivated for its showy, bright-red blossoms. Poppyseed is used as an article of food, and the oil, which can be extracted from the seeds, is edible and is also used as an oil-painting medium.

POPULAR FRONT, a reconciliation of Communists with other political forces. The united front of the 1930's was an alliance between Communist and leftwing Socialist groups, but the popular front took in a greater part of the political spectrum. The union of Communist parties with other political parties was a method that the Communists have used in the past to gain advantages. The sincerity with which Communists work with those of differing opinions can be judged by a study of the Communist nations, where only the Communist parties can function.

The popular-front tactic was contemplated by the Comintern (Communist International) as early as 1931, when Dmitri Manuilsky advocated a more conciliatory policy. The chance to put the popular front into effect came on Feb. 6, 1934. On that day the extreme rightwing political groups in France attempted a coup. The coup was unsuccessful, but it brought the Socialists and Communists into an alliance that was formally declared on July 27, 1934, following a trip to Moscow by Maurice Thorez, head of the French Communist party. The Communists began an attempt to attract middle-class support, and several months later the Radical Socialists were brought into the popular front. Léon Blum complained that the Communists were infiltrating Socialist organizations, including the trade unions. The Socialists were to have more and more reason to complain of the popular front. In 1936 the popular front was successful in forming a government under Socialist Léon Blum. The Communists stayed out of the government, however, and toward the end of 1936, their activities, which included numerous strikes, seemed to be directed at displacing Blum. This occurred in June, 1937. A Radical Socialist government was set up, lasting until March, 1938. Blum again formed a government, but a series of strikes sponsored by the Communists caused his government to fall in April. The last popular-front demonstration occurred on July 14, 1938, but no speakers appeared, for the Communists, Socialists, and Radical Socialists could not agree on a program.

In Spain a popular front was formed to protect the republic from the insurgent generals in January, 1936. The Communists, a small party in Spain, joined in defense of the government. Indeed, the Soviet Union was the only nation actively to supply the Spanish government.

Unfortunately, the Soviet political police, then known as OGPU, were introduced in Spain. The idea, possibly, was to make Spain the first of the so-called popular democracies that were to appear in eastern Europe following World War II. Through the OGPU, many Communist political opponents—anarchists, Trotskyists, and Socialists—who also fought for the republic, were ruthlessly eliminated.

Popular-front tactics were introduced elsewhere in the world between 1935 and 1938. Except in Spain, France, and China, the Communist parties were too insignificant to do more than propagandize. In the United States a number of people were attracted to the "liberalized" party for a time. The bloody purges of 1936 in the Soviet Union, however, tended to disenchant those new adherents who could judge objectively.

POPULAR MUSIC, the music that is accepted by the public and that the public often recognizes by hearing only a few bars of the melody or a few words of the lyric. In recent decades the term has come to mean those tunes that are written in the 32-bar so-called ballad idiom, with relatively simple melody pattern and rhythm. Such tunes can be further categorized (country and western, rhythm and blues, and so forth) according to characteristics of the lyric, rhythm, or melody or according to the purpose for which they were written.

Taste in music varies in different countries and changes gradually and constantly in all countries. Certain operatic arias are well enough known to be considered popular music in Italy even today. The waltzes of Johann Strauss were probably the most popular music of 19th-century Europe. Even small regions may develop a distinctive style of music, such as the flamenco music of Andalusia, in Spain, and the calypso music of the British West Indies.

Popular music in the United States before the Civil War included a number of patriotic songs, religious songs, and to a certain extent the classics. However, most of the music with which the American public was familiar was of what is now termed the folk tradition. Many of the musical forces that shape popular music today (with the notable exception of jazz, which arose at the turn of the century) were present when Stephen Foster, the first well-known popular-song writer in the United States, began to compose. Many of Foster's songs were broadcast to the people by means of the minstrel show, at that time a very popular form of music-hall entertainment, which served as a forerunner of vaudeville and the musical revue. (See JAZZ.) Even at that time popular music was an integral part of the entertainment world.

About 1880 the music-publishing business, heretofore scattered throughout the United States, became concentrated in Union Square,

The disc-jockey program is a primary means of presenting popular music to the public.

Courtesy of WNEW Radio, New York

George Shearing is an English pianist and composer of popular music.

New York, then the entertainment center of the country. The writers and publishers of Union Square were convinced that a song could be produced and sold like any other commodity; that a song could be manufactured to suit the prevailing taste; and that it had to be sold to the people. Important to the songwriting industry at that time was the song plugger (song promoter), whose task it was to have the song performed in public, preferably by a well-known entertainer. About 1900 the center of the songwriting industry gravitated to 28th Street, in New York, between Fifth and Sixth avenues, an area that soon became famous as Tin Pan Alley. Among the many composers associated with Tin Pan Alley were George M. Cohan, George Gershwin, Jerome Kern, Irving Berlin, and Hoagy Carmichael. The trade was revolutionized by the development of the mass-communications media, especially the radio, the phonograph, and the sound motion picture. Gradually the smaller publishing houses were absorbed by the Hollywood motion picture producing companies and by the radio-network corporations. Revenue gained from Broadway stage royalties and the sale of sheet music was slight in comparison to the potential income in the recording business. By 1930 Tin Pan Alley ceased to exist.

An important event in the development of the songwriting industry in America was the founding in 1914 of the American Society of Composers, Authors, and Publishers (ASCAP). To this organization institutions (clubs, radio stations, ballrooms, and so forth) paid a fee for the use (for profit) of music written and published by ASCAP members. The fee was divided as royalties among ASCAP members. The radio industry set up the rival organization Broadcast Music Incorporated (BMI) in 1940 during a dispute over a contract between the networks and ASCAP.

Today music becomes popular for a variety of reasons. A song becomes accepted most often through repetition—by being played innumerable times on radio, jukeboxes, and television. The public then buys the records and sheet music and requests orchestras and disc jockeys to repeat the piece of music. The entertainer or band introducing the piece of music is also important and may often determine its success. A certain song sometimes becomes associated with an entertainer or with a band. For example, Bing Crosby is associated with "When the Blue of the Night Meets the Gold of the Day"; Perry Como, with "Prisoner of Love"; Sophie Tucker, with "Some of These Days"; and the Glenn Miller band, with "Tuxedo Junction." Some songs enjoy a seasonal popularity. "Easter Parade" and "White Christmas" are revived each year for the appropriate seasons. Numerous popular songs were taken from the classics. For example, Ernesto Lecuona's "Malagueña" was transformed into "Crossroads," and a theme from Peter Tchaikovsky's First Piano Concerto became "Tonight We Love." "I'm Always Chasing Rainbows," "Till the End of Time," and "No Other Love" were all based on themes found in the piano compositions of Chopin. Some tunes become popular merely because of novel lyrics or melody or an unusual recording technique. By far the greatest number of the so-called pop standards (songs that have retained their popularity over a long period of time) have come from either Broadway productions or from the scores of motion pictures. A large number of these standards were composed by a relatively small number of writers, most of whom were associated with Tin Pan Alley, Broadway, and Hollywood. This group includes George Gershwin, Vincent Youmans, Sigmund Romberg, Hoagy Carmichael, Jerome Kern, Cole Porter, Richard Rodgers, and Irving Berlin. While some composers also write lyrics, others collaborate with lyricists.

Noted lyricists included Ira Gershwin, Lorenz Hart, and Oscar Hammerstein 2d. Popular music, or more correctly, commercially popular music, commenced to grow up during the late-19th century and the early decades of the 20th century in Europe and elsewhere as various mediums of mass communication became established. At the turn of the century the chief outlet for popular music in the European countries was the music hall or beer garden, an establishment that functioned somewhat like the American minstrel show or vaudeville. Among the music-hall entertainers to gain renown outside their native countries were Sir Harry Lauder, the Scottish singer and comedian, and Maurice Chevalier, French song-and-dance man. The form of the operetta was more or less set in the late 19th century by Gilbert and Sullivan, the British librettist-composer team whose works are still popular throughout the English-speaking world. In more recent decades this idiom, which has been the vehicle of numerous popular songs, was expanded through the work of several European composers and lyricists, including German-born Kurt Weill and Englishman Noel Coward.

With the advent of the radio and the rapid growth of the phonograph-record and motion picture industries, it became possible for a type of music, an entertainer, or even an individual piece of music to attain international popularity. Shortly after World War I, jazz, a type of music of American origin, became popular in Europe and, subsequently, throughout the world. A comparable but less significant development, which has occurred in more recent years, has been the widespread acceptance of Afro-Cuban and Latin-American rhythms and dances, such as the cha-cha and the rhumba and samba. As with the spread of the jazz idiom, the chief broadcasting mediums have been the radio, the phonograph record, and the dance band. The numerous singers of popular songs who have gained an international audience include Charles Trenet, Yves Montand, and Edith Piaf of France; Dave King and Vera Lynn of England; Bing Crosby, Frank Sinatra, and Ella Fitzgerald of the United States; Lotte Lenya of Austria; and German-born Marlene Dietrich. Similarly, the popularity of a number of songs such as the French "La Vie en Rose" and "La Mer" and the Italian "Volare," once only national, is now worldwide.

POPULATION. The population of the world was about 2,900,000,000 in 1960. Before man settled down to an agricultural life, there were probably less than 20,000,000 people scattered over the globe. The population of the world has increased ever since. By the middle of the 18th century there were about 1,000,000,000 people in the world, and in 1925 the world population was estimated as 1,907,000,000.

Each rise in population occurred after some major advance or change in the way of living or working. The substitution of an agricultural life for a nomadic existence, the growth of commerce, the movement toward the city, the invention and use of machinery, and the technical revolution have brought about such changes. In the 20th century medicine gave the greatest boost to population. People lived much longer than ever before. The average life of a Stone Age man may have been about 20 years. The average 20th-century American or European could expect to live about 70 years, or his full biblical three score and ten.

The population increase has given rise to problems. In 1954 the first United Nations World Population Conference was held at Rome to discuss these population problems. The conference was sponsored by the United Nations. The major problem is how to feed a world population that increases at the rate of about 150,000 a day. Malthus wrote an *Essay on the Principle of Population* in 1798. He said that food production increased arithmetically. This meant that twice as much food would be produced on twice as

much good land. But population, said Malthus, increased geometrically; twice as many people would have many more than twice as many children as their parents had. Malthus thought that mankind might eventually starve. This idea has not proved to be correct. Mankind has been much more ingenious at producing food than Malthus had thought. Yet scientists are still worried about man's ability to produce enough food to feed such an increasing number of people. They also wonder whether man can find enough space and resources on the earth to maintain himself in comfort and health.

POPULIST PARTY, an American political party founded in 1891 by a movement of farmers, Westerners, workers, and small businessmen. During the financial panic of 1873, the prices of farm products had fallen so low that middle-western and southern farmers burned their crops as fuel rather than send them to market. The party representatives met in Omaha, Neb., drew up a political platform, and nominated James Baird Weaver for president. They advocated the free coinage of silver and the issuance of more paper money, a graduated income tax, government ownership of railroads, the election of senators by popular vote, eight-hour working days, postal banks, and pensions. The party made a very strong showing. Weaver received over one million votes and 22 electoral votes including all the votes from Kansas, Colorado, Idaho, and Nevada, and 1 vote each from North Dakota and Oregon. In addition, the party

elected a few representatives to the House of Representatives and the Senate. In 1896 they endorsed the Democratic nomination of William Jennings Bryan for president. With the defeat of Bryan the Populist party declined rapidly in strength although a few representatives remained in Congress for several years.

PORCELAIN. See CHINA.

PORCUPINE, a member of either of two families of the order Rodentia, possessing modified hairs, known as quills, that are shed like other hairs and serve as protection against enemies. One family is native to the Old World and the other to the New World. The largest living porcupine is the African crested porcupine, a member of the Old World family. The New World family includes small South American species that have prehensile tails. The large species common in North America measures up to 3 feet in length.

The yellow-haired porcupine can climb trees.

The porcupine in the eastern United States is more blackish than the one in the western United States and has many yellow hairs on its head. The porcupine's food is mainly plants, which it collects in the early morning, at dusk, or in the moonlight. It eats tree bark and may do damage by girdling trees.

The porcupine is dangerous because of its quills. The tail is the porcupine's principal weapon of defense. When it slaps its enemies with its tail, some of the tail quills, which are loosely attached, are apt to be driven into the enemy. There is no truth in the old tale that the porcupine shoots its quills at its enemies; but when it slaps its tail against a hard object, quills may be loosened and flipped some distance. The quills are barbed at the end and, once embedded in the flesh, are difficult to dislodge.

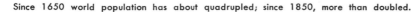

Since 1650 world population has about quadrupled; since 1850, more than doubled.

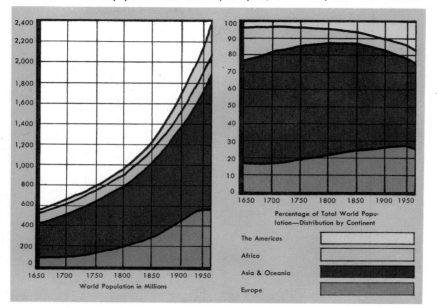

Percentage of Total World Population—Distribution by Continent

The Americas

Africa

Asia & Oceania

Europe

World Population in Millions

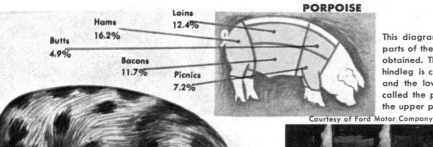

Hams 16.2%
Butts 4.9%
Loins 12.4%
Bacons 11.7%
Picnics 7.2%

This diagram (left) of a hog of the meat type shows the parts of the animal from which the various cuts of pork are obtained. The pork from the upper portion, or thigh, of a hindleg is called a ham. Bacon is obtained from the belly and the lower portions of the sides of the hog. The cut called the picnic, which is similar to ham, is obtained from the upper portion of a front leg.

Courtesy of Ford Motor Company

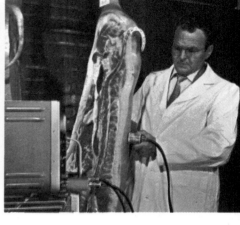

Courtesy of Ford Motor Company

Courtesy of Ford Motor Company

The carcasses of butchered hogs are shown at right. The man is using an electronic device to measure the thickness of the fat on a hog carcass.

PORK, the meat of swine, including various cuts, processed meats, and edible byproducts. Pork offers special opportunities for economy and nutrition. Present-day preferences are toward more lean meat and less fat in pork cuts.

Pork may be bought in a wide variety of forms. The chief lean cuts are ham, pork shoulder, picnic, Boston butt, pork loin, and tenderloin. Ham, the largest of pork cuts, is also the most versatile. It may be bought fresh or in a number of cured forms and styles. Fatter cuts of pork include bacon, salt pork, and jowls. Other common cuts include Canadian bacon, spareribs, neckbones, backbones, and hocks.

Processed meats include various kinds of canned meats—such as canned whole, half, and quarter hams—chopped spiced ham, sausages, frankfurters, wieners, luncheon meats, and vinegar-pickle products,

such as pickled pigs' feet. The most important edible byproduct of pork is lard, used as a shortening in cooking. Variety meats, such as pork liver, hearts, kidneys, brains, and tongues, are also classed as edible byproducts.

Pork, because it may be used as both fresh and cured meat, is the most versatile of meats. It is also higher than other meats in content of water-soluble vitamins, especially vitamin B_1, or thiamin. Pork is also higher in content of essential fatty acids.

The highest grade cuts of pork are obtained from young, well-fed hogs weighing from 180 to 250 pounds; most meat from older hogs goes to make sausage and other processed meats. Several new, meat-type breeds of hogs have been developed in recent years. These breeds produce a greater percentage of lean meat than do older breeds.

PORPOISE, an animal found in the North Atlantic and North Pacific oceans. Though shaped like a fish, the porpoise, of which there are several kinds, is a true mammal: warmblooded, breathes air, brings forth its young alive, and suckles them. It is generally 4 to 6 feet long, bluish black above and whitish beneath, and has a triangular fin near the middle of the back. The skin is smooth and destitute of hair.

Porpoises travel in schools and may frequently be seen rolling and tumbling about in the water as they come to the surface to breathe, which they do with a puffing sound. When rolling in the water, they look like great black pigs. As a result of this resemblance, sailors of old often referred to them as hogfish or as sea hogs.

Porpoises are related to dolphins but are smaller. Both porpoises and dolphins are related to whales. Porpoises swim in schools, which sometimes travel alongside moving ships. The frequent leaping of swimming porpoises suggests frolicsome play.

PORTER, COLE (1893-), an American composer of musical comedy, was born in Peru, Ind., the child of a wealthy family. He began his musical training by studying the violin at six years of age and taking up the piano two years later. Porter was educated at Yale University, where he wrote two famous school songs, "Yale Bull Dog Song" and "Bingo Eli Yale." After a year at Harvard law school he transferred to the Harvard music school. He met there Lawrason Riggs with whom he wrote his first produced musical, *See America First.*

After World War I, in which he served with the French Foreign Legion, Porter lived in Paris. He studied there with the French composer Vincent d'Indy, and in 1923 he wrote five songs for the *Greenwich Village Follies.*

Porter's first success was *Paris*, a 1928 hit that starred Irene Bordoni. Since then he has been one of the most productive composers of musical comedy. His hits include *The Gay Divorce, Anything Goes, Leave It to Me, Panama Hattie, Silk Stockings,* and *Kiss Me, Kate.*

In 1937 Porter's leg was crushed in a fall from a horse. He spent the next seven years either in bed or in a wheelchair and underwent 30 painful operations. The leg was amputated in 1958.

PORTER, WILLIAM SYDNEY. See HENRY, O.

PORTLAND, the largest city and the commercial and shipping center of Oregon. In 1960 it had a population of 372,676. Exports from Portland include wool, lumber and paper products, grain, livestock, and processed foods. Chief imports include burlap, sugar, copra, and iron and steel. The city has shipyards, flour and paper mills, canneries, meat-packing plants, and industries producing aluminum, wood products, and chemicals.

Portland is a cultural and educational center and is the seat of Reed College and the University of Portland. Its annual Rose Festival draws many visitors. The city is situated near many scenic attractions, a number of which are accessible by way of the Columbia River Highway, which runs east along the river.

The city was settled in 1845 and developed rapidly during gold-rush days. Hydroelectric power from Bonneville Dam, the construction of which was completed in 1937, stimulated industrial growth.

PORTUGAL, a country in southwestern Europe, on the western side of the Iberian Peninsula, bounded by Spain on the east and north and by the Atlantic Ocean on the west and south. It is about 125 miles wide and 360 miles long. The total area, including the islands of the Azores and Madeira, is more than 35,000 square miles. The population is about 9,000,000. The capital is Lisbon; other chief cities are Oporto, Setúbal, and Coimbra.

The surface is generally mountainous except for lowlands in the river valleys, which widen toward the coast. The mountain ranges are mainly continuations of those of Spain. The major rivers are the Douro, the Tagus, and the Guadiana. The climate is generally moderate, with the heaviest rainfall in the north. The south has a more Mediterranean type of climate, with dry summers and winter rains. Portugal's chief farm products are wheat, corn, barley, oats, potatoes, and French beans. Oranges, olives, and grapes are also major agricultural products. About 27 percent of the land is forested. The cork trees of the mountain slopes, especially in the south, provide the major export product of Portugal. Other important forest products are turpentine and resin. Sheep, cattle, and pigs are raised, and winemaking and fishing are major industries. The sardine

The national flag of Portugal, adopted in 1910, and the coat of arms are shown below.

Fish are sold in the square of Caxias, a picturesque fishing village near Lisbon. Fishing is one of the chief industries of Portugal.

industry is centered at Setúbal, about 20 miles southeast of Lisbon. The chief manufacture is textiles, and Portugal's porcelain tiles and china are world famous. The country's rich mineral resources are largely undeveloped, but coal, copper pyrites, tin ore, zinc ore, and wolframite are mined. The chief exports are crude cork, sardines, wines, olive oil, resins, turpentine, and wolfram.

The great majority of the people are Roman Catholic. Almost one-half of the population is illiterate, although elementary education is compulsory. Among the leading universities are the University of Coimbra, founded in 1290; the University of Lisbon, founded in 1290 and restored in 1911; and the University of Oporto, founded in 1911. Portugal is a corporative republic. The president is elected for seven years, and the one-chamber legislature of 120 members is elected every four years. Another body, the corporative chamber, deals with labor, economic, and social matters.

In ancient times Portugal was inhabited by the Lusitanians, who were conquered by Rome in the 2d century B.C. The Visigoths conquered the country in the 5th century and ruled until the arrival of the Moslem Moors in the early 8th century. The territory in the north between the Minho and Douro rivers was reconquered in the 11th century by the ruler of León and

Joseph Muench

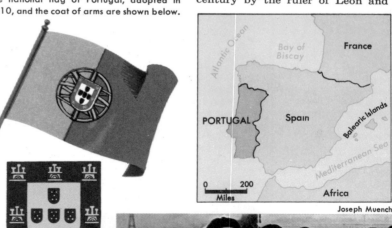

Jane Werner Watson

Nazaré, a popular fishing port and bathing resort, is on Portugal's west coast.

Castile. In 1095 it was given to Henry of Burgundy as the County of Portugal and became an independent kingdom under Alfonso I. The rulers of Portugal carried on the war against the Moors. They gradually pushed them southward, and in the 13th century they drove them entirely out of the country.

In the 15th and 16th centuries Portuguese navigators took the lead in voyages of discovery to Africa, Asia, and South America. Trade was developed with Africa, India, and the East Indies, and Brazil was settled by Portuguese colonists. From 1580 to 1640 the country was under the rule of the kings of Spain. After regaining her independence, Portugal was no longer a major world power, having lost much of her empire to the Dutch and the British, although still holding her colonies in Africa. Since 1654 Portugal's foreign relations have been based on close ties with England. In 1822 Brazil declared her independence and became an empire under Pedro I, the son of the Portuguese king. In 1908 King Charles and his heir were assassinated, and in 1910 a republic was declared. Portugal entered World War I in 1916 on the side of the Allies. Law and order, which had broken down in the early 19th century, was only reestablished in 1928 by Antonio Oliveira de Salazar, finance minister in a new government. Four years later he became prime minister and,

for all practical purposes, dictator. The nation remained neutral in World War II and in 1943 permitted the Allies to establish naval and air bases in the Azores. The Portuguese overseas territories include Goa, Dãmao, and Diu in India; Macao on the coast of China; part of the island of Timor in the East Indies; the Cape Verde Islands in the eastern Atlantic; and Portuguese Guinea, São Tomé, Príncipe Island, Angola, and Mozambique in Africa. Portugal is a member of the United Nations and the North Atlantic Treaty Organization. For detailed map, see SPAIN.

PORTUGAL

Area: 34,200 sq. mi. (continent), 1,200 sq. mi. (islands)
Population: 9,000,000
Capital: Lisbon
Largest cities: Lisbon, Oporto, Setúbal, Coimbra
Highest mountain peaks: Malhão, on continent (6,532 feet)—Pico, on Azores (7,611 feet)
Chief rivers: Tagus, Douro, Guadiana
Climate: Mild winters, warm summers—heavy rainfall in north, much lower winter rainfall in south
National flag: Green, red—armillary sphere and shield in center
National anthem: *A Portuguesa* (The Portuguese)
Form of government: Republic
Unit of currency: Escudo

Language: Portuguese
Chief religion: Roman Catholic
Chief economic activities: Agriculture (including livestock raising), fishing, forestry, mining
Chief crops: Wheat, corn, potatoes, beans, grapes, olives
Chief minerals: Coal, copper, sulfur, tungsten, tin
Chief exports: Cork, sardines, wine, rosin and turpentine, tungsten ore, pyrites, olive oil
Chief imports: Iron and steel, petroleum, foodstuffs (including sugar, codfish, coffee, wheat), cotton, machinery and vehicles, coal, fertilizers

PORTUGUESE AFRICA, four overseas territories of Portugal in Africa, including Angola and Portuguese Guinea on the west coast, Mozambique on the east coast, and São Tomé Island and Príncipe Island in the Gulf of Guinea. Since 1951 each of the territories has had its own governor and autonomy in financial and administrative matters. It is the policy of the Portuguese government to encourage the immigration of Portuguese settlers to the territories.

Angola is a large, thinly settled region on the west coast of central Africa, bordered by the Congo Republic on the north, Southwest Africa on the south, and Northern Rhodesia on the east. It is 1,000 miles long at the coast and over 700 miles wide, with a total area of 481,351 square miles. The population is about 4,000,000. The capital is Luanda; other large towns are Benguela, Mossâmedes, and Lobito. Most of Angola consists of a high plateau (average elevation over 3,000 feet) sloping sharply to a narrow coastal lowland in the west and sloping gradually to the Congo and Zambezi basins in the east. Along the coast the northern part has an unhealthful tropical climate, and the south is dry. The most healthful area is the upland plateau region, which has an average annual temperature of between 65° and 70° F.

The principal crops are coffee, corn, sugar, palm oil, cotton, wheat, tobacco, cacao, and sisal. Cattle raising and sheep raising are important. Angola has large diamond deposits. Coffee, diamonds, and corn are the chief exports.

Angola and the Congo region were discovered by the Portuguese in 1482, and the first colony was established in 1491. Luanda was founded in 1575. The area was taken by the Dutch in 1640 and was occupied by them until 1648. A prosperous

Martin S. Klein

The city of Lourenço Marques has one of the finest harbors in southern Africa. It is located on Delagoa Bay in Mozambique.

slave trade with Brazil was carried on from the 17th century to the 19th century.

Mozambique stretches 1,700 miles along the southeastern coast of Africa opposite the large island of Madagascar, and its widest point east to west is 400 miles; the total area is 297,731 square miles. The population is about 6,000,000, including about 66,000 Europeans. Most of the Africans are of Bantu stock, with much Arabic blood. The capital is Lourenço Marques; other cities are Beira and Mozambique. Mozambique lies mainly in the large east African coastal plain, but there are highlands in the north and west around Lake Nyasa. The Zambezi River, one of the great rivers of the world, flows across the center of the territory. The climate is tropical and subtropical along the coast and is more moderate in the interior highlands.

Soils in the south and central portions are generally poor, and in those regions corn is the principal crop. However, there are areas of rich soil in the river valleys, where sugarcane is raised on a large scale. The chief farming region is the north, where cotton, coconuts, tea, rice, and peanuts are grown. Exports include sugar, tea, copra, cotton, and sisal. Both Mozambique and Angola profited by the program of economic development undertaken by the Portuguese government after World War II.

The Portuguese established settlements along the Mozambique coast in the 16th century. The territory was used mainly as a source of slaves until the late 19th century, when the slave trade was abolished. From 1891 to 1942 the central portion of the territory was controlled by the Mozambique Company under charter from the Portuguese government. In the latter year the charter expired, and the government took over the administration.

Portuguese Guinea is a triangle of territory of 13,948 square miles at the western tip of Africa, bounded by Senegal on the north and the Republic of Guinea on the east and southeast. It has a population of about 500,000, including about 2,000 Europeans. The capital is Bissau. It is a low delta region crossed by several streams. The tropical climate is unhealthful, with an annual rainfall of about 80 inches. Lining the coast and the banks is a thick jungle, in which elephants, hippopotamuses, and panthers roam. The principal products of the region are almonds, rice, copra, palm oil, peanuts, rubber, and beeswax. Cattle and hogs are raised. Rice milling and palm-oil processing are the chief industries.

Portuguese Guinea was discovered in 1446 by Nuno Tristão. It became a separate colony in 1879.

Príncipe and São Tomé, discovered in 1470 by the Portuguese, are two volcanic islands in the Gulf of Guinea on the west African coast; they form a single territory under a Portuguese governor. São Tomé almost touches the Equator, and both islands have heavy tropical vegetation. They export cacao, coffee, and coconuts.

PORTUGUESE MAN-OF-WAR, a

colonial jellyfish, so named because it looks like a ship in full sail on the sea's surface and because it was first seen near Portuguese colonies in America. Sometimes great numbers swim together, and their bladder-like floats, brilliant blue or orange, give the surface of the ocean the appearance of a splendid flower garden. The float, a delicate, sac-

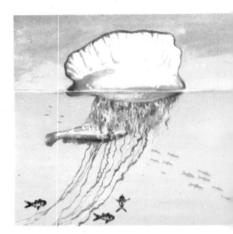

The Portuguese man-of-war

like bladder about 6 inches long and filled with air, is drawn out into two points at opposite ends. Above it is a kind of comb running lengthwise, and on its under surface is a tangle of various tentacles, some long and threadlike and some with grapelike clusters of little bodies like bells or pears. All these various parts constitute a colony or a compound animal, each part representing a separate animal that performs some of the necessary functions of life, just as do the organs in a single animal.

When a Portuguese man-of-war is driven by the wind along the surface of the ocean, its long tentacles stretch out behind, sometimes for 30 to 50 feet. Some of these tentacles are provided with poisonous, stinging threads, which paralyze any animal with which they come into contact. They are dangerous even to man and produce bad swellings on those who touch them. Even half-dead, stranded Portuguese men-of-war are dangerous to handle, for their sting burns like fire and leaves a lasting irritation.

POSEIDON. See NEPTUNE.

POSTAL SERVICE, a service for delivering written messages. The postal service is one of man's hardest won and most beneficial accomplishments. Letterwriting dates from the 4,000-year-old clay tablets of Babylon, but the first record of any system for transmitting written messages was made in the 5th century B.C., when Herodotus, a Greek historian, wrote of men on horseback who carried messages written on bronze tablets.

In 1464 King Louis XI of France established the forerunner of a public postal system with regular messengers carrying messages. Their arrivals were announced by golden horns. In those days the postman was hailed as the king's courier, a man of such importance in the community that his journey was delayed only at the hazard of extreme punishment. Like most early postal systems the service started by Louis XI was restricted to use by high officials of the court. It was more than a half-century later that postal service was first made available to the public. This service was inaugurated between Vienna and Berlin, but the costs were so high that only the wealthy could afford the service. The first postal system in England was established in 1523. Its use was initially limited to members of the royal family.

During the time of Queen Elizabeth I of England the warning phrase "Haste, Post, Haste, for Thy Lyfe, for Thy Lyfe, Haste" was often written on letters to remind the postboys of their duty. The postboys, with post horns and mailpouches across their saddlebags, were the carriers of the Elizabethan Age and for about 200 years thereafter. Regulations required that the post horn be blown four times in every mile. During the summer the postboys were required to ride at

Postal service, once too expensive for all but the rich, is now within the means of all.

7 miles per hour; during the winter, at 5 miles per hour.

From the 17th to the early 19th century most countries ran their postal system for profit. The postage was paid by the recipients of letters. Because of the expense some people returned their letters unread and others evaded payment. Research by Sir Rowland Hill produced suggestions for reform. As a result England reorganized its postal system in 1840 and lowered postage rates. As part of the reform, it

introduced the postage stamp as the sign that the sender had paid costs. Soon these reforms spread to many other countries.

Another important advance in postal service was the organization of the Universal Postal Union (U.P.U.) in 1874. Before this time sending international mail was both complicated and expensive. Each country had to have a special treaty with every other country to which its citizens sent mail, and each nation through which a letter passed

This chart shows the history of a first-class letter, **1.** It is taken to a mailbox, **2;** collected, **3;** and rushed to the post office, **4.** Here it is postmarked, **5;** classified by state, **6;** and sent to a secondary case, **7,** where it is tied into a bundle with letters to the same city, **8.** It is put into a pouch, **9;** dispatched, **10;** and given a truck, train, or airplane ride, **11.** At its destination it is put into the proper station separation, **12;** the correct carrier route, **13;** and rushed, **14,** to the post office station. Here it is separated according to the address, **15.** Finally, it is delivered by a carrier, **16.**

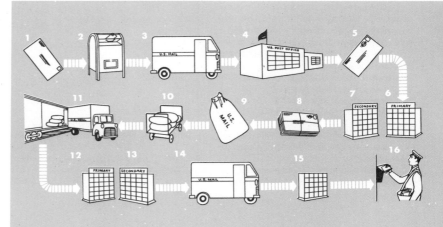

Monkmeyer

This is the lobby of a modernized post office in Washington, D.C. Notice the new open-type counters where stamps are sold.

Monkmeyer

In the modernized post office in Washington, D.C., a Mail Flo system conveys letters rapidly and efficiently between sorting areas.

Monkmeyer

Each sorting-machine operator sorts 3,000 letters an hour to some 300 destinations.

on its way charged for transporting it. After the establishment of the U.P.U. all member countries were regarded as part of one huge postal district; postage was paid in the country from which a letter was sent; the country of destination delivered the letter without charge; and for a certain fee each country that sent mail had the right to use the postal systems of all countries through which the mail traveled on its way to its destination. Since 1948 the U.P.U. has been an agency of the United Nations. Almost all the nations of the world belong to the U.P.U.

Postal services and methods have constantly increased. Present-day

services include delivery of packages, banking by means of postal-savings accounts, insurance, and issuing of money orders. Delivery facilities may range from dogsled (in remote parts of Alaska) through trains, airplanes, pneumatic tubes

OCCUPATION: Letter Carrier

NATURE OF WORK: Delivery of the mails

PERSONAL FACTORS—ABILITIES, SKILLS, APTITUDES: Good physical condition, good eyesight, and average intelligence are needed, as well as the ability to drive an automobile.

EDUCATION AND SPECIAL TRAINING: Applicant must pass a physical examination and a basic civil service test plus a driver's test.

WORKING CONDITIONS:

1. **INCOME:**
   COMPARED WITH OTHER CAREERS WITH EQUAL TRAINING: Average
   COMPARED WITH MOST OTHER CAREERS: Average
2. **ENVIRONMENT:** Mostly outdoors; subject to weather
3. **OTHER:** Regular hours; usual government benefits; good opportunities; allowance for uniform

RELATED CAREERS: Post office clerk, mail sorter, postal inspector

WHERE TO FIND MORE INFORMATION: U.S. Post Office Department, 12th Street and Pennsylvania Avenue NW, Washington 25, D.C.

(as in Paris), and special subways between main sorting offices and the railroad stations (as in London). In many countries the post office departments also run the national telegraph and telephone services. Throughout the world, postal departments are experimenting with mechanical devices to speed up the mail. These include automatic sorting machines and even an electronic system that transmits the contents of a letter almost instantaneously to its destination hundreds of miles away.

POSTER, a sign or placard put up by advertisers or government officials to attract public attention. As a form of commercial art, the poster is fairly young; but as a means of making public announcements, posters are centuries old; they were certainly known to the Romans. Much later, in the 18th century, printed handbills were used for various advertising purposes, such as promoting the sale of tea and tobacco and listing the time schedules of stagecoaches. Many of these printed handbills were ornamented with engravings.

The modern type of commercial poster began to appear in Paris in the 1860's. It advertised theatrical celebrities, foods, and household goods. Manet and Bonnard made designs for posters, but the most skilled artist in this craft was Toulouse-Lautrec. His bold, simple designs and bright colors were easy to see at a distance. They were pleasing to look at and often amusing in a satirical way. People of the theater were his usual subjects.

Contemporary posters do not have the wit and verve of Toulouse-Lautrec's productions, although in design they are similarly clear and simple. Clean-cut, bold lettering is looked upon as a prime requisite.

Posters can be made, as Toulouse-Lautrec made his, by forming lithographic prints from a design carved

This circus poster dates from 1832. It is possibly the oldest poster in America.

in stone. Metal plates are more often used in this process nowadays. Some artists cut out designs from colored paper and then paste them to a cardboard background. The method usually followed by commercial artists involves the use of an opaque watercolor called poster color. The artist first draws a design on prepared cardboard and then paints the appropriate areas with poster color. This pigment is easier to apply to cardboard than is transparent watercolor, and it photographs better. The original design may be engraved by hand on a metal plate or transferred to it photographically.

POST OFFICE DEPARTMENT, UNITED STATES, the department of the U.S. government that is responsible for carrying and delivering the mail throughout the United States and for sending it abroad. The Continental Post Office was established in 1775 by the Continental Congress. Benjamin Franklin became the first postmaster general. In 1789 the Constitution gave Congress the power to establish a post office. Samuel Osgood became the first postmaster general under the Constitution. He was in charge of 75 post offices. By 1960 the postmaster general had charge of over 35,000 post offices.

The Jeffersonians and the Federalists, who differed on so many policies, also differed on the question of the post office. Alexander Hamilton had wanted the post office to make money for the government.

The Jeffersonians, however, decided to use the proceeds from the post office to improve mail delivery on the frontier.

By Jackson's time stagecoaches were commonly used as mail carriers. One of the most colorful of mail carriers was the famous pony express in the year 1860. Railroads were first used as mail carriers in 1835. Rates were high; it cost 25 cents to send a one-page letter 400 miles. At that price the average American sent only two letters a year. However, rates were reduced, and in 1847 the first postage stamps were issued. City delivery service was introduced in 1863. Special delivery came into being in 1885. The isolation of farmers was lessened by the rural free delivery, established in 1896. Before World War I, postal savings, village delivery, and parcel post had extended the services of the postal system. Mail between New York and Washington, D.C., was carried by airplane in 1918. The Post Office Department operated its own planes until 1928. Certified mail was added to the department's many services in 1955. By 1957 the postal service employed half a million workers and took in 2.5 billion dollars each year.

The Post Office Department is run by the postmaster general, who is appointed by the president. In 1829 President Jackson made the office of postmaster general a Cabinet post, which it has been ever since. The Post Office Department became an executive department in 1872. See PONY EXPRESS.

With the advent of the automobile, billboards became popular. Such posters are boldly lettered and depict eye-catching features, such as the pretty girls on this poster.

The minuteman on this well-known poster became a familiar sight during World War II.

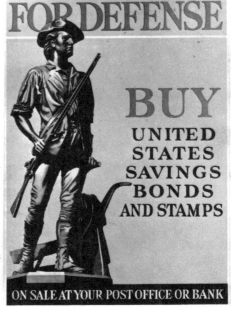

POSTURE is the arrangement of the parts of the body as a whole. Important muscles involved in maintaining a correct upright posture are located in the neck, the jaw, the back, the abdominal wall, the knees, and the ankles. Impulses from the inner ear and various areas in the brain alter the tone of these muscles. This makes possible slight adjustments required for maintenance of an upright posture for a long period of time. (See BALANCE.) Good posture is important for general health as it maintains a proper balance among internal organs. A person should develop proper posture in standing and sitting. For example, standing with one hip higher than the other and sitting with the shoulders bent should be avoided. The most important causes of abnormal posture are deformities of the spine, including a loss of elasticity and flexibility. Such deformities may be caused by inflammation of the bones, tuberculosis, or injuries. However, no general cause of abnormal curvatures of the spine, such as in humpback and in swayback, is known. In these cases an original softness of the bones involved, accompanied by muscular weaknesses, allows for the appearance of permanent deformities as the body develops. Such conditions as knock knees, flat feet, and obesity contribute to acquired bad posture. In such cases the strain on certain joints may lead to a form of arthritis. Cases of acquired poor posture can usually be improved with proper training.

For good standing posture the head is held erect, with shoulders squared, back straight, abdomen drawn in, and the feet pointing straight ahead. When sitting, the back should be straight, with the head, shoulders, and hips in vertical alignment.

POTASH, any one of several compounds formed by the union of potassium with other elements. It derives its name from the fact that it was first obtained from the ashes left in pots after burning wood or plants. It is used as a fertilizer and in the manufacture of hard glass, soap, drugs, dyes, photographic film, and many other products.

Before World War I the production of potash was a German monopoly. The war cut off the supply to the Allies, and the United States was forced to find another source. With the help of the U.S. Geological Survey, potash was discovered in California and Maryland. Besides these two sources, potash is also derived from deposits of potassium salts mined in New Mexico and from alunite in Utah.

POTASSIUM, an element, is a member of the family of alkali metals (Group IA in the periodic table). Its chemical symbol is K. Potassium in its pure state is a silver-white metal that can be easily molded or cut. Its density at 20° C. is 0.86. Potassium is an excellent conductor of heat and of electricity. All common potassium salts are soluble in water.

Potassium oxidizes (combines with oxygen) instantly when it is exposed to air. Unoxidized potassium is often stored by putting it in a container and covering it with kerosene. Kerosene does not contain any oxygen and does not absorb oxygen as do many other liquids. Potassium reacts violently with water to form hydrogen gas and potassium hydroxide, KOH, a powerful base.

Potassium makes up a little less than $2\frac{1}{2}$ percent of the earth's matter. Because of its high chemical activity potassium is never found in its pure state. It is found in com-

Courtesy of Ford Motor Company

Grapes grown in soil deficient in potassium (top) and grapes grown in a normal soil (bottom) are shown in the picture above.

The usual plant symptom of a lack of potassium is reduced growth. The small tomatoes below grew in potassium-deficient soil.

Courtesy of Ford Motor Company

pounds with oxygen, sulfur, carbon, chlorine, bromine, and nitrogen. The most important sources of potassium are layers of potassium salts that were deposited when ancient inland seas evaporated. Evaporation deposits are found near Stassfurt, Germany, in the western Ural Mountains of the U.S.S.R., and in the Permian basin near Carlsbad, N.M. Important deposits of another type are found in the coastal deserts of Chile. Still another source of potassium is brine that is obtained from inland salt seas or from brine wells. Potassium salts are produced in South Africa by evaporation of sea water. Potassium salts are obtained from ancient sea deposits in Spain, France, Israel, Poland, and Australia. Large deposits found in Yorkshire, England, lie 4,000 feet beneath the ground.

Potassium is a necessary ingredient of all plant and animal tissue. It helps utilize food for growth and energy. One of the important uses of potassium in the form of soluble compounds is in fertilizers for potassium-poor soils. (See FERTILIZER.) The compounds commonly used as fertilizers are potassium chloride,

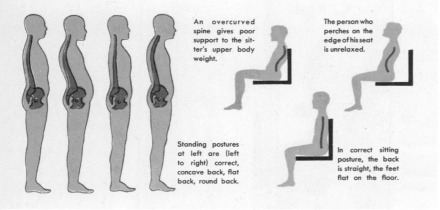

An overcurved spine gives poor support to the sitter's upper body weight.

The person who perches on the edge of his seat is unrelaxed.

Standing postures at left are (left to right) correct, concave back, flat back, round back.

In correct sitting posture, the back is straight, the feet flat on the floor.

KCl, and potassium sulfate, K_2SO_4.

Potassium chloride is the starting material for the manufacture of most potassium compounds. Potassium hydroxide, KOH, is used as a chemical reagent. It is also used in making soap and is used in some batteries. Potassium nitrate, KNO_3, is often called saltpeter. It is used in black gun powder, explosives, matches, and fireworks and in curing meat. Both potassium iodide, KI, and potassium bromide, KBr, are used in medicines and in photographic emulsions. Potassium carbonate, K_2CO_3, often called potash, is used in the manufacture of glass and soap. See POTASH.

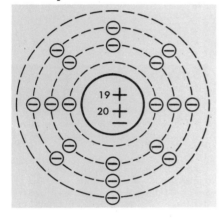

This diagram of a potassium atom shows how the 19 electrons (−) are arranged around a nucleus of 19 protons (+) and 20 neutrons. Potassium has atomic number 20; the atomic weight of the most abundant isotope is 39.

Potassium chloride is refined from brine pumped from wells in Searles Lake in southern California. The lake surface is usually dry and covered with a salt crust, as in this picture.

American Potash and Chemical Corporation

POTATO, a well-known tuberous plant native to the Western Hemisphere. It is called the white, or Irish, potato to distinguish it from the sweet potato. Next to rice, potatoes are the most widely eaten food in the world. Germany is the greatest potato-growing country in the world. The principal potato-growing states in the United States are Maine, Idaho, California, New York, Colorado, Minnesota, Pennsylvania, Wisconsin, North Dakota, Michigan, and Florida. The potato has been greatly changed and improved by horticulturists, and the varieties are multiplied and changed constantly. The plant was introduced into Spain by Peruvian explorers in 1538 and then spread through Europe. Potatoes consist principally of water (approximately 78 percent), starch (18 to 20 percent), and protein (approximately 2 percent). The plant thrives best in a well-watered, sandy loam. The potato plant is a member of the nightshade family and is closely related to the eggplant, tomato, and pepper. The potato plant has fibrous roots and also a number of underground stems, which become fleshy and swollen at their tips and form the potatoes. Thus, potatoes are not roots, even though they do grow underground, but are tubers that form on the ends of the stems. The eyes of the potato are little buds, which, if given the right opportunity, grow into leafy branches. That is what happens when potatoes sprout in the late winter or spring.

Potatoes are usually raised by planting pieces of potatoes, each containing one or two good eyes.

POTATO PRODUCTS

Potatoes can be converted into many commercial products, including potato chips and frozen french-fried slices; dry flour, granules, and flakes; canned potatoes; and alcohol and vodka.

In 1853 potato chips were produced by accident. Aunt Katy, an Indian cook in Saratoga, N.Y., was heating a pot of doughnut fat and slicing potatoes at the same time. A slice of fresh potato fell into the fat, and by the time Aunt Katy managed to skim the slice out, it was brown and delicious. Of course she made some more and called them saratoga chips. The potato-chip industry spread all over the United States, and in 1938 the National Potato Chip Institute was organized to conduct research in qualities of cooking, standards for oils, varieties of potatoes, and problems of saltiness and freshness.

Potato flour for bread and soups and potato flakes and granules for instant mashed potatoes compete successfully with other flours and with fresh potatoes. Canned potatoes are also available.

Potatoes are a source of alcohol and also have possibilities as a fuel, some of which has been produced in Germany. But 10 tons of potatoes produce only 255 gallons of alcohol, whereas 10 tons of grain produce 670 gallons. A powerful alcoholic drink, vodka, once made exclusively from rye and barley, may also be made from corn and potatoes.

POTOMAC RIVER, the stream that flows past the U.S. capital, Washington, D.C. It is formed by two branches that start in the Allegheny Mountains in West Virginia and unite 15 miles southeast of Cumberland, Md. From there the river flows northeast and then southeast along the Maryland–West Virginia border and the Maryland-Virginia border to Chesapeake Bay southeast of Washington. It is 285 miles long and about 8 miles wide at its mouth. Large vessels can go up the river as far as Washington, 115 miles above the mouth. Just above Washington are the Great Falls of the Potomac. The river's upper course flows through a deep gorge near Harpers Ferry, W.Va. The Potomac is noted for its beauty.

POTSDAM CONFERENCE, a meeting of the Big Three (Great Britain, the U.S.S.R., and the United States) held from July 17 until Aug. 2, 1945, to negotiate major policies for the peace settlements after the defeat of Germany. Continuing the war-planning discussions previously held at the Iranian capital of Teheran and at the Crimean resort of Yalta, the conference brought together Joseph Stalin, Harry S. Truman, and Clement Attlee, who replaced Winston Churchill as British prime minister on July 28.

The conference called upon Japan to surrender unconditionally and drew up the Potsdam Agreement with regard to defeated Germany. By this agreement Königsberg (now Kaliningrad) and the adjacent area, formerly the northern part of East Prussia, were placed under Soviet administration. Poland's administrative boundaries were extended

1. Coil pottery: Roll the moistened clay into a long rope, and coil it several times to form the base of the vase. Build up the sides of the vase as shown, and smooth out the ridges. Cut a piece of cardboard according to the desired outline form, and use it as a guide in giving the vase its final shape. 2. Hand-modeled pottery: Thrust the thumbs into a lump of clay and spread it outward. Shape it as desired; let it dry before baking or firing.

westward to the Oder and Neisse rivers to await the peace settlement. The agreement provided for the evacuation of Germans living in Poland, Czechoslovakia, and Hungary.

The powers also agreed to destroy every vestige of German military power; to extirpate all the organs of the Nazi party; to deprive Germany of all heavy industry not needed in a peace economy; to permit the excess industrial equipment to be used for reparations, much of which was promised to the Soviet Union; and to bring to justice the German war criminals. Numerous other questions were referred to the five-power Council of Foreign Ministers (including France and China), which was set up by the Big Three to continue negotiations for the peace settlements.

POTTERY AND POTTERY MAKING, the art and science of creating stonelike dishes and other objects out of clay. This raw material, which is plastic when blended with water, becomes a totally different substance, pottery, when slowly fired up to higher than 1000° F. and then slowly cooled. So inert to the destructive forces of water, frost, and soil is pottery that pieces of it made by men and women thousands of years ago are still found in perfect condition. Pottery making seems to have evolved independently wherever tribes settled down in the vicinity of clay deposits.

The four stages in making pottery are molding the damp clay, decorating the damp-clay object, firing the clay object into biscuit ware, and glazing the porous biscuit ware.

In working with clay the pottery maker can have the thrill of reproducing some of the experiences of mankind from the ages before the dawn of recorded history. The six basic methods of pottery shaping are: building up by means of the soft, coiled rope of clay; using a basket as a frame, on which the clay is daubed; scooping out a lump of clay while fashioning the outside with the fingers; pressing the clay around a soft mold and letting it dry; throwing clay on a potter's wheel; and casting heavy liquid clay as slip in a mold.

After the clay object has been shaped and dried to the consistency of heavy leather, decoration, in the form of incising or painting, is generally applied. Many large objects, such as jars or casks, are built up in sections and then cemented together with slip at this stage.

Clement Attlee, Harry Truman, and Joseph Stalin participated in the Potsdam Conference.
UPI

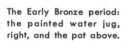

Archaeologists learn much about the customs of ancient peoples from the kinds of pots they used. The pots below range from the Bronze Age to the Iron Age.

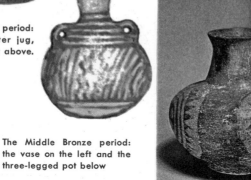

The Early Bronze period: the painted water jug, right, and the pot above.

The Middle Bronze period: the vase on the left and the three-legged pot below

Laura Gilpin

Maria Martinez (above), one of the United States most skillful modern Indian potters, lives and works in San Ildefonso, N.M. The Arkansas vase (left) is an example of Indian pottery.

Museum of the American Indian—Heye Foundation

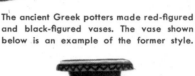

Washing stand, left, and table bowl, above, are from the Iron Age I period.

The Late Bronze period: the yellow bowl, lower left, and the pitcher, lower right

The work of reconstructing ancient pottery from the fragments uncovered through archaeological excavation requires considerable knowledge and skill.

Agora Museum, Athens, Greece

Iron Age II period: the bronze pitcher above and the loop-handled pot left.

The ancient Greek potters made red-figured and black-figured vases. The vase shown below is an example of the former style.

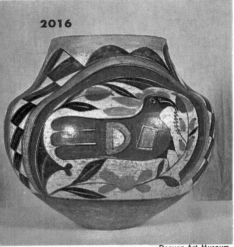

Denver Art Museum

This jar is typical of Pueblo pottery.

Firing pottery, first brought to perfection by the Chinese in their manufacture of porcelain, requires much in the way of experiment, skill, and observation. Each clay has its own fusion point, ranging from 752° F. to about 2500° F.

If too low a temperature is used, the clay reverts to its porous, fragile condition; if too high a temperature is used, the clay object melts down into a lump. Temperatures in pottery making are measured not in degrees but by ceramic cones of various resistances to heat, which soften and bend as the heat rises.

Glaze is the decorative and protective glassy covering melted onto pottery in the second firing. Unfired glaze is a very fine powdered type of special glass, frequently beautifully colored, mixed in water to a thick, creamy consistency. This material is painted onto porous biscuit ware and is melted to a smooth, impervious surface.

With an electric kiln that costs less than $100 the amateur pottery maker can strive to match the skill of the Chinese masters of the Ming Dynasty or the equally beautiful creations of the Incas.

POULENC, FRANCIS (1899-   ), French composer, born in Paris. His musical education, which consisted almost entirely of private lessons in piano technique and classical composition, was cut short by military service in World War I. His first significant composition, a rhapsody scored for piano, string quartet, flute, clarinet, and voice, was written in 1917. Influenced by the aesthetic ideas of composer Erik Satie and writer Jean Cocteau, Poulenc soon joined "The Six," a group of young French composers who shared a dislike for the romanticism of the impressionist school of music. With his colleagues, Poulenc sought frankness and plainness of musical expression. To achieve his purpose he frequently drew upon the popular music performed in the carnival and the music hall. Typical of his work are *Le Gendarme incompris*, written in the manner of the *opera buffa*, and *Les Biches*, a ballet. He also wrote songs, piano pieces, and chamber music.

The style of this modern black-on-black jar originated in San Ildefonso, N.M.

Laura Gilpin

The New York Historical Society

POULTRY, a general name for all kinds of domesticated fowl, including the chicken, the duck, the turkey, the goose, the guinea fowl, the pigeon, and the pheasant. See CHICKEN.

Major poultry products are eggs, meat, and feathers. Feathers and goose down are used in various proportions to stuff pillows but are of minor commercial importance. However, since 1940 the annual consumption of eggs per person in the United States has risen from 319 to 348, an increase of 11 percent; the annual consumption of roasters, broilers, and fryers per person has risen from 14 to 28 pounds; and the consumption of turkey, from not quite 3 pounds per person per year to almost 6 pounds. Behind this spectacular increase in the consumption of poultry products lies a revolution in production and marketing methods, which has not yet run its course.

Egg production per hen per year has risen since 1925 from 90 to 180. This rise has been accompanied by a drastic fall in labor costs and food costs per dozen eggs. From 1946 to 1956 retail egg prices rose by less than 5 percent, while the general price level almost doubled.

Falling costs have also been achieved in the production of broilers and fryers. In 1942 farmers had to feed 470 pounds of food to make 100 pounds of meat, whereas 14 years later they needed only 317 pounds of food. During the same years farm income from poultry and eggs rose about 9 percent.

The shift to turkey as a year-round source of meat has been due to the tremendous improvement in

A 19th-century Wedgwood-china pitcher

The teapot and sugar bowl on the left were made in England during the 19th century for sale in the United States. These pieces are decorated on one side with Robert Fulton's famous steamboat, the *Clermont*, and on the other side with a large sailing ship.

This jungle fowl, a member of the pheasant family, is the ancestor of domestic poultry. It resembles the domestic chicken. It still exists in a wild state in the oriental regions.

Courtesy of Poultry Tribune

African Geese

Ring-Necked Pheasant

Rouen Ducks

Single-Comb Buff Minorca

Pigeon

White Holland Turkeys

Courtesy of Poultry Tribune

These variations in comb are examples of hereditary variations.

the breeding of small turkeys and to the cure and control of many poultry diseases, especially pullorum disease and blackhead. These diseases used to kill not only millions of chickens but also many flocks of turkeys.

Other advances in the poultry-products industries are the production of millions of disease-free, day-old chicks in commercial hatcheries; the separation of cockerels from pullets when one day old; the raising of the cockerels intensively for meat; and cleaner packaging, icing, and deep freezing.

Poultry raising may be done either on a large commercial scale or simply as a backyard enterprise to satisfy the poultry needs of a single family. The first rule for getting a good profit from poultry is to have high-quality birds that have been hatched early in the year. Most poultry raisers buy these chicks when they are a day old. The next rule is to keep them growing so that they will reach egg-laying maturity before the beginning of cold weather. Cleanliness is essential in raising chicks, as they are not very sturdy and are subject to several diseases. They should be raised apart from old stock and should be kept on clean land. Since small, bare yards soon become contaminated, it is better to raise chicks in a house with an outside wire-floored sun porch that will keep them entirely off the ground.

Chicken houses should be light, comfortable, and dry. They should have a good supply of fresh air but be free from drafts. The building should have a southern or southeastern exposure, and the number of windows and openings and the amount of ventilation should be regulated according to the climate. The site of the house should be well drained. Concrete floors are preferred. The house should be large enough to allow about 4 square feet of floor space for each bird. Roosts should be at the back of the house about $2\frac{1}{2}$ feet from the floor.

Chickenfeed has several ingredients, ordinarily including ground yellow corn, ground wheat, wheat bran, wheat middlings, soybean meal, alfalfa meal, fishmeal, ground limestone, steamed bonemeal, salt mixture, riboflavin supplement, cod-liver oil, and vitamin B_{12} supplement. These are mixed in different proportions for chicks and adult chickens. Ordinarily, feeds are purchased already mixed, although operators of large poultry farms may mix their own feeds.

POWER, as a physical concept, is defined as the rate at which work is done. A weight may be lifted a certain distance in one minute or one hour; the work done in either case is the same, but the power developed is different. Since work is equal to force $\times$ distance, power is equal to (force $\times$ distance) $\div$ time. See ENERGY; FORCE; WORK.

In engineering, the horsepower is defined as doing work at a rate equal to lifting 550 pounds of weight 1 foot per second. In the metric system the watt is the unit of power and is equal to 1 newton-meter per second, or 1 joule per second. In electrical units wattage is equal to voltage $\times$ amperage. Since the watt is a small unit, the kilowatt (1,000 watts) is often used. The watt was named after James Watt, who was the first person to measure power. See HORSEPOWER.

Any type of power can be measured in either horsepower or kilowatts. A 100 horsepower automobile engine is also a 74.6 kilowatt engine. Electric light bulbs could be rated in horsepower instead of watts. An electric power company charges its customers for kilowatt-hours of electricity. This unit is equal to power $\times$ time and is thus a unit of work rather than of power.

POWER, in mathematics, is the product resulting from repeated multiplication of a number by itself. The operation of raising a number to a power is thus a special case of multiplication in which all the factors are equal. The operation is indicated by an exponent, a small number to the right and toward the top of the base number. The rules for multiplying and dividing powers and raising them to powers are called the laws of exponents.

Powers are referred to by the number of times one number—the base—is used as a factor. For example, the number 4 multiplied by itself 3 times is called the third power of 4, or 4 cubed. This expression is written 4^3, where 4 is the base and 3 is the exponent. The second power of 5, or 5 squared, is written 5^2.

There are five laws of exponents, governing multiplication, division, power of a power, power of a product, and power of a quotient. The law of exponents for multiplication states that two or more powers having the same base may be multiplied by adding the exponents and raising the common base to that power. For example,

$$6^2 \times 6^3 = 6^{2+3} = 6^5$$

Conversely, division on powers of the same base is done by subtracting exponents. Thus,

$$4^4 \div 4^2 = 4^{4-2} = 4^2$$

To raise a power to a power, multiply the exponents. For example,

$$(2^3)^2 = 2^{3 \cdot 2} = 2^6$$

The final two laws of exponents state that the power of a product is equal to the product of the powers of the factors, and the power of a quotient is equal to the quotient of the powers. Thus,

$$(2.3^2.5^{3(2)} = 2^{1 \cdot 3}.3^{2 \cdot 2}.5^{3 \cdot 2}$$
$$= 2^2.3^4.5^6$$

and

$$\left(\frac{3}{4}\right)^3 = \frac{3^3}{4^3}$$

In work with the laws of exponents, powers that require special explanation occur. Zero exponents arise in division of powers: for example, $4^3 \div 4^3 = 4^0$. The expression "zero power" may at first seem meaningless. However, since any number divided by itself equals 1, $4^3 \div 4^3$ must equal 1, and thus 4^0 must also equal 1. The zero power of any number except zero is found equal to 1. Similarly it is found that the first power of any number must be the number itself; or, in other words, every number written without exponent carries the exponent 1 understood. A number with a negative exponent is equal to 1 divided by the same number with the corresponding positive exponent. (For example, $8^{-2} = \frac{1}{8^2}$.) Fractional exponents indicate roots; thus, $9^{1/2} = \sqrt{9}$, and $27^{1/3} = \sqrt[3]{27}$. See ROOT.

POWHATAN (1550?-1618), an American Indian chief. He was leader of the powerful federation of Powhatan Indians of the Algonquian group, whom the English settlers named after the chief. The confederation, which at its height in the early 17th century consisted of about 30 tribes, occupied about 200 settlements centered in the Tidewater area of Virginia. Differences between the white settlers of the English colony and the Indians were settled temporarily by the marriage of Pocahontas, Powhatan's daughter, to the Englishman John Rolfe in 1614. After Powhatan's death hostilities were resumed. In 1637 the Indians wiped out all white settlements except Jamestown. Soon afterward, however, the decline of the federation commenced. By the end of the 17th century most of its territories had been lost, and in the early 18th century the federation was dissolved.

The Prague Palace and St. Vitus Cathedral, shown above, are notable buildings in Prague.

PRAGUE, city and capital of Czechoslovakia, in central Bohemia, on the Moldau River, 170 miles south of Berlin. The population is about 1,000,000. It is a picturesque city, situated on both banks of the river, and is known as the City of a Hundred Spires. The river is spanned by 12 bridges. Charles Bridge, over 1,600 feet long and dating from 1357, is guarded by two towers, the buttresses of which are adorned with many statuary pieces and groups. The ancient walls were torn down to make room for boulevards and gardens. The city is divided into two sections known as the Old Town and the New Town. There are important manufactures of heavy machinery, automobiles, aircraft, railroad rolling stock, clothing, furniture, foodstuffs, chemicals, electrical equipment, smoked meats, and fancy leather articles.

Charles University of Prague was founded in 1348 and has always been known as an outstanding center of European scholarship. It has a large library, an astronomical ob-servatory, museums, and botanical gardens. Other structures of note are the 9th-century Hradcany Castle, St. Nicholas Church, the Church of Our Lady of Victory, Clementinum Library, Waldstein Palace, the 13th-century Town Hall, the 15th-century Power Tower, a 13th-century synagogue, St. Vitus

This prairie dog is standing by its burrow.

Cathedral, the National Theater, and Masaryk, or Strahov, Stadium.

Prague was founded about the 9th century, and by the time of King Wenceslaus I of Bohemia it had become an important town. It was made the capital of Bohemia in 1336. In the early part of the 16th century it was famous as a center of scientific research, with such scholars as Johannes Kepler and Tycho Brahe. The city was captured by the French in 1742 and by the Prussians in 1744 during the War of the Austrian Succession. In the 19th century it became the center of Czech nationalism, and in 1918 the Czechoslovakian republic was proclaimed here. From 1939 to 1945, during World War II, it was occupied by the Germans. It suffered considerable damage but was rapidly rebuilt.

PRAIRIE. The prairies are tracts of level or rolling, grassy, generally treeless land. In contrast to the short grasses of the steppes, prairie grasses are tall. The humid Pampas of Argentina can be considered prairies. In central North America they extend from Ohio in the United States across southern Michigan, Illinois, Indiana, Wisconsin, Iowa, Minnesota, and west of the Missouri River, to the foothills of the Rocky Mountains. In Canada the area is smaller, stretching from a point east of Winnipeg, Manitoba, to the Rocky Mountains. The soil is deep and fertile, but west of the Missouri irrigation is often required. The prairies are subject to severely cold winters and often to arid summers. The prevailing wind is from the west, and it loses much of its moisture as it passes over the Rocky Mountains.

PRAIRIE CHICKEN. See GROUSE, PTARMIGANS, PRAIRIE CHICKENS.

PRAIRIE DOG, a name given to squirrel-like burrowing rodents of western American prairies. Their cry somewhat resembles the bark of a small dog. They have also been called barking squirrels. They are about 1 foot long; the color varies from a cream to a brown. They formerly made large communities on the prairies; now their numbers have been greatly reduced. Each burrow has a little hillock at its entrance. Passages connect the burrows, which are sometimes shared by the burrowing owl.

PRAIRIE SCHOONER. See COVERED WAGON.

PRAXITELES (flourished 4th century B.C.), Greek sculptor, born in Athens. Although Praxiteles was one of the greatest of all sculptors, little is known about his life. It is fairly certain, however, that he spent most of his years in Athens and that he also worked in a number of cities in Asia Minor. The terminating date of his sculpturing was about 332 B.C. He was survived by two sons, both of whom were sculptors.

Although various authorities have set his total number of works at 60 or more, the marble statue of Hermes with the infant Dionysus (preserved near the site of its excavation at Olympia, Greece) is generally believed to be the only original Praxiteles in existence. Copies of this and other works—statues of Aphrodite, Apollo, Eros, and satyrs —are housed in museums throughout the world. "Aphrodite of Cnidus," known to us through copies alone, has long been admired as Praxiteles' greatest achievement.

PRAYER WHEELS, cylinders or wheels revolved with the aim of obtaining spiritual or magical benefits. Ancient peoples often associated the wheel with the sun. The Rig-Veda, religious poetry of early Hinduism, speaks of the sun as a wheel that nothing can stop and that gives existence to all things. The wheel was also likened to the sun by the Latins, the Celts, the Teutons, and other groups. Gradually, the wheel, among certain peoples, came to represent the cosmos.

Nowhere were prayer wheels more in evidence than in Tibet, the country of Lamaism. Small cylinders of silver attached to wooden handles were spun by monks, who recited a formula engraved on the cylinder, *"Om mani padme Hum"* ("O the jewel in the lotus"). Larger cylinders of brightly colored wood were placed near monasteries. People passing by could turn these cylinders by means of a handle. Many cylinders contained written prayers or religious manuscripts, and it was believed that the person revolving the prayer wheel would derive the same spiritual benefit as if he had read the texts or recited the prayers contained in the cylinder. Prayer wheels in the form of water wheels were built on streams, and they turned out spiritual benefit continuously for the person who constructed them.

Lamaism derived its idea of the prayer wheel from Buddhism. Buddhist texts do not mention prayer

This beautiful silver prayer wheel was made by a skilled Tibetan craftsman.

wheels, but the wheel is often given a spiritual significance.

A type of prayer wheel was sometimes placed on wooden pillars at the entrance of Japanese pagodas. In parts of France (Brittany) wheels decorated with bells were sometimes placed near images of the saints. The turning of the wheel in honor of the saint afforded spiritual benefit to the worshiper.

PRAYING MANTIS. See MANTIS.

As the earth's axis precesses, the north celestial pole gradually moves in a circle around the constellation Draco. Today it is near the star Polaris in Ursa Minor, the Little Dipper. In about 12,000 years the pole will reach the opposite side of the circle near the brilliant star Vega in Lyra.

PRECESSION, in astronomy, the gyration of the earth's axis in relation to the celestial sphere. This gyration, which takes about 26,000 years to complete one cycle, causes gradual changes in the apparent positions of heavenly bodies and in the time of the equinoxes.

The rotation of the earth has caused it to bulge slightly at the Equator, so that the earth's shape is that of an oblate spheroid rather than that of a sphere. This equatorial bulge is tilted $23\frac{1}{2}$ degrees from the plane of the ecliptic, or the plane of the earth's orbit around the sun. The attraction of the sun and the moon acts on the equatorial bulge, tending to bring the Equator in line with the ecliptic. But because the earth is spinning, the Equator and the ecliptic do not actually line up; instead, the gyration called precession occurs. This gyration is similar to the gyration of a spinning top, set up by the attraction of gravity.

Precession is manifested in several interesting phenomena. One is the movement of the celestial poles, the points where the earth's axis meets the celestial sphere. Thus all the stars gradually change their positions upon the celestial sphere though not relative to each other. Several thousand years ago a different star from Polaris lay near the north celestial pole. The precession of the earth's axis also caused the equinoxes to move forward, or precess, making the year of our seasons 20 minutes shorter than a full sidereal year. See YEAR.

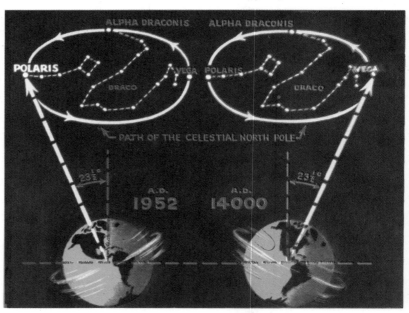

PRECIPITATION, in weather and climate, a general term covering all forms of moisture falling from the sky. The word *rainfall* is often used to refer to all kinds of precipitation. When the Weather Bureau offers an average annual rainfall measurement of 42.16 inches for Washington, D.C., this water measurement includes rain, sleet, snow, and hail. On the U.S. Weather Bureau maps precipitation is shown by shading. See ATMOSPHERIC CONDENSATION; CLOUD SEEDING; DEW; HAIL; MONSOON; RAIN; RAINFALL MEASUREMENT; SLEET; SNOW.

PREFIX, in morphology, an affix of one or more letters or syllables that precedes the radical element (root or stem) of a word. The infix and the suffix are other types of affixes. (See SUFFIX.) Examples of prefixes in English are *re-* in *refill,* *bi-* in *biplane,* and *in-* in *incomplete.* The prefix limits, or modifies, the idea or object represented by the stem. Prefixes cannot normally stand alone as independent words; some of the abstract relations indicated by prefixes are negation (*non-, dis-, im-, in-, a-*), position in space and time (*ante-, pre-, re-*), and number (*bi-, tri-*). Eskimo, Yana, Nootka, and Hottentot are languages that do not use prefixes at all. Languages in which prefixation is very important include English, French, German, Russian, Latin, Hebrew, Apache, Navaho, Hupa, and the Bantu languages of Africa.

PREMATURE BABY, a baby that is born more than two weeks before the expected time. Because it is difficult to determine the exact time a baby is due, all babies weighing less than $5\frac{1}{2}$ pounds are considered premature. All such babies need special care.

After the 28th week, or roughly about $6\frac{1}{2}$ calendar months of pregnancy, a baby's chances of living, if prematurely born, increase with each month. A 7-months' baby has a fair chance of surviving premature birth; an 8-months' baby, even better chances. The most dangerous time of a premature baby's life is in the first few days. With every day that goes by, the chances for his survival increase tremendously. At the present time premature babies have a better chance than ever before because of the widespread knowledge of improved ways of taking care of such babies.

Premature babies need special care because they are not so strong and their bodies are not so ready to get along in the world as those of larger babies. They may need to live in an incubator for a while, where there is carefully regulated temperature and humidity. When it is necessary to make it easier for a baby to breathe, oxygen is introduced into the incubator. Very tiny, weak babies are often fed through a tube at first or through a medicine dropper. If they are very tiny, premature babies should not be handled any more than is absolutely necessary. Small babies need to be especially carefully protected against infection, so only those workers whose duties lie entirely within the premature nurseries are allowed to handle them. Most premature babies are not sent home until they weigh $5\frac{1}{2}$ to 6 pounds.

When premature babies start to gain, they seem to be in a hurry. As compared to full-term babies they sometimes make extrafast gains.

Naturally, it takes premature babies a while to catch up in size with babies who had the advantage of a longer time to develop. Sitting, standing, walking, and talking all come along in proportion to the amount of time such a baby is "behind" a baby who was born at full term.

PREPOSITION, in English grammar one of the traditional parts of speech. A preposition may be one word (*at, by, for, from, in, of, on, to, with*) or a compound ("in front of," "with respect to," "in spite of," "according to"). The preposition connects substantives (nouns and pronouns) with other grammatical elements of a sentence, such as other substantives (We took *a drive* in *the country*) or verbs (It *was put* on *the floor*). Prepositional relations are abstract relations, the commonest of which is that of space and time (*above, behind, during, until, since, after*).

Of the two grammatical elements a preposition joins, one follows it in the sentence and is called the object of the preposition. The object may be a word (He went to *Chicago*), a phrase (She lives in *a big red house*), or a clause (He pointed to *where the bottle had fallen*). When the object is a pronoun, the objective form is used: "with *her*." "for *him*," "to *them*."

The preposition, its object, and the object's modifiers together constitute a prepositional phrase, which may function grammatically as an adjective (The tree *in the yard* is an elm), as an adverb (We ran *beside the road*), or as a substantive (*On the table* is the best place for it).

It is not absolutely necessary for the preposition to precede its object. Most grammarians agree it is necessary in some instances to place the preposition at the end of the sentence to avoid awkwardness of expression or to conform to idiomatic practice: For example, "He is the man whom I bought the book from." "He is the man I talked with" is more colloquial than "He is the man with whom I talked."

PRESIDENT OF THE UNITED STATES, the chief executive officer of the United States, is elected for a term of four years and cannot be elected to more than two terms. He must be at least 35 years of age, have been a resident of the United States for 14 years, and be a "natural-born" citizen. He is provided with an official residence and is paid a salary of $100,000 per year plus an expense account of $50,000 per year. He may veto legislation passed by Congress, which can repass it over his veto only by means of a two-thirds majority vote in both houses. With the consent of the Senate he has the power to make treaties and appoint cabinet officers, Supreme Court justices, foreign representatives, and many other officials. He is commander in chief of the armed forces and may grant reprieves and pardons. He can be removed from office only by the impeachment of Congress for treason, bribery, and other high crimes. In case of the president's death or removal from office by resignation or inability, the vice president takes over the office. In case both men resign or become disabled, the order of succession to the presidency, as established by act of Congress in 1955, is as follows: the speaker of the House of Representatives, the president pro tempore of the Senate, the secretary of state, the secretary of the treasury, the secretary of defense, the attorney general, the postmaster general, the secretary of the interior, the secretary of agriculture, the secretary of commerce, the secretary of labor, and the secretary of health, education, and welfare.

In 1792 Congress enacted a law providing that the president begin his term of office on March 4, following his election. This law was superseded by the 20th Amendment (1933), which established that "the terms of the President and the Vice-President shall end at noon on the 20th day of January."

PRESIDENTS
OF THE
UNITED STATES

George Washington
president 1789–1797

John Adams
president 1797–1801

Thomas Jefferson
president 1801–1809

James Madison
president 1809–1817

James Monroe
president 1817–1825

John Quincy Adams
president 1825–1829

Andrew Jackson
president 1829–1837

Martin Van Buren
president 1837–1841

William Henry Harrison
president 1841

John Tyler
president 1841–1845

James K. Polk
president 1845–1849

Zachary Taylor
president 1849–1850

Millard Fillmore
president 1850–1853

Franklin Pierce
president 1853–1857

James Buchanan
president 1857–1861

Abraham Lincoln
president 1861–1865

Andrew Johnson
president 1865–1869

Ulysses S. Grant
president 1869–1877

Rutherford B. Hayes
president 1877–1881

James Garfield
president 1881

Chester A. Arthur
president 1881–1885

Grover Cleveland
president 1885–1889, 1893–1897

Benjamin Harrison
president 1889–1893

William McKinley
president 1897–1901

Theodore Roosevelt
president 1901–1909

William Howard Taft
president 1909–1913

Woodrow Wilson
president 1913–1921

Warren G. Harding
president 1921–1923

Calvin Coolidge
president 1923–1929

Herbert Hoover
president 1929–1933

Franklin D. Roosevelt
president 1933–1945

Harry S. Truman
president 1945–1953

Dwight D. Eisenhower
president 1953–1961

John F. Kennedy
president 1961–

PRESIDENTS OF THE UNITED STATES

Name	Lifetime	Party	In Office	Important Events
Washington, George	1732-1799	Federalist	1789-1797	Bill of Rights—Neutrality Proclamation—Whisky rebellion—Jay's Treaty
Adams, John	1735-1826	Federalist	1797-1801	Naval war with France—Alien and Sedition Acts
Jefferson, Thomas	1743-1826	Dem.-Rep.	1801-1809	Louisiana Purchase—Embargo Act—*Marbury* vs. *Madison*
Madison, James	1751-1836	Dem.-Rep.	1809-1817	Battle of Tippecanoe—War of 1812—Hartford Convention
Monroe, James	1758-1831	Dem.-Rep.	1817-1825	Era of Good Feelings—Missouri Compromise—Monroe Doctrine
Adams, John Quincy	1767-1848	Dem.-Rep.	1825-1829	American System—Erie Canal completed
Jackson, Andrew	1767-1845	Democratic	1829-1837	Spoils system—Nullification controversy—Bank veto—Republic of Texas
Van Buren, Martin	1782-1862	Democratic	1837-1841	Panic of 1837—Abolitionist controversy—Independent Treasury Act
Harrison, William Henry	1773-1841	Whig	1841	
Tyler, John	1790-1862	Whig	1841-1845	Webster-Ashburton Treaty—Oregon Dispute
Polk, James	1795-1849	Democratic	1845-1849	Texas annexed—Mexican War—Wilmot Proviso—Gold discovered in California
Taylor, Zachary	1784-1850	Whig	1849-1850	Free-Soil Party—Compromise of 1850
Fillmore, Millard	1800-1874	Whig	1850-1853	Fugitive Slave Law—Clayton-Bulwer Treaty—First Railroad to Great Lakes
Pierce, Franklin	1804-1869	Democratic	1853-1857	Gadsden Purchase—Perry's reopening of Japan—Republican Party founded
Buchanan, James	1791-1868	Democratic	1857-1861	Dred Scott decision—Panic of 1857—Secession of the Confederate states
Lincoln, Abraham	1809-1865	Republican	1861-1865	Civil War—Emancipation Proclamation
Johnson, Andrew	1808-1875	Democratic	1865-1869	Reconstruction Acts—13th and 14th Amendments—Purchase of Alaska—Impeachment of Johnson
Grant, Ulysses	1822-1885	Republican	1869-1877	Ku Klux Klan—Credit Mobilier—Panic of 1873—Civil Rights Act
Hayes, Rutherford B.	1822-1893	Republican	1877-1881	Great Strike of '77—Defeat of radical Republicans—Samoan treaty
Garfield, James A.	1831-1881	Republican	1881	Assassination of Garfield, July 2, 1881
Arthur, Chester A.	1830-1886	Republican	1881-1885	Pendleton Act—Agrarian discontent—International Prime Meridian Conference
Cleveland, Grover	1837-1908	Democratic	1885-1889	A. F. of L. organized—Interstate Commerce Act—Hatch Act—First Pan-American Conference
Harrison, Benjamin	1833-1901	Republican	1889-1893	Sherman Antitrust Act—Populist Party—Panic of 1893
Cleveland, Grover	1837-1908	Democratic	1893-1897	Forest Reserve Act—Venezuelan Boundary Dispute
McKinley, William	1843-1901	Republican	1897-1901	Spanish-American War—Gold Standard Act—Open Door Policy
Roosevelt, Theodore	1858-1919	Republican	1901-1909	Muckrakers—Pure Food and Drug Act—National Conservation Commission—Hay-Bunau-Varilla Treaty—Roosevelt Corollary—Portsmouth Peace Conference
Taft, William H.	1857-1930	Republican	1909-1913	Mann-Elkins Act—Progressive Movement
Wilson, Woodrow	1856-1924	Democratic	1913-1921	16th, 17th, 18th, and 19th Amendments—Federal Reserve Act—Clayton Antitrust Act—Federal Farm Loan Act World War I—League of Nations
Harding, Warren	1865-1923	Republican	1921-1923	Washington Armament Conference—Budget and Accounting Act—Veterans Bureau—Teapot Dome Scandal
Coolidge, Calvin	1872-1933	Republican	1923-1929	Billy Mitchell Trial—Sacco-Vanzetti Case—Dawes Plan—Naval Disarmament: Geneva Conference—Kellogg-Briand Pact
Hoover, Herbert	1874-	Republican	1929-1933	Panic of 1929—Young Plan—London Naval Conference—Veterans Administration Act—Hoover Debt Moratorium—Reconstruction Finance Corporation
Roosevelt, Franklin D.	1882-1945	Democratic	1933-1945	Good Neighbor Policy—The New Deal—TVA—Gold Reserve Act—WPA—NLRA—Social Security Act—Fair Labor Standards Act—World War II—Atlantic Charter—Yalta Conference
Truman, Harry S.	1884-	Democratic	1945-1953	United Nations—Potsdam Conference—UNRRA—Marshall Plan—NATO—Berlin blockade—Korean War—Presidential Succession Act—22nd Amendment—Taft-Hartley Act—Cold War
Eisenhower, Dwight D.	1890-	Republican	1953-1961	New states: Alaska, Hawaii—Summit Conference—Hydrogen bomb, atom-powered submarine, ICBM, earth satellite
Kennedy, John F.	1917-	Democratic	1961-	

PRESSURE, in physics, is defined as the force exerted by a fluid on a specific area, at right angles to the surface. Common units of pressure are the dyne per square centimeter and the pound per square inch. Atmospheric pressures are usually measured in millimeters of mercury or in bars. One bar is 1,000,000 dynes per square centimeter. See ATMOSPHERIC PRESSURE.

The pressure changes of a mass of gas as its volume and temperature change are expressed by the general gas law. The general gas law is obtained by combining Boyle's gas law and Charles's gas law. (See BOYLE, ROBERT; GAS.) The law can be stated as

$$\frac{P'V'}{T'} = \frac{PV}{T}$$

In this statement of the gas law P' is the original pressure, and P is the final pressure. V' is the original volume and V the final volume. T' and T, the original and final temperatures, are measured on the absolute, or Kelvin, temperature scale ($273°$ K. $= 0°$ C.).

Liquids do not react to pressure changes as do gases. (See FLUID; LIQUID.) Pressure gauges may not show absolute pressures. They may show only pressures above some standard pressure or may show the pressure of only one material in the system.

Partial pressure is the part of the total pressure of a system that is due to one component. If two gases that do not react chemically with each other are put in the same container, the actual pressure on a wall of the container is caused partly by one of the gases and partly by the other gas.

Vapor pressure is the pressure exerted by a vapor. A vapor consists of liquid molecules that have acquired enough energy to escape from the body of a liquid. The vapor pressure of a particular liquid varies according to the temperature. The vapor pressure of a liquid is an indication of the difference between the number of molecules that are escaping from a liquid and the number that are being recaptured. See VAPOR.

Osmotic pressure is the pressure of a solution necessary to stop the flow of a pure solvent through a semipermeable membrane between a solvent and a solution. When the solution pressure is equal to the osmotic pressure, the solvent will not flow through the separating membrane into the solution. See OSMOSIS.

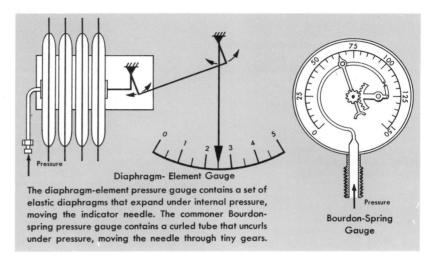

Diaphragm- Element Gauge

The diaphragm-element pressure gauge contains a set of elastic diaphragms that expand under internal pressure, moving the indicator needle. The commoner Bourdon-spring pressure gauge contains a curled tube that uncurls under pressure, moving the needle through tiny gears.

Bourdon-Spring Gauge

PRESSURE GAUGE. Two types of mechanical pressure gauges are in common use to measure the pressure of water, steam, gas, or compressed air. The simplest one is merely a bent tube with some type of liquid filling the bend. If the gas supply is connected to one end of the tube, the pressure will force the liquid up into the other part of the tube. The distance the liquid is forced to move can be measured as an indication of the gas pressure. Where pressures are high, mercury is used as the liquid in this instrument, known as a manometer. See MANOMETER.

A more complex gauge, and one used for great pressures, is the Bourdon gauge, which can be used to measure pressures of a thousand pounds or more. This gauge consists of a flattened metal tube bent in the shape of a circle. One end of the tube is closed, and the other is fitted to a pipe joining it to a pressure system. As pressure is applied to the tube, it tends to straighten out, which causes a system of levers and cogwheels to move a needle over a scale. See ALTIMETER; BAROMETER.

For the measurement of very low pressures thermal (hot-wire) gauges or ionization gauges often are used. The thermal gauge operates on the principle that the heat loss from an electrically heated coil of wire or filament changes as the pressure changes. The amount of heat lost is measured electrically. Some ionization gauges contain a hot filament, a grid, and a plate. They are essentially a triode electron tube with the glass cover removed. Electrons are emitted from the heated filament and ionize molecules of the gas whose pressure is being meas-

ured. The ions formed go to the plate of the tube and set up a flow of current. The flow of current is proportional to the number of ions that reach the plate. The number of ions formed is proportional to the number of molecules present per volume, which is equivalent to the pressure. Therefore the flow of current measures the pressure. Another type of ionization gauge uses radioactive material to emit electrons that ionize gas molecules.

PRESSURE-SENSITIVE MATERIAL, a class of adhesives, usually in the form of tape, that by its high degree of tackiness on one or both sides adheres to or bonds together instantly and easily wood, metal, leather, paper, cloth, or plastic. Pressure-sensitive tapes produce no physical or chemical change in the

When sanding part of a wood surface, mask adjacent areas with pressure-sensitive tape.
Grand Rapids Varnish Corp.

surfaces of the materials to which they are applied. On removal by a light pull, these tapes leave surfaces clean.

Some types of tape are made with adhesive material on both sides. Rolls of these types of tape generally require a layer of non-adhesive material between the sticky surfaces of the tape. Pressure-sensitive materials are also manufactured in liquid form to be spread on surfaces that when partially dried make a bond when laid together.

Cloth, plastic film, tough paper, or even asbestos is used as a backing. To the backing is applied the tacky material such as rubber, synthetic rubber, or one of the many other natural and synthetic adhesive compounds. Research on new backing materials and new tacky materials is intensive.

Pressure-sensitive materials are used as masking tapes in painting, stenciling, and sandblasting, and as insulation in electric motors. Manufacturers use colored pressure-sensitive tapes to identify parts and materials. Shippers of machinery and household appliances such as refrigerators use pressure-sensitive tape to prevent the sliding of shelves and the opening of doors in transit.

One pressure-sensitive industrial tape has a backing reinforced with either nylon or glass threads. This type is superior to steel strap used to bind corrugated paper boxes because the tape binds the entire surface it clings to instead of putting a crushing pressure on the corners of the boxes.

PREVAILING WESTERLIES, winds that blow out of the poleward sides of the subtropical belts of high pressure. They begin about 35 to 55 degrees both north and south of the Equator. Air descends at the horse latitudes, which are about 35 degrees north and south of the Equator. This air tends to blow toward the poles, but the rotation of the earth forces these winds to veer to the right in the Northern Hemisphere and to the left in the Southern Hemisphere. Thus, the area between the horse latitudes and the subpolar lows, in the vicinity of the polar circles, is one of prevailing westerlies. In the Northern Hemisphere these winds blow over great land areas whose surface irregularities cut down their speeds. In the Southern Hemisphere, between latitudes 40 to 50 degrees south, the westerlies blow unimpeded over the ocean and are known at the tip of South America as the roaring forties.

The weather in the Temperate Zones, north and south, is dominated by the westerlies. They are subject to many interruptions by storms and irregular, intermittent winds from all directions near the earth's surface, but the prevailing direction is from the west. This is the area where cold polar air from the high latitudes and warm, moist, semitropical air meet and form cyclones and anticyclones. Because of the prevailing westerlies, these cyclones and anticyclones move from west to east across the United States. See WIND CIRCULATION.

PRICE, the rate at which a commodity or a service exchanges for money. The crucial factor in prices is the relationship between prices. For many purposes it does not matter that commodity A is worth $10.00 and B is worth $5.00. What is important is that B costs half as much as A. Relative prices play a large part in determining how much of A, B, and all other products will be purchased. This in turn, indicates how much of each will be produced and by what methods. The three functions of the price system are to distribute consumer goods, to direct production, and to direct the use of economic resources.

Price is a very handy way to measure the economic value of very different goods. Without the concept of price it would be hard to compare the economic value of a cow with that of a diamond. With price, however, a person need only say that the cow costs $100 and the diamond $1,000. In the same way, a pair of shoes can be easily compared with a coat, a ton of coal, or a typewriter.

How are these prices decided? Custom has a strong effect on price. People are used to paying 5 cents or 10 cents for candy bars. For that reason a rise in the cost of producing candy might be reflected in the size of the bar rather than in the price. Another factor in deciding price is supply and demand. The producer will try to earn as much as he can, and the buyer will look for the lowest price he can find. Their compromise in the market results in the setting of price.

When the prices of goods that an average family buys are compared with the money the family earns over the same period, a cost-of-living index can be established. If wages rise and prices remain the same, the cost of living for the family decreases. But if prices rise more quickly than wages, a higher cost of living will result for the family. The cost of living indicates a price-wage relationship that is the same as the single wage term "real wages." See MONEY; SUPPLY AND DEMAND.

PRIESTLEY, JOSEPH (1733-1804), an English liberal clergyman and natural scientist who discovered oxygen. Born near Leeds, Yorkshire, he was educated at an academy dominated by Nonconformist religious ideas. He later became a Nonconformist clergyman. The name Nonconformist was then given to Protestant ministers who dissented from the doctrines and practices of the established Church of England. In 1755 he became the minister of a small church in Suffolk.

While performing the duties of

This general diagram of wind circulation in the Northern Hemisphere explains the origin of the prevailing westerlies. Air rises at the Equator and is carried aloft northward. At about latitude 30 degrees the air piles up and forms a high-pressure area. Some air descends to the earth's surface, where a portion moves northward. The rotating earth deflects the northward-moving winds so that they blow from the west as prevailing westerlies.

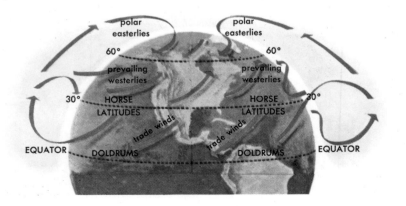

The versatile Englishman Joseph Priestley

his ministry and writing popular tracts on controversial religious subjects, Priestley was conducting experiments in chemistry and electricity in his own laboratory. About 1774 he obtained pure oxygen by heating mercuric oxide and collecting the oxygen as it was emitted. He discovered from further experiments that this gas stimulated combustion and was important in animal respiration. However, not realizing the exact nature of this strange new gas, he called it dephlogisticated air. He subsequently discovered and isolated other gases, including carbon dioxide, nitrogen, ammonia, and sulfur dioxide.

Because of Priestley's Nonconformist religious views and his sympathies with the French Revolution his house and church were pillaged and burned by an enraged mob in 1791, and his books, manuscripts, and scientific instruments were destroyed. Because of this persecution he and his family moved to the United States in 1794. There he resumed his scientific experiments, associated with Benjamin Franklin, George Washington, and Thomas Jefferson, and continued to write about his Nonconformist religious views.

PRIME MERIDIAN. See LATITUDE AND LONGITUDE.

PRIMITIVE ART. The term *primitive* is applied to art produced in a primitive culture, either past or present. The term is also applied to the earliest stage in the development of an art form. Modern artists' work that resembles primitive art is generally classified as neoprimitive or pseudoprimitive. The term *primitive* has been extended to include the work of children and folk art.

When dealing with the art of a primitive culture the distinction be-

tween fine art and applied art virtually disappears. In the primitive culture art was not produced as an end in itself. The objects that we admire from the standpoint of aesthetic appeal were created to fulfill a specific purpose. The carving on a wooden war club was considered secondary to the war club's utility. Because the decorations were executed with such a high degree of craftsmanship and artistic taste, the club is today considered an object of art. The very object that the archaeologist or the anthropologist studies because of its cultural relevance is admired by the lover of art.

The primitive artist is characterized by his ignorance of the academic theories and techniques of art —such as perspective, foreshortening, and so forth—which are generally considered fundamental. Consequently, his art, particularly his pictorial art, impresses us with a certain air of simplicity and directness. As in nonprimitive art, styles range from the realistic to the abstract, from naturalism to symbolism. Much primitive art is marked by an amazingly sophisticated sense of design and by great skill.

Primitive cultures of today produce art that is little different from that produced by prehistoric peoples. Such cultures exist in isolated parts of Africa, Australia, New Zealand, South America, and Oceania.

However, primitive art is not produced exclusively in a primitive culture. For example, during the Middle Ages the fine arts—sculpture and painting in particular—passed through a stage of relative primitivism. It was not until the

Renaissance that these forms commenced to regain their classical level of academic development.

Primitive art has had a significant influence on modern art, as can be seen in the works of such artists as Henri Rousseau and Paul Gauguin. Although the primitive influence

Courtesy of Milwaukee Public Museum

Fish and kangaroo are commonly depicted in Australian bark paintings. Bark drawings appear on the walls of huts in western Arnhem and have some religious significance.

may be quite apparent in a particular work of art, its creator may have been well trained in the academic tradition. This conscious attempt, however successful, to imitate the so-called primitive style is generally considered to be the major factor separating the neoprimitive, or pseudoprimitive, from the genuine primitive.

"Grandma" Moses is one of the best known modern American primitive painters.

Brown Brothers

Museum of the American Indian——Heye Foundation

This is a painted Arkansas pottery vase.

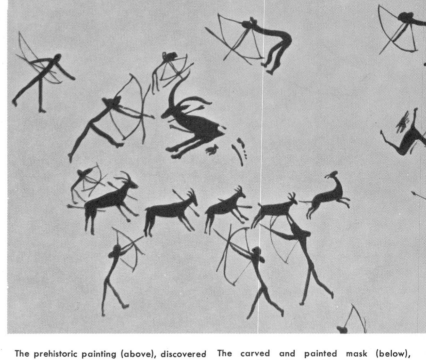

The prehistoric painting (above), discovered on the wall of a cave in Valencia, Spain, shows men on a hunting expedition.

The carved and painted mask (below), representing a demented man, was made by Indians of North America's northwest coast.

American Museum of Natural History

A Zapotecan clay figure from Mexico

Below is a mural decoration from a prehistoric Hopi kiva.

Museum of Northern Arizona

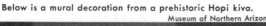

This is a primitive carving of a rooster.

Eliot Elisofon

Laura Gilpin

The painting above, by To-Pove, shows Pueblo people working in the fields.

Carved wooden masks, like the one shown below, are very common in Angola.

Portuguese Overseas Ministry

Above is a painted pottery bowl from San Ildefonso, N. M.

Laura Gilpin

Photo, Jose R. Sarmiento, Philippine Tourist & Trav. Assoc., Inc.

From Luzon, left, a statue of an Igorot granary god

Museum of Navajo Ceremonial Art, Inc.

Below is a painting of a Navaho feather dance. The work is by the 20th-century Navaho artist Harrison Begay.

PRINCE EDWARD ISLAND is the smallest and one of the most picturesque of the Canadian provinces. One of the Maritime Provinces, it covers an area of approximately 2,000 square miles in eastern Canada. The island is situated in the Gulf of St. Lawrence and is separated by Northumberland Strait from New Brunswick and Nova Scotia. Its greatest length is 145 miles, and it has a width up to 35 miles. Charlottetown is the capital and the chief city. Prince Edward Island has a population of approximately 100,000.

The coastline of the island is very irregular, presenting a succession of deep bays and inlets between projecting headlands. Broad sand beaches extend for miles along the northern shore, while a sandstone cliff rises on the south shore. Its surface, devoid of steep hills, is gently rolling and intensively cultivated. Red sandy-loam soil gives the landscape a colorful appearance. The island has many short rivers, but none of them is navigable. The island has a maritime climate. Charlottetown's average temperature in January is 28° F., and in July it is 62° F.

The temperate climate and rich soil are beneficial to farming, the chief pursuit of three-fourths of the population. Cattle and poultry raising, dairying, and the production of potatoes (the chief crop), turnips, and fruit are carried on. Wheat, oats, barley, and feed crops are produced. The lobster and oyster fisheries are also important.

Lacking minerals and appreciable timber resources, the manufacturing industry of Prince Edward Island is largely confined to processing the food products of the farms and fisheries. Fox farming was once a thriving industry. Ranching still exists, but only on a small scale.

The shield of Prince Edward Island displays the heraldic lion of England, as do the shields of Quebec, New Brunswick, Saskatchewan, and Newfoundland. The oak trees symbolize the forests on the island.

The chief recreational area of the island is along the north shore at Prince Edward Island National Park. Nearly 25 miles of sandy beaches attract many visitors.

Jacques Cartier is credited with the discovery of Prince Edward Island in 1534. Settled by the French in the first half of the 18th century, the island was ceded by France to Great Britain in 1763. In 1798 its name was changed from Ile Saint Jean to Prince Edward Island in honor of Queen Victoria's father. The island was at first a part of the colony of Novia Scotia, but in 1873 it was admitted to the Dominion as a province. It is governed by a lieutenant governor and a legislative assembly, whose 30 members serve for a term of five years.

PRINCE EDWARD ISLAND

Shield: British lion at top—below one large oak tree and three oak saplings on an island
Flag: Shield on Canada's red ensign
Flower: Lady's-slipper
Capital: Charlottetown
Largest city: Charlottetown
Area: 2,184 sq. mi.
Rank in area: 12th (including territories)
Population: 100,000
Chief university: St. Dunstan's University
Chief rivers: Hillsborough, Yorke
Average temperature: Charlottetown, 28° F. (Jan.), 62° F. (July)
Average annual rainfall: 40 inches
Chief economic activities: Agriculture (including dairying), fishing
Chief crop: Potatoes
Chief manufactures: Processed food and fish
Notable attractions: Prince Edward Island National Park
Important historical dates:
  1534 Island visited by Jacques Cartier
  1719 First settlement at Port La Joie established by French
  1763 Island ceded to Great Britain by France
  1769 Detached from Nova Scotia
  1798 Name changed from Île Saint Jean to Prince Edward Island
  1873 Membership in federation

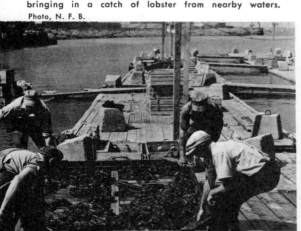

Fishing is an important industry on Prince Edward Island, the smallest province of Canada. These fishermen are bringing in a catch of lobster from nearby waters.
Photo, N. F. B.

Many fur-bearing animals are found on Prince Edward Island, including the beaver, raccoon, fox, and mink. The animals are both trapped and raised. These silver foxes are being raised on a fur farm.
Malak-Annan Photo Features

An early example of printing is Chinese block printing. All characters and designs were hand-carved in a single block.

PRINTING, the method of producing an impression from type or plates on paper or any other suitable material. The first known printing was the Chinese block print. The first European woodblock prints were made sometime late in the 14th century; whether the technique was learned from the Chinese or developed independently in Europe is not known. While words as well as pictures could be cut onto a woodblock, the process was necessarily slow and laborious and was therefore virtually limited to reproducing pictures rather than texts.

HISTORY

The man who made possible the printing of books was Johann Gutenberg, a German goldsmith who lived in Mainz. Gutenberg's great contribution was the perfecting of movable type and the process of casting it. This type could be arranged, by hand, in frames; comparatively little time was needed to set up a whole page, and corrections and alterations could be made with ease. Gutenberg also adapted the wine press, used for pressing grapes, to printing. He began his experiments in the 1440's; in 1452 he began working on his first book, a Vulgate Bible, which was published sometime before August, 1456. See GUTENBERG, JOHANN.

The new process rapidly spread throughout Europe. Until that time all books had been laboriously handwritten by scribes, which process was of course most expensive. Printing made possible mass production of books, thereby greatly lowering the cost of their production. This in turn made it possible for many more people to buy them; consequently, the market for books increased significantly. The importance of this development cannot be overestimated. By making the Greek and Roman classics and the works of the humanist authors available to a large public in many countries, printing contributed, probably more than any other single factor, to the development and spread of that remarkable phenomenon that is known as the Renaissance.

Of the early printers one of the most important is Aldus Manutius, who established his firm, now generally referred to as the Aldine Press, in Venice, Italy, about 1490. Aldus' enthusiasm for the Greek and Roman classics prompted him to publish a series of compact, inexpensive editions, which soon were imitated throughout Europe. In France the leading printer and publisher for many years was the firm of Estienne, founded in Paris about 1502. William Caxton established printing in England in 1476 and published editions of such English medieval masterpieces as Chaucer's *Canterbury Tales*, as well as English translations of classical works.

Among Aldus' contributions to printing were the introduction of the italic type style and the establishment of the roman and italic styles as standard. Aldus adopted roman and italic simply because their letters were the narrowest of any type style then known; by using them he saved money, since they enabled him to get more words onto a page. The success of Aldus' books prompted other printers to adopt his type styles, which eventually became standard throughout most of Europe. The type in which this encyclopedia is set is a modern version of Aldus' roman style; *italic type is also used occasionally, as here.* Germany was the only European country that did not adopt roman and italic but instead developed its own style, a style called *Fraktur.* This style, which is characterized by ornate, heavy, black letters, predominated in the German-speaking countries until well into the 20th century, when it was finally abandoned.

In addition to contributing greatly to the spread of classical and humanistic literature, printing played an important part in the development of modern languages. During the Middle Ages education had been limited almost entirely to members of the clergy, and consequently Latin had been the only written language of any importance. Each spoken language had many dialects, and on the rare occasions when such a language was written, it was spelled according to the pronunciation of the writer. Thus, for

With the development of movable type by Johann Gutenberg in the 15th century, books became plentiful in Europe. An entire page of print could be quickly composed and printed.

Brown Brothers

William Caxton submits his first proofsheet to the abbot of Westminster in 1477. In the half century after Gutenberg's work the movable-type printing press spread through Europe.

example, the written English of Chaucer, a 14th-century Londoner, is vastly different from that of his great contemporary in the north of England, the so-called William Langland. When the introduction of inexpensive printed books, together with the spread of education to the middle classes, created a demand for books in the language of the people, it was the printers more than any others who set the standards of the developing printed languages. Thus London English, Parisian French, Florentine Italian, and Saxon German became the standard literary forms of their respective languages and gradually displaced the local dialects. Regional accents remained, as they do to this day, but they were overshadowed by the written, printed, and increasingly spoken standard languages. This fact is of immense importance not only to literature

but also politically, for the establishment of nationwide languages in place of local ones made people more conscious of their nations, whereas their previous concern had been principally for their counties or provinces. The gradual development of this national consciousness is one of the most important developments in modern history.

For over three centuries after Gutenberg's invention there were few important changes in printing techniques. Type continued to be both cast and set by hand, and the hand-operated press was not significantly improved upon. The Industrial Revolution, however, affected printing as it did virtually all manufacturing processes, so that by 1850 a number of inventions had revolutionized printing.

The first important development was Nicolas Louis Robert's invention in 1798 of a mechanical method

of manufacturing paper, a process that previously had been done by hand. In 1804 Lord Stanhope introduced an improved printing press and the following year the stereotype. (See STEREOTYPE.) Koenig's powered press, first used in 1810, increased the number of pages that could be printed in an hour from 300 to 1,100, and the introduction of the rotary press in 1848 increased that number to 48,000. In 1822 William Church invented a letter-founding machine that more than doubled the amount of type that could be cast in an hour. In 1840 the process of manufacturing inexpensive paper from woodpulp was developed.

Near the end of the 19th century Ottmar Mergenthaler's Linotype (1886) and Tolbert Lanston's Monotype (1889) revolutionized typesetting, the only important phases of printing that were still being done by hand. See LINOTYPE; MONOTYPE.

The first color printing in Europe was the color printing of woodcuts, which began late in the 15th century. But the beginnings of modern color printing lay in the work of Jacques Le Blon, an 18th-century engraver. Working on the basis of Newton's recent discoveries concerning the composition of light, Le Blon reduced the number of inks required for full-color reproduction from seven to three (red, blue, and yellow), sometimes with the addition of black. Process work involved in modern color printing originated at the end of the 19th century. In four-color process work color art is separated into red, blue, yellow, and black components by means of color filters, and separate photo-engravings are produced to print each of the colors. See PHOTOENGRAVING.

The first printing press in the United States was brought from England in 1638.

Brown Brothers

This pressroom is equipped with single-color and multicolor lithographic offset presses.

PRINTING METHODS

There are several processes used in printing. Each represents a different way in which the ink is transferred onto the paper. While an average job may be printed by any of these processes, much depends upon individual characteristics of that particular job and the effect desired.

Generally there are five different methods of printing. They are letterpress, offset lithography, gravure, collotype, and silk screen.

Letterpress. This is a raised-surface method of printing. The ink is transferred directly to the paper from type, engravings, or other materials. One can detect a letterpress-printed job by examining it under a strong magnifying glass. The ink has a tendency to squeeze out on the edges of the printed surface. There are three major kinds of letterpress equipment: flatbed cylinder press, platen press, and rotary press.

Offset Lithography. In offset a thin zinc or aluminum plate is used. It has a finely grained flat surface that has an affinity for water and onto which the image has been exposed. The offset process is based on the principle that grease and water do not mix. As the plate (which has already been inked) revolves, it contacts the water rollers first. Water will adhere to the grained, nonprinting areas only and will not adhere to the greased printing-surface areas. The reverse happens when the plate next comes in contact with the ink rollers. The inked image is first transferred on the rubber blanket cylinder and then to the paper.

Gravure. Contrary to raised surface in letterpress and flat surface in offset, the gravure process uses a depressed surface, also referred to as intaglio. The copper cylinders are etched with square depressions of different depth that hold the ink. As the cylinder revolves in a thin base ink, the doctor blade, which is in contact with the cylinder, wipes the ink off the raised nonprinting areas. The impression cylinder brings the paper in contact with the etched cylinder and sucks the ink out of the depressions onto the paper. Another form of intaglio printing is steel engraving as used in printing postage stamps or currency. Letterheads and wedding invitations are also printed by the intaglio process.

Collotype. This fine old process was invented in France over a hundred years ago and is also known as the photogelatin process. It produces a printing surface in gelatin backed by a glass or a metal plate. A photograph or a line illustration can be reproduced without the aid of mechanical screens. The gelatin, containing a bichromate to make it sensitive to light, is exposed in contact with a photographic negative. In a whirler the emulsion under heat changes to a brittle, hard substance. No screen of any kind is used in making collotypes. The image, of fine grain, is produced by the reticulation of the gelatin itself. Beautiful reproductions are made by this method, but the process is somewhat slow. The plates are delicate, which limits the number of the impressions.

Silk Screen. The silk-screen process is the most practical method of printing on metal, glass, cloth, cork, plastics, and so forth. It is probably the oldest of the printing processes used by the Chinese and Japanese centuries ago. It is a method of printing through a stencil that is affixed to a porous ground or screen of silk. The layer of ink deposited is much thicker and more opaque than in any other printing process. The colors are brilliant and have a hand-painted appearance.

Regardless of which method is used, the copy must be set in type. This process is called composition. There are several kinds of composition: linotype, monotype, Ludlow, handset, and photocomposition. For economical and practical purposes text copy is machine set. If it is linotype composition, the type is cast as a complete slug, and if any corrections are to be made, the whole line is reset. Monotype composition consists of individual letters that are assembled in lines. Monotype casting machines cast type from perforated ribbons. These ribbons are first punched on keyboard machines, each combination of perforations representing a certain character. Monotype machines are also capable of setting larger display type up to certain sizes. Ludlow composition consists of matrices set by hand. The line is then inserted into the Ludlow machine, and the case is made. In all three methods the type is cast from fresh metal, and after it has been used, it is melted again. Hand composition is generally used for setting headings in larger type or for special jobs where foundry type (type made of extra-hard metal) is required.

Photocomposition is a fairly new process in printing. The characters are on film, and they are assembled in lines somewhat like linotype. They are then projected on film for reproduction.

Sometimes special effects are achieved for headings by using artwork and hand lettering. This is costlier, but the extra expense is usually justified by the rich appearance of the job. After the type has been set, it is compiled into galleys and proofread against the copy for possible errors. After the corrections have been made, the type is then made up into pages, folios are added, and the job is ready to be printed by the process selected for it.

When a person is called a printer, it does not necessarily mean that he actually prints the job. He may be a production man, a compositor, a vice-president of the printing company, or a bindery foreman. Modern printing is one of most important trades of the present day. It is made up of a large number of different trades that need knowledge and skill that can be gained only by special training and experience in preparation for thorough craftsmanship. This encyclopedia includes entries on many aspects of printing. See FACSIMILE PRINTING; LITHOGRAPHY.

LETTER PRESS
(RELIEF PRINTING)

HIGH SURFACE

HALFTONE CUT-OUT NEGATIVE

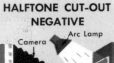
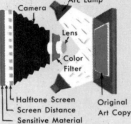

Camera — Arc Lamp — Lens — Color Filter — Halftone Screen — Screen Distance — Sensitive Material — Original Art Copy

NOTE: SCREEN IS USED AT THIS OPERATION

METAL PRINTING OPERATION

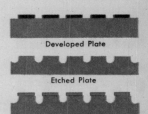

Arc Lamp — Vacuum Printing Frame — Halftone Negative — Sensitized Metal Plate

Transparent — Opaque — Light Source

Metal Plate Light Sensitive Coating

COLOR ETCHING

Developed Plate

Etched Plate

Ink Plate

OFFSET LITHOGRAPHY
(PLANO PRINTING)

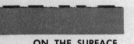

ON THE SURFACE

CONTINUOUS-TONE CUT-OUT NEGATIVES

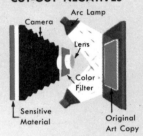

Camera — Arc Lamp — Lens — Color Filter — Sensitive Material — Original Art Copy

NOTE: SCREEN IS NOT USED AT THIS OPERATION

HALFTONE POSITIVE OPERATION

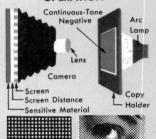

Continuous-Tone Negative — Arc Lamp — Lens — Camera — Screen — Screen Distance — Sensitive Material — Copy Holder

Screen — Halftone

COLOR CORRECTION
HALFTONE ETCHING

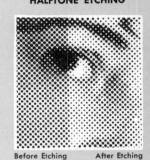

Before Etching — After Etching

GRAVURE
(INTAGLIO PRINTING)

BELOW SURFACE

CONTINUOUS-TONE CUT-OUT NEGATIVES

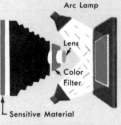

Arc Lamp — Lens — Color Filter — Sensitive Material

NOTE: SCREEN IS NOT USED AT THIS OPERATION

CONTINUOUS-TONE POSITIVE OPERATION

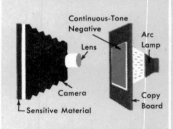

Continuous-Tone Negative — Arc Lamp — Lens — Camera — Sensitive Material — Copy Board

NOTE: SCREEN IS NOT USED AT THIS OPERATION

COLOR CORRECTION
CONTINUOUS TONE

Before

After

SILK SCREEN
(STENCIL PRINTING)

THROUGH SURFACE

LINE OR HALFTONE NEGATIVES

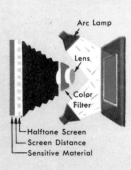

Arc Lamp — Lens — Color Filter — Halftone Screen — Screen Distance — Sensitive Material

OVERLAY DRAWINGS

Black — Yellow — OR — Green

HAND CUT STENCIL

SILK SCREEN

PRESS PLATES ELECTROTYPING

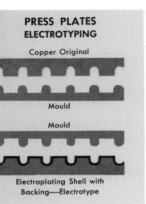

Copper Original

Mould

Mould

Electroplating Shell with Backing—Electrotype

LOCK-UP FORM

PRINCIPLE OF RELIEF PRINTING PRESS

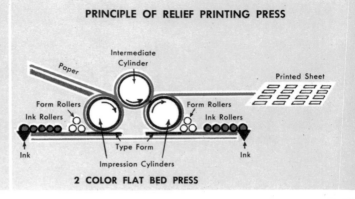

Intermediate Cylinder

Paper

Printed Sheet

Form Rollers

Ink Rollers

Form Rollers

Ink Rollers

Ink

Type Form

Impression Cylinders

Ink

2 COLOR FLAT BED PRESS

PRESS PLATE MAKING

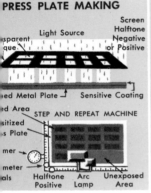

Screen Halftone Negative or Positive

Light Source

Transparent
que

ed Metal Plate — Sensitive Coating

ed Area
sitized
s Plate

mer

meter
als

STEP AND REPEAT MACHINE

Halftone Positive

Arc Lamp

Unexposed Area

DEVELOPING OF IMAGE ON PRESS PLATE

(Deep Etch)

Unexposed Area

Grained Metal Plate

Exposed Area

Developed Image

Etched Area

Unexposed Coating Removed and Ink Applied to Image

Ink Receptive Area

Grained Metal Plate

PRINCIPLE OF THE OFFSET PRESS

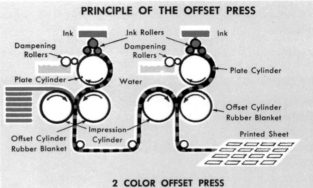

Ink

Ink Rollers

Ink

Dampening Rollers

Dampening Rollers

Plate Cylinder

Water

Plate Cylinder

Offset Cylinder Rubber Blanket

Offset Cylinder Rubber Blanket

Impression Cylinder

Printed Sheet

2 COLOR OFFSET PRESS

CARBON TISSUE PRINTING

(2 Exposures)

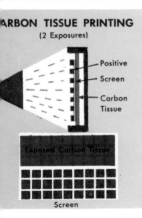

Positive

Screen

Carbon Tissue

Exposed Carbon Tissue

Screen

CARBON LAYED ON CYLINDER

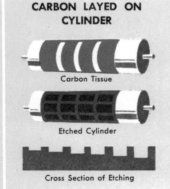

Carbon Tissue

Etched Cylinder

Cross Section of Etching

PRINCIPLE OF THE GRAVURE PRESS

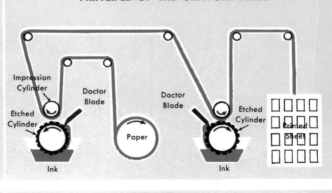

Impression Cylinder

Doctor Blade

Doctor Blade

Etched Cylinder

Etched Cylinder

Paper

Printed Sheet

Ink

Ink

STENCIL EXPOSURE

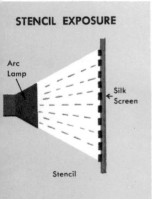

Arc Lamp

Silk Screen

Stencil

DEVELOPED AND MOUNTED STENCIL

SILK SCREEN

PRINCIPLE OF STENCIL PRINTING

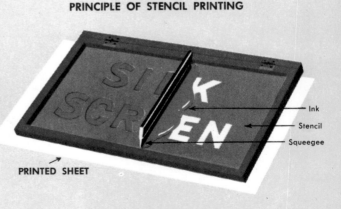

SILK SCREEN

Ink

Stencil

Squeegee

PRINTED SHEET

PRINTING PRESS

For over 300 years printing presses were all very much alike, though they differed in size. Today there are a great many different types of presses. The main types of printing presses are platen presses, flat-bed presses, sheet-fed rotary, and web-fed rotary.

In the platen press the pressure is applied by a flat platen, or heavy pressure plate, that is brought down upon sheets of paper, pressing them against the type in the form, which lies on the bed of the press under the platen. Most commercial printing is done on these small platen presses. The first one was invented by George Phineas Gordon, of New York, about 1858. The machines are able to produce 1,000 to 3,600 impressions per hour, depending on the type of job and whether it is fed by hand or is automatically fed.

Special small hand presses, a variation of the platen type, are used for pulling proofs before printing begins and are called proof presses.

In the cylinder press the pressure is not applied by a flat surface but by a heavy cylinder, or roller, though the printing plates are flat. All cylinder presses, whether horizontal or vertical in movement, operate on similar principles. The type forms are locked in iron or steel frames and placed on the bed of the press. The printing surfaces of the type, or printing blocks, are inked by several rollers, which are fed with the proper amount of ink from a separate ink fountain. The paper is brought around the impression cylinder, and after the impression is made, an automatic-carriage delivery unit gathers the sheets. Some modern cylinder presses have a capacity of 20,000 impressions per hour.

In the rotary press curved stereotype or electrotype plates are locked on a shaft, or roller, and pressure is applied on the plates by other rollers. On the sheet-fed press the paper is fed to the press in sheets. On the web-fed press the paper is drawn by the press from a continuous roll, or web, which may contain several miles of paper. Most newspapers are printed on web presses; they can be printed at the amazing rate of 144,000 per hour. Magazines, catalogs, and newspaper supplements are also the product of high-speed rotary presses.

The first rotary press was invented by an American, William Bullock in 1856. Offset and photogravure presses resemble rotary and cylinder presses in many respects, but they have added rollers and other devices that make them more complex in design.

The many ink rollers in a lithographic press, above, distribute ink in an even layer to the surface of the lithograph press plate. The sheet-fed lithographic offset press, below, prints in two colors. The large, eight-color rotary offset press, right, is designed to print magazine covers. Running at a rate of 1,000 feet of paper per minute, this press can print 100,000 magazine covers from 1 ton of paper in less than half an hour. This rotary offset press weighs 174 tons.

Courtesy of Harris-Intertype Corp.

Courtesy of Harris-Intertype Corp.

The large, web-fed relief press, above, can print both sides of the paper simultaneously as it passes through the press. The high-speed eight-color gravure press, right, can print accurate, full-color illustrations on inexpensive paper. On modern presses, below, empty paper rolls can be replaced without stopping the press.

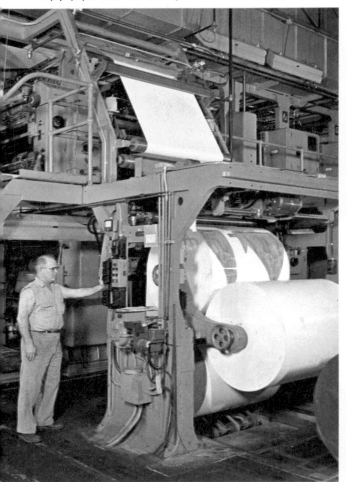

The silk-screen process is a stencil printing method. The screen press below can print a heavy film of ink on many materials.

Courtesy of General Research, Inc.

OCCUPATION: Platemaker

NATURE OF WORK: Making offset, rotogravure, and photoengraved printing plates of illustrations and copy

PERSONAL FACTORS—ABILITIES, SKILLS, APTITUDES: An aptitude for science, ability in art, good eyesight, and good physical condition are needed. Manual dexterity and attention to detail are helpful.

EDUCATION AND SPECIAL TRAINING: An apprenticeship of five or six years, with at least 800 hours of related classroom instruction, is required.

WORKING CONDITIONS:
1. INCOME:
   COMPARED WITH OTHER CAREERS WITH EQUAL TRAINING: Average to high
   COMPARED WITH MOST OTHER CAREERS: Average
2. ENVIRONMENT: Indoor benchwork
3. OTHER: Regular hours; usual benefits; rush seasons; unionization

WHERE TO FIND MORE INFORMATION: American Photoengravers Association, 166 West Van Buren Street, Chicago 4, Ill.; National Association of Photo-Lithographers, 317 West 45th St., New York 19, N. Y.

This platemaker is preparing a rotogravure press cylinder.

OCCUPATION: Pressman

NATURE OF WORK: Duties are to make ready and then to tend the presses while they are in operation.

PERSONAL FACTORS—ABILITIES, SKILLS, APTITUDES: Mechanical aptitude, physical strength and endurance, and some art ability are needed.

EDUCATION AND SPECIAL TRAINING: An apprenticeship of two to four years (varies with the type of press) is required. On-the-job training and related classroom instruction are included.

WORKING CONDITIONS:
1. INCOME:
   COMPARED WITH OTHER CAREERS WITH EQUAL TRAINING: Average
   COMPARED WITH MOST OTHER CAREERS: Average
2. ENVIRONMENT: Noisy pressroom; occupational hazards
3. OTHER: Physically demanding work; night shifts; unionization; usual benefits; good opportunities

WHERE TO FIND MORE INFORMATION: International Printing Pressmen and Assistants' Union of North America, Pressmen's Home, Tenn.

Courtesy of Harris-Intertype Corp.

This operator is setting a line of type on an Intertype (similar to a Linotype).

OCCUPATION: Linotype Operator

NATURE OF WORK: Setting type by using automatic machine

PERSONAL FACTORS—ABILITIES, SKILLS, APTITUDES: An aptitude in English and mathematics, imagination, and artistic ability are needed. Manual dexterity is helpful.

EDUCATION AND SPECIAL TRAINING: An apprenticeship of up to six years is usually required. Printing courses in vocational or high schools are helpful.

WORKING CONDITIONS:
1. INCOME:
   COMPARED WITH OTHER CAREERS WITH EQUAL TRAINING: Average
   COMPARED WITH MOST OTHER CAREERS: Average to high
2. ENVIRONMENT: Noisy plant
3. OTHER: Regular hours; possible shifts; usual benefits; unionization; good opportunities

RELATED CAREERS: Hand compositor, Monotype operator, Monotype-caster operator, Intertype operator

WHERE TO FIND MORE INFORMATION: International Typographical Union, 2820 North Meridian Street, Indianapolis 6, Ind.; Printing Industry of America, Inc., 5728 Connecticut Avenue NW, Washington 15, D.C.

This pressman attends a sheet-fed offset press that prints in single color.

OCCUPATION: Compositor

NATURE OF WORK: Setting of type by hand or machine

PERSONAL FACTORS—ABILITIES, SKILLS, APTITUDES: Aptitude in English and mathematics, imagination, and artistic ability are needed.

EDUCATION AND SPECIAL TRAINING: An apprenticeship of up to six years is required. Printing courses in vocational schools or high schools are helpful.

WORKING CONDITIONS:
1. INCOME:
   COMPARED WITH OTHER CAREERS WITH EQUAL TRAINING: Average
   COMPARED WITH MOST OTHER CAREERS: Average to high
2. ENVIRONMENT: Noisy plant; long hours of standing
3. OTHER: Regular hours; possible shifts; usual benefits; good opportunities; unionization

RELATED CAREERS: Linotype operator, Monotype operator, makeup man

WHERE TO FIND MORE INFORMATION: International Typographical Union, 2820 North Meridian Street, Indianapolis 6, Ind.; Printing Industry of America, Inc., 5728 Connecticut Avenue NW, Washington 15, D.C.

PRISM, commonly a small, wedge-shaped piece of glass used to refract or reflect light passing through it. The prism is used in binoculars, periscopes, and spectroscopes.

Prisms refract (change the direction of) light beams and their different wavelengths (colors) in varying degrees. Refraction occurs because the velocity of light is less within the prism than it is in air. The entering beam is bent toward the normal (a line that makes a right angle with the face of the prism). The angle formed by the entering beam and the normal is called the angle of incidence; the angle formed by the beam and the normal after bending is called the angle of refraction. The degree that light is bent depends on its wavelength in addition to the slower velocity caused by the prism. The longest wavelengths, the red colors, are bent the least; the shortest wavelengths, the blue colors, are bent the most. This results in a beam's being divided into colors, with the reds on one side and the blues on the other. A series of colored bands, called a spectrum, is thus formed.

A light beam moving within a prism is reflected when it strikes the surface at a certain angle. Upon striking the surface the beam is bent away from the normal, and the angle of refraction is always larger than the angle of incidence. If the angle of incidence increases, the angle of refraction increases and always remains larger. Finally, the angle of refraction becomes a right angle, and the light beam skims the surface of the prism. The incident angle at which this occurs is called the critical angle. When a light ray inside the prism strikes the surface at an angle greater than the critical angle, it does not enter the air but is reflected back into the prism. Since none of the light enters the air, the reflection is complete and is called total reflection. It is similar to a mirror's reflection but greater.

Because of their greater reflecting power, prisms are used in binoculars and periscopes. Spectroscopes, which are used to analyze unknown materials, also contain prisms.

Laws of probability can be demonstrated by coin throws. With three coins there are eight possible results. The probability of getting three heads or three tails is one-eighth. The probability of getting either one head or one tail is three-eighths.

PROBABILITY, the likelihood that an object or event will have a given property. Mathematical probability is found by determining the number of ways in which an object or an event may occur and the number of ways in which it may occur with the given property, and then dividing the second number by the first. Empirical probability is computed by considering a number of cases (objects or events) and then dividing the number that have the given property by the total number considered.

The term *probability* is used very loosely in everyday life. In the study of probability the word is used only in the sense of "the probability that an object, A, will have the property, B." This is denoted by the symbol, $P\{A|B\}$, and is found by the formula

$$P\{A|B\} = \frac{n(AB)}{n(A)}$$

where $n(A)$ is the number of objects, A, in a given set of objects and $n(AB)$ is the number of objects, A, having property B. Probability is always expressed by a number between 0 and 1. If the given property always occurs, its probability is 1; if it never occurs, its probability is 0.

How mathematical probability is figured may be seen from the solution of a simple problem: What is the probability that, in one toss, a coin will fall heads? Two distinct objects may result from the toss—a coin with heads up or a coin with tails up. Thus $n(A) = 2$. Only one of the two objects A has the given property; thus $n(AB) = 1$. According to the formula the probability that the coin will fall heads is $\frac{n(AB)}{n(A)} = \frac{1}{2}$.

Probabilities involving more than one property are found by using the addition rule or the product rule.

Addition Rule. If two properties are mutually exclusive—that is, if the occurrence of one rules out the occurrence of the other—the probability of the occurrence of one or the other is the sum of their separate probabilities. For example, the probability that a card drawn from a pack of 52 will be a king is $\frac{4}{52}$, or $\frac{1}{13}$; the probability that it will be a queen is likewise $\frac{1}{13}$. The probability that the card will be either a king or a queen is found by adding the two probabilities: $\frac{1}{13} + \frac{1}{13} = \frac{2}{13}$.

Product Rule. The probability of a combination of two or more independent properties is given by the product of their separate probabilities. Properties are said to be independent if the occurrence of one does not affect the occurrence of another. Coin tossing provides a good example of independent properties; whether a coin falls heads or tails in one toss does not at all depend on how it fell in any previous toss. Thus the probability that a coin will fall heads in five consecutive tosses is $\frac{1}{2} \times \frac{1}{2} \times \frac{1}{2} \times \frac{1}{2} \times \frac{1}{2} = \frac{1}{32}$.

If the occurrence of one property affects the occurrence of another, the two properties are considered dependent. The probability of a combination of dependent properties is the product of their relative probabilities—the probabilities of each of the properties as affected by

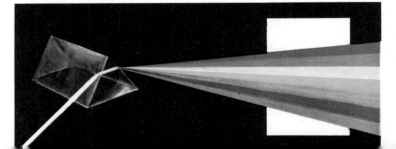

As a beam of white light passes through a prism, different wave lengths of light are refracted at different angles and form the familiar color spectrum.

the other properties. For example, let us compute the probability that 4 cards drawn from a pack of 52 will all be aces. The probability that the first card drawn will be an ace is $\frac{4}{52}$. But if the first card is an ace, only 3 aces will remain among 51 cards left in the pack. Thus the probability that the second card drawn will also be an ace is $\frac{3}{51}$. Similarly the probability that the third card drawn will be an ace is $\frac{2}{50}$, and the probability that the fourth card will be an ace is $\frac{1}{49}$. The probability of the combination—the probability that all 4 cards will be aces—is $\frac{4}{52} \times \frac{3}{51} \times \frac{2}{50} \times \frac{1}{49} = \frac{24}{6,497,400}$ or $\frac{1}{270,725}$.

Empirical probability is probability computed by experimental or statistical methods. The empirical probability that one card drawn from a pack of 52 will be either a king or a queen may be found by making a number of separate draws, recording the results, and dividing the number of cards that are kings or queens by the total number of cards drawn. In a great number of draws made entirely at random the empirical probability will tend to be very close to the mathematical probability. Exactly what would happen if the number of draws were increased to infinity is still a topic of debate among mathematicians. See BERNOULLI'S THEOREM.

Empirical probabilities are used in several fields where unpredictable properties make purely mathematical probabilities practically impossible to compute. Life insurance rates are based on empirical probabilities computed from statistics on deaths.

PROCLAMATION OF 1763 provided for the organization and government of the American territory the English had acquired from the French as a result of the French and Indian War. The provinces of Quebec, East Florida, and West Florida were created out of this territory. English law was proclaimed in Quebec, but because the laws of England were very anti-Catholic at the time, the French Canadians were deprived by these laws of most of their civil and political rights. It was hoped that the proclamation would resolve the conflict between the interests of the Indians in the new territory and interests of the colonists and fur traders. While the proclamation was being formulated, settlement of European lands the Indians thought were theirs and the fur traders' cheating brought on Pontiac's Conspiracy. The Proclamation of 1763 tried to solve the problem by forbidding colonists to settle west of the Appalachians and requiring Indian traders to be licensed by colonial or military governors. Neither the prohibition on settlement, which was intended to be temporary, nor the regulations regarding Indian trade were effective. American frontiersmen were not to be stopped in their search for more fertile land farther west, and many fights with the Indians resulted. The colonial governors would not cooperate in the licensing system, and the traders' abuse of the Indians remained as bad as ever.

PROFIT AND LOSS. Profits are returns to entrepreneurs (or enterprisers) for the successful functioning of a business. If the business is unsuccessful, the entrepreneur may lose the money he invested. The entrepreneur's part in the functioning of a capitalist economy is the taking of risks. He seeks profits through business units that are called single proprietorships, partnerships, and corporations.

Profits in a business are what is left over from the gross income after all costs have been deducted. Not too infrequently a company's annual costs may exceed its annual gross income. In that case, the company has lost money in its operations. A typical statement of profits and losses might be the Westinghouse Electric Corporation's report of its operations in 1949. This company's total income from its products, services, and other sources was about $950,000,000. This was the gross income. From this figure the costs of operation were deducted. The greatest costs were materials and services from other companies and wages and salaries. Other costs were employee insurance, pensions, social security taxes, federal taxes, other taxes, interest on loans, depreciation, and future expenditures on current operations. The costs in this particular year amounted to about $883,000,000. The net income for the year was about $67,000,000 ($950,000,000 minus $883,000,000).

What does the net income of a corporation consist of? In the first place, some owners engage in managing their own enterprise. The return to them of the money they would have had to pay another manager cannot be called profit. The second part of the net income is somewhat more difficult to understand. If the corporation had to rent its buildings and land or borrow money, it would have had to repay rent and interest. But if the corporation owns its own buildings and land and furnishes its own capital, it is logical to consider part of the net income a return in interest and rent rather than pure profits. It is just as if a corporation had lent its money and rented its land to another company. The part of the net income that is left over after paying wages of management and interest and rent on its own capital and property comprise the pure profits of the corporation. Some economists divide pure profits into necessary and surplus profits. The necessary profit is the income necessary to attract the investments of entrepreneurs and is the return normally expected for assuming risk. Surplus profit is simply an added return beyond what is necessary to attract investors. Surplus profit will be temporary unless there is some degree of monopoly, which prevents free entrance into the industry. Unless monopoly exists, other entrepreneurs will enter the business until the surplus profit disappears.

The profits and losses of individual entrepreneurs are a feature of the capitalist economy. However, even in socialist economies profits and losses may be figured to see whether a company is operating efficiently. See INCOME; STOCKS AND BONDS.

PROGRESSIVE CONSERVATIVE PARTY, CANADIAN, one of the two major political parties of Canada. It began to take shape as early as 1854 and formed governments of the federation from 1867 to 1873 and again from 1878 to 1896. Its founder and first great leader was Sir John A. Macdonald. In general, the party (commonly called Conservative) stood for a united country, industrial development protected by tariffs, and close association with Great Britain.

The Conservatives were returned to office in 1911 on the issue of a trade agreement with the United States that would have allowed raw materials from Canada to be sold in the United States without paying a duty. Sir Robert Borden led the party at that time. A coalition including some of the Liberals was formed in 1917 and remained in power until the elections of 1921. The Conservative party did not win another general election until 1930, and this government lasted until 1935. The party remained out of power from that year until 1957. At that time the Conservatives returned to office under the leadership of John Diefenbaker.

PROGRESSIVE PARTY, the name of several third-party movements in the United States. Progressive party movements include the Progressive party that supported Theodore Roosevelt for the presidency in 1912, the Progressives who supported Senator Robert M. LaFollette in 1924, and the Progressive party that supported Henry Wallace in 1948. None of these attempts to elect Progressive party candidates was successful, but the movements represented important trends in American politics.

At the Republican national convention of 1912 a battle developed between the conservatives and the more radical wing of the party. The conservatives backed President William Howard Taft for reelection. The dissatisfied radicals decided to back former president Theodore Roosevelt. They formed the Progressive party. Its symbol, a bull moose, gave the party its popular name. The platform of the new party stressed social reforms such as social insurance, safety and health standards in industry, workingman's compensation, and a minimum-wage law for women. In fact, except for the consideration also shown for big business, the platform was generally a farmer-labor platform. Roosevelt received 4,126,200 popular votes in the election—a number larger than the Republican slate received but less than the Democratic slate. The Progressive party was therefore largely responsible for the election of Woodrow Wilson to the presidency in 1912.

In 1924 reformist elements in the Middle West backed Senator Robert M. La Follette for president. The La Follette supporters were not actually a party, but were a coalition of political forces that included the Socialist party, Farmer-Labor party, trade unions, and the executive council of the American Federation of Labor. The Progressives drew about 4,822,000 popular votes, but this was only 16 percent of the total as compared with Roosevelt's 27 percent in 1912.

A Progressive party led by Henry Wallace and Senator Glen Taylor was formed in 1948. The party advocated domestic reform, but foreign policy was its chief interest. Generally, it favored a more conciliatory policy with relation to the Soviet Union. Henry Wallace won 1,157,218 popular votes, which was only 2 percent of the total. He finally left the party after criticizing its radical members for their unswerving support of the Soviet Union.

PROHIBITION, the banning of the manufacture and sale of alcoholic beverages. Prohibition was, in the United States, a nationwide policy after the ratification of the 18th Amendment to the Constitution on Jan. 29, 1919. This amendment prohibited the manufacture, transportation, importation and exportation, or sale of any alcoholic beverage in the United States. It went into effect in January, 1920. The Volstead Act, an extension of the wartime measure banning the distilling and brewing of any beverage containing over .05 percent alcohol, reinforced the 18th Amendment. The amendment was repealed in 1933 by the 21st Amendment.

Temperance crusaders had been protesting the use of alcoholic beverages in the United States since the founding of the nation. Toward the middle of the 19th century, temperance advocates began to turn to legal measures. In the period from 1846 to 1855, 13 states prohibited alcoholic beverages, although 9 of these states repealed their law later. Kansas wrote a prohibition measure into its constitution in 1880, and new life was injected into the prohibition crusade. The Prohibition party, founded in 1869, the Woman's Christian Temperance Union, founded in 1874, and the Anti-Saloon League of America, organized in 1895, were instrumental in the prohibition movement.

By the time of World War I there were prohibitory laws in 26 of the states. The war gave a further stimulus to the Anti-Saloon League of America, which began to espouse prohibition as a patriotic measure. The stress on patriotism was effective. The Lever Act was passed in 1917 to prohibit the use of grain for distilling and brewing. The 18th Amendment was passed by Congress in December, 1917, and submitted to the states, three-fourths of which ratified it by January, 1919.

The Prohibition Bureau found that enforcement of the amendment was virtually impossible where public opinion was against it. Liquor was brewed and sold illegally through speakeasies. Much opposition stemmed from the uncompromising insistence on the banning of wine and beer as well as hard liquor. The worst effect of prohibition was the increase in bootlegging, which was controlled by notorious gangsters. The report in 1931 of a commission appointed by President Herbert Hoover indicated that the enforcement of prohibition was not possible without huge expenditures. The Democratic party advocated the repeal of the 18th Amendment in the presidential campaign of 1932, and this was quickly accomplished by the passage and ratification of the 21st Amendment in 1933. Prohibition has been a matter of state laws since that time. See TEMPERANCE MOVEMENT.

PROKOFIEV, SERGEI (1891-1953), Russian composer, born in Sontsovka. Entering the St. Petersburg Conservatory in 1903, he studied under a number of renowned musicians, including Anatoli Liadov and Nikolai Rimski-Korsakov. At the age of 19 he won the Rubinstein prize with his first piano concerto. Four years later he won the conservatory's highest award for piano playing. A brilliant pianist, he appeared in public concerts throughout his career, often as the interpreter of his own compositions. Before permanently settling in the U.S.S.R. in 1931, Prokofiev lived for a time in England, France, Japan, the United States, and Germany.

These men are enforcing the provisions of the 18th Amendment by destroying casks of illegal liquor. Enforcement of prohibition proved difficult, and the amendment was repealed.

UPI

In 1921 two of his major works were performed for the first time: the ballet *Buffoon*, danced by Serge Diaghilev's company in Paris; and the opera *The Love for Three Oranges*, sung in Chicago.

From the beginning Prokofiev's music aimed primarily at the expression of simple and primitive emotions. It is remarkable for its originality, and audacity, for its use of satire and playfulness, and for its tunefulness. Difficult to classify, his music is an intriguing fusion of classical and more modern elements.

In addition to *Buffoon* and *The Love for Three Oranges*, Prokofiev's best known works include the opera *War and Peace*, the musical fairytale *Peter and the Wolf*, the cantata *Alexander Nevsky*, the ballet *Romeo and Juliet*, the suite *Lieutenant Kije*, the Classical Symphony, and the *Scythian Suite*. He composed six symphonies, five piano concertos, seven operas, and a great deal of incidental music.

PROMETHEUS, in classical mythology, a Titan. The name of Prometheus means "forethought," and the name of his brother Epimetheus means "afterthought." According to one myth, Prometheus was the creator of mankind. Jupiter gave him this task because Prometheus sided with him in the war against the Titans. Prometheus angered Jupiter by bringing fire from the sun and giving it to man. Angry, Jupiter had Prometheus bound to a rock in the Caucasus. He did this not only to punish Prometheus but also because Prometheus was the only one who knew the answer to a prophecy that told who would dethrone Jupiter.

Chained to the rock, Prometheus was unyielding. Many tortures were devised by Jupiter, but Prometheus kept his silence. According to one version of the myth, Chiron the centaur took Prometheus' place on the rock and was accepted by Jupiter as a substitute. Throughout history Prometheus has symbolized unyielding strength that resists oppression. Aeschylus wrote a trilogy about Prometheus, but only one play, *Prometheus Bound*, survives.

PRONOUN is a word used instead of a noun. It refers to a thing, person, or place without naming it. In the sentences "*Who* knows anything about *this?*" and "*He who* does not love *himself* cannot love *others*," all italicized words are pronouns. Not one of them names what it stands for. If a pronoun refers to a previously mentioned word, that word is called the antecedent of the pronoun. In the sentence "The *man* was very ill, and the doctor gave *him* no hope," *man* is the antecedent of *him*. Pronouns may be classified as personal, possessive, reflexive, intensive, demonstrative, interrogative, relative, and indefinite.

Personal pronouns refer to persons already known. They are divided into pronouns of the first person (*I, me, we, us*), of the second person (*you, thou, thee*), and of the third person (*he, him, she, her, it, they, them*). In the second person there are no separate pronouns for singular and plural. *You* and *it* are the only personal pronouns that can be either subject or object in a sentence. The third person singular is divided into masculine, feminine, and neuter pronouns (*he, she, it*). Since *he, she, we,* and *I* are subjective forms, a sentence like "It amused she" is incorrect.

The possessive pronouns, such as *mine, yours, thine, his, hers, ours,* and *theirs*, indicate ownership. They correspond closely to the personal pronouns.

Reflexive pronouns refer to the subject of the sentence of which they are the object. They are formed by adding *-self* or *-selves* to the objective form of the personal pronoun, as in "He is hurting *himself.*" "*Each other*," as in "They fought *each other*," is called a reciprocal pronoun.

Intensive pronouns look like reflexive pronouns but are used for emphasis only, as in "He *himself* told me so." They should not be used as simple personal pronouns. In the sentence "They took Martha and me," *myself* should not be used for *me*.

Demonstrative pronouns (*this, that, these, those*) are, as it were, pointing to things: "*That* is the thief, and *those* are his victims." Demonstrative pronouns are inflected only for number; the form is the same for all genders.

Interrogative pronouns (*who, whose, whom, what, which*) always ask for identification of something or someone. *Whom* is the objective form of *who*, and in formal language it should be used as such, as in "*Whom* was he addressing?"

Relative pronouns look like demonstrative or interrogative pronouns but have a different function. In subordinate clauses of a sentence they refer to an antecedent in the main clause. In "We own *nothing that* we value," *nothing* is the antecedent of the relative pronoun *that*. Antecedent and pronoun may occur in various cases. In very informal language *whose* may occasionally replace *of which*: "They belong to a generation whose preoccupation is fun."

Indefinite pronouns point out objects indefinitely or less clearly than demonstrative pronouns do. Often they are somewhat vague, as in "*It* rains." To this class belong such pronouns as *each, both, some, all, any, either, neither, other, another, such, each other,* and *one another.*

PRONUNCIATION, the action of pronouncing, the way of voicing an articulate sound of spoken language. Alphabetical spelling usually follows pronunciation, but in some languages, like Spanish, it does so much more closely than in English. To record the sounds of a language accurately the phonetic alphabet is used. Society formulates standards of correct pronunciation. Besides the officially correct, there may be dialectical pronunciations. The study of pronunciation belongs to linguistics, the science of language.

In the course of time, changes of pronunciation often take place. Middle English, which was used during the Middle Ages, was pronounced very differently from 20th-century English. One of the reasons that modern English spelling sometimes seems illogical is that some words are spelled according to their past pronunciation. Phonetics is the study of pronunciation. Linguists have discovered that languages change pronunciation according to phonetical laws of change.

To pronounce the language correctly is as important as to spell it correctly. Just as does bad spelling, bad pronunciation gives an unfortunate impression of stupidity or indifference. Correct speech is the ordinary speech of intelligent, well-educated society. How correct speech sounds depends on where one lives. English correctness is American affectation; a Yankee pronunciation is sometimes unacceptable in the south; and Castilian Spanish does not sound right in Mexico.

PROOFREADING is reading of printed matter against manuscript in order to detect and mark errors to be corrected by the printer. The printed matter is called proof; the manuscript from which the printer sets the type is called copy. (The term *proofreading* is also sometimes used loosely to mean the careful rereading and correction of handwritten or typed manuscript.)

A proofreader needs a good eye to detect errors in spelling, irreg-

This proofreader works in a publishing house.

ular spacing, and broken letters. A knowledge of printing processes and kinds of type is helpful, and familiarity with the subject matter makes the work easier.

Sometimes the proofreader works alone, comparing the proof with the copy. Often, however, the proofreader is assisted by a copyholder, who reads the copy aloud while the proofreader watches the proof and marks on it any deviations from copy.

Needed corrections are indicated by proofreader's marks, which are symbols used to shortcut instructions to the printer. Some of these marks are also used in editing manuscript to be sent to the printer. Manuscript should be double spaced; copyreader's marks and other small corrections may then be inserted between the lines.

Sometimes the proofreader is asked to check the proof for errors in grammar, punctuation, and usage. The proofreader either corrects such errors or queries them in the margin for decision by the author or editor.

HOW TO PROOFREAD

In proofreading alone, look first for typographical errors, such as bad spacing, broken type, poor alignment, improper word division, and letters or words set in the wrong kind of type. Then check the proof against the copy.

Mark each error twice—once in the line of type (usually by a caret or a line) and also in the margin (usually by a proofreader's mark). In the book method of proofreading align the marginal mark with the line in which the error occurs. Do not draw a line from the error to the margin. Do not obliterate any

type. Align the marginal mark with the line in which the error occurs. If there are only a few errors in a line, mark them all in the same margin, and separate them by slant lines. If there are a number of corrections in the line, use both margins. In the guideline method the error in the type is connected to the marginal symbol with a line. Use ink or a dark pencil. Soft lead pencil marks are hard to read.

Initial the proof in the upper right-hand corner. If only a few corrections are to be made, indicate that the proof is approved "as corrected." If there are many corrections, ask the printer to submit another proof after making the corrections. When that revised proof comes to you, check it against the previous proof, but proofread only the reset lines. Be sure to proofread the whole line, however, for while correcting one error the printer sometimes makes another. Also look at the preceding and the following lines to be sure the reset line has been properly placed.

OCCUPATION: Proofreader

NATURE OF WORK: Reading of proof sheets to catch errors and mark for correction

PERSONAL FACTORS—ABILITIES, SKILLS, APTITUDES: A good knowledge of spelling, English grammar, and punctuation, a retentive memory, an aptitude for detail and accuracy, and good hearing and eyesight are needed.

EDUCATION AND SPECIAL TRAINING: A high-school graduate should have courses in English, grammar, and spelling; on-the-job training as a copyholder; and a knowledge of the proofreader's special symbols and marks.

WORKING CONDITIONS:
1. INCOME:
   COMPARED WITH OTHER CAREERS WITH EQUAL TRAINING: Average
   COMPARED WITH MOST OTHER CAREERS: Low to average
2. ENVIRONMENT: Printing shop, pressroom, or publishing house
3. OTHER: Regular hours; benefits; unionized in some shops; hard on eyesight; moderate opportunities but little advancement

RELATED CAREERS: Compositor, editorial assistant, copyholder, copyreader

WHERE TO FIND MORE INFORMATION: National Editorial Association, 222 North Michigan Avenue, Chicago 1, Ill.; American Institute of Graphic Arts, 5 East 40th Street, New York 16, N. Y.

PROPAGANDA, an oral or written means to change opinions. Propaganda is not meant to inform. Its first task is to convince, rather than to educate. The propagandist sets about to strengthen opinions already favorable to his; to change opinions that are against his; and to arouse the indifferent to form favorable opinions. The object of the propagandist may be to sell toothpaste, to convince people of the value of democracy, or to convince men that the earth is flat. As the propagandist conducts his campaign, he learns where his opposition lies. Then he is able to direct his propaganda toward his opponents with greater effect. There are ways to test the value of propaganda techniques to see that they are doing the job. Speeches are tried out before small groups before they are delivered before large audiences. Propaganda campaigns are tested on the radio and television and then in magazines and newspapers to see which has the greatest effect on a particular audience. Questionnaires are often sent out to gauge the effectiveness of propaganda. Often, however, it is almost impossible to determine the effect of propaganda, because there is usually propaganda on every side of a question. Therefore, propaganda may cancel itself out. This is why dictators want to monopolize propaganda.

Propaganda is no new invention. Election appeals were found on Pompeii's walls. One purpose of St. Augustine's *The City of God* was to persuade the pagans to embrace Christianity. Samuel Adams directed committees of correspondence during the American Revolutionary War to persuade the Americans to fight the British. "Memphis Blues," one of the first songs by W. C. Handy, was written as propaganda for an election campaign. Modern propaganda has taken advantage of improved communications—radio, television, telephone, and the airplane. People are also better educated generally than they once were; it is therefore easier to reach them through propaganda but somewhat more difficult to convince them.

Propaganda is a tool. In itself it is neither good nor bad. It can be used for evil purposes, as when Joseph Paul Goebbels directed his Nazi propaganda campaign in Germany. Propaganda can also be used for good—to bring out the vote or to prevent accidents. In any case, propaganda will not disappear so long as people want to convince one another of something.

PROPELLER, a device for pushing or pulling a craft through air or water. When a propeller (an adaptation of the screw) whirls around, it screws itself forward.

A propeller has two or more blades joined at a central hub. Each blade has a cross section similar to that of an airplane wing. Each blade has a twist from its outside tip to where it is fastened to the hub. The edge of the blade that strikes the air or water first is the leading edge; the other is the trailing edge.

The pitch of a propeller is the distance it moves forward in one revolution if there is no slippage. If the blades are almost parallel to the plane of the propeller, the propeller has a low pitch; if the blades are at a large angle, the propeller has a high pitch.

Airplane propellers usually have long, narrow blades. Light, slow-speed airplanes have propellers made of laminated wood. Larger and faster airplanes have propellers of solid aluminum alloy or hollow steel.

Small airplanes have propellers with two blades; large ones have three-bladed or four-bladed propellers.

The angle of the blades, and therefore the pitch of the propeller, can be varied on some airplane propellers. Propellers on which the blade angle can be changed by the pilot during flight are called controllable-pitch propellers. Propellers that automatically change the blade angle to suit flight conditions are called automatic propellers. All modern high-powered airplanes that use propellers have automatic propellers. Multiple-engine airplanes have propellers that can be feathered; the blades can be brought to such an extreme pitch that they are parallel to the line of flight. When an engine is shut off during flight because of some emergency, feathering the propeller prevents damage to the engine and makes the plane easier to control. Counterrotating propellers are used with very powerful engines. A six-bladed, counterrotating propeller has one three-bladed propeller rotating in one direction and, behind it, another three-bladed propeller rotating in the opposite direction. Two three-bladed propellers are more efficient than one six-bladed propeller.

Marine propellers, often called screws or screw propellers, usually have shorter, broader blades than airplane propellers and are made of cast steel or manganese bronze. Outboard motors and small, high-speed craft may have two-bladed propellers. Three-bladed propellers are common, and many ships have four-bladed or five-bladed propellers. Small ships may have only one propeller; larger ships have two or more. When a ship has two propellers, the one on the right side of the ship rotates clockwise, and the one on the left rotates counterclockwise. Marine propellers, like airplane propellers, can be made so that the pitch can be varied. Some can be reversed in pitch. Such propellers eliminate the need of a reverse gear in the ship's power transmission.

H. Grubstein—Photo Researchers

The three-bladed, adjustable-pitch, metal propellers (above) are fitted to a four-engine airliner. With adjustable-pitch propellers an airplane pilot can cruise at the most economical propeller setting, below, **A.** When the pilot increases his altitude, **B,** he alters the pitch of the propellers to produce more "bite" on the air. As he climbs into thinner air, **C,** he increases the pitch still more to compensate for the reduced air density.

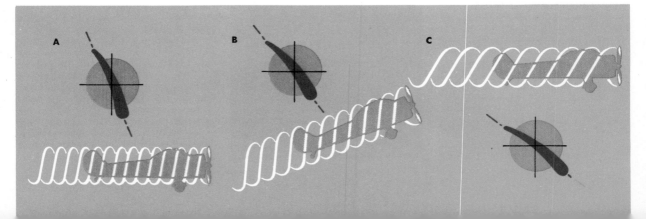

PROPHET, a term derived from the Greek word meaning "to proclaim," "to foretell." In ancient Greece, Rome, and elsewhere prophetesses, called sibyls, were consulted about various matters concerning future happenings. These sibyls, like the shamans of Siberia, the medicine men of the American Indians, or the dancing dervishes of the Near East, often worked themselves into a frenzy by wild dancing and music before uttering an oracle or prophecy. Other prophets, like the Magi of Babylonia, used crystal gazing and astrology in predicting the future, while the augurs of Rome recommended, from the entrails of animals, the right time for battle. The modern fortunetellers are descendants of these early prophets.

A different kind of prophetic inspiration was claimed by the great Hebrew prophets, Isaiah, Jeremiah, Ezekiel, and Daniel, and by the founder of Islam, Mohammed. These prophets considered themselves the mouthpieces of God, chosen to deliver God's message to a people or peoples. Their message was often not a prophecy about a particular action to be taken or avoided but was aimed at the changing of the religious and moral life of men. The sacred books of Christianity and Islam include many passages thought to have been written by prophets under divine inspiration.

PROSERPINA, the only daughter of Ceres, was abducted by Pluto, lord of the underworld, who wished to make her his queen. Ceres mourned and wandered over the earth, asking where her daughter was. She was finally told by the Sun, and she was so saddened that the whole earth dried up. Alarmed and wishing peace, Jupiter told Ceres that she could have her daughter back if Proserpina had taken no food in the underworld. Ceres agreed to this, and Mercury was sent for Proserpina. When her daughter came up, Ceres discovered that Proserpina had eaten a pomegranate seed while in the underworld and therefore must return. It was Jupiter who made the compromise that allowed Proserpina to spend the winter with Pluto and the summer with Ceres. See CERES.

The Greek name for Proserpina was Persephone. Proserpina was sometimes identified with Hecate, the goddess of the underworld. Hecate represented the terrors and darkness of the night and was believed to wander about at nighttime, invisible to all except dogs, who barked to tell of her approach.

Wilson & Macpherson Hole

Carl Niemann (left) and Nobel-laureate Linus Pauling (right), both of the California Institute of Technology, pose with a model of an amino acid, one of the building blocks of proteins. Blue balls represent nitrogen atoms; black, carbon; red, oxygen; and white, hydrogen.

PROSTHESIS is an artificial part of the body, such as an eye, arm, leg, or denture, that is used to replace one congenitally absent or lost through disease or injury. Artificial eyes are now usually made of plastic. If attachment to the eye muscles is possible, the movement of the prosthesis may be coordinated with that of the normal eye. Artificial limbs are made of leather, wood, fiber, metal, or plastic material. They may be attached by means of straps, lacings, or sockets. The suction socket is held to the stump by means of negative pressure and is used where amputation occurred above the knee. A special type of prosthesis is the cineplastic prosthesis, used where less harnessing is required; it is especially useful when the hand is secured at the wrist. The hook or artificial hand is controlled by a surgically constructed muscle loop to which direct attachment is made by pins and a cable. With training under an experienced physical and occupational therapist, the amputee attains good facility.

PROTECTIVE COLORATION. See ANIMAL COLORING.

PROTEIN, a class of complex organic substances essential to the life and structure of all plant and animal tissue. All proteins contain carbon, hydrogen, nitrogen, and oxygen, and some contain other elements, such as sulfur, phosphorus, and iron. They are almost the only source of nitrogen that man and animals can use in their bodies. Proteins are essential in the diet of man and animals for the building of new tissue and the repairing of damaged tissue.

In man, proteins in the form of food are gradually converted by enzymes such as pepsin, trypsin, and erepsin into water-soluble substances known as amino acids. After being absorbed through the intestinal walls, these substances are transformed into proteins that normally make up the bulk of muscles and other tissues of the body. See NUTRITION.

Protein molecules are made of smaller molecules of amino acids. Twenty-three amino acids have been isolated; there are indications that more exist. Some proteins contain additional groups, such as carbohydrates and metals. All proteins are very large molecules with molecular weights of 30,000 to several millions. Because of their large size, they belong to the class of substances known as colloids.

Animals are ultimately dependent on plants for amino acids, and thus protein, for only plants can form amino acids from simple inorganic forms of nitrogen. Plants are dependent upon nitrogen-fixing bacteria, which convert free atmospheric nitrogen into usable forms (nitrates), or upon fertilizers.

The Leipzig Disputation in 1519 between Martin Luther (right) and Johann Eck (left) revealed the depth of the growing split between Luther and the Roman Catholic Church.

PROTESTANT, a member of any of a number of Christian churches that trace their origins to the Reformation. The meaning of the term "to protest" has come to be largely negative. At the time of the Reformation and into the 18th century, however, the term conveyed the meaning "to declare openly a fact, an opinion, or a resolution." The Protestant churches disagree with certain doctrines of the Roman Catholic Church and present a positive theology of their own.

John Wycliffe in England and John Huss in Bohemia were pre-Reformation Protestants. However, the initial impetus was given Protestantism by Martin Luther, John Calvin, and Huldreich Zwingli. The term itself was derived from the "Protestio" issued by the reforming members of the Second Diet of Speyer in 1529. The group declared that they would not abide by the decision of the Roman Catholic majority of the diet, that they would continue their innovations, and that they would not allow the Mass in their realms. The positive doctrines of these princes and representatives of cities was presented in the Augsburg Confession (1530), which was an authoritative Lutheran document. As revised by Melanchthon, the Augsburg Confession was also adopted by some Calvinist groups in Germany. Only after the first period of the Thirty Years' War did Calvinists and Lutherans unite under the name Protestant. The Church of England adopted the designation Protestant in the 17th century, but not until the common opposition to the policies of the Stuart kings did the Puritans join with the Church of England in the use of the name. The name Protestant has come to apply commonly to all non-Roman Catholic groups that can trace their origins, however remotely, to the Reformation.

In the United States there are over 200 Protestant denominations. They include, among others, the Baptists, founded by Roger Williams in 1738; the Disciples of Christ, founded by Thomas Campbell in 1804; the Methodist churches, founded by John Wesley in 1729; the Presbyterian churches, which derive their theology from John Calvin and the Scottish reformer John Knox; the Protestant Episcopal church, which had its origin in the Church of England; and the United Church of Christ, founded by a union of the Congregational Christian Churches and the Evangelical and Reformed Church in 1957. Other Protestant groups include the Brethren churches, the Reformed churches, the Friends, the Adventists, the Mennonites, the Moravians, the Churches of God, and a number of Eastern churches.

The Protestant churches share with the Roman Catholics the belief in one God, the Creator of the world; the belief that God's will is revealed in the life and resurrection of Jesus; and the belief that men are accountable to God and bear a responsibility to one another. A central theme in many Protestant groups is justification by faith, which means that the acceptance of Christ's sacrifice is the sole ground for God's forgiveness. Good works are performed only through God's goodness. The salvation of man depends entirely on God's mercy, which is beyond man's understanding. Most Protestants accept the Bible as the Word of God, a religious authority that no human agency could contain. Protestants, in their understanding of man's approach to God, believe that the religious act is a direct encounter with God. See REFORMATION.

PROTON, one of the basic atomic particles and the fundamental unit of positive electric charge. See ATOM.

A proton has a charge that is equal but opposite to that of an electron. (See ELECTRON.) The electrical charge carried by a proton is 4.803×10^{-10} absolute electrostatic units.

All atomic nuclei contain one or more protons. The atomic number of an element is the number of protons an atom of the element has in its nucleus. The nucleus of a hydrogen atom contains one proton; the atomic number of hydrogen is 1. The nucleus of a uranium atom has 92 protons; the atomic number of uranium is 92.

The mass of a proton is 1.67×10^{-24} grams. A proton has 1,837 times as much mass as an electron.

Artificially accelerated protons are often used to bombard atomic nuclei to induce nuclear disintegration. See PARTICLE ACCELERATOR.

PROTON SYNCHROTRON. See PARTICLE ACCELERATOR.

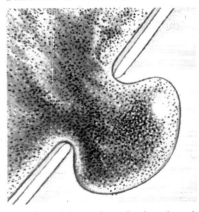

Protoplasm is seen here flowing through a microscopic hole. Most of its structures are colorless or nearly colorless.

PROTOPLASM, the living substance of which all animals and plants are composed. Protoplasm is thick, semiliquid, and jelly-like. Its color is like that of cloudy water, and it is semitransparent.

The details of protoplasm structure cannot be seen by looking at an animal or a plant with the naked eye. A small portion of animal or plant tissue, such as a bit of raw beef or green leaf, must be viewed through a microscope. Upon so doing, we will see a network or mosaic of semitransparent cells, each filled with a clear liquid that is slightly thicker than water. This liquid, which seems to waver and flow within the cell, is protoplasm. The protoplasm of a cell is divided into two parts: One of these parts is a small, round, oval structure called the nucleus; the other part is the cytoplasm that surrounds the nucleus. The membrane that encloses the entire cell is likewise composed of living protoplasm. Plant cells have in addition to the living cell membrane a heavy outer cell wall that is composed of nonliving but highly complex starches. These starches are collectively known as cellulose.

Cells from every living part of an animal's body—its skin, muscles, fat, blood, bone marrow, and nerves —contain protoplasm that is essentially the same but that differs slightly in color and consistency and in the kinds of proteins contained therein. The protoplasm of plant cells appears essentially the same as that of animal cells except for the differences in their color and consistency.

Protoplasm is found only within the cells of living animals and plants. It is the only substance on earth that is known to possess life, and no living organism has ever been discovered that is not composed of protoplasm. It is involved in all of the activities that characterize living animals and plants—warmth, breathing, eating, sensation, intelligence, and reproduction.

Protoplasm consists chiefly of proteins, carbohydrates, and fats, which are organic compounds consisting chiefly of the elements carbon, oxygen, hydrogen, and nitrogen. It is the extremely complex organization and interaction of these elements and compounds within protoplasm that result in life in both animals and plants. As yet biologists know only a little about the internal secrets of protoplasm, but the increase of such knowledge through research will answer many perplexing questions about the causes and fundamental nature of life.

PROTOZOA, tiny animals of only one cell or a group of similar cells forming a colony. Whereas multicellular animals have different kinds of cells for different functions, protozoa perform all of their life functions within a single cell. This cell is, however, not unlike those of multicellular animals. It has a distinct nucleus, controlling many of its functions and containing structures called chromosomes, which carry inherited characteristics and pass them on to the offspring. Surrounding the nucleus is a jelly-like cytoplasm, which makes up the main

body of the cell. The animal is then enclosed in a thin, pliable membrane.

Protozoa are frequently divided into groups according to their method of locomotion. The amoeba group moves by extending temporary finger-like processes called pseudopodia (false feet). Another group, to which the paramecia belong, is covered with short hairlike structures called cilia, which act as little "oars." Still another group, the most primitive, has one or more long hairlike structures called flagella, which whip back and forth. A fourth group has no locomotor structures, since they are all parasites. The protozoan that causes malaria belongs to this group.

An amoeba obtains its meal of single-celled plants and animals by encircling them with its pseudopodia, thus forming a little pocket, or vacuole, around the food. It then secretes enzymes into the vacuole to digest the food. Some protozoa have green pigment called chlorophyll,

just as plants do, and thus are able to manufacture much of their food.

Protozoa respond to stimuli by moving away from strong light or touch by a needle, but they respond to contact with food by engulfing it. Extremely minute fibers within the cytoplasm apparently carry stimuli to various parts of the body.

Although protozoa are not recognized as males and females, they reproduce by various methods. Some merely split into two small cells, each of which grows to adult size. This is a method of asexual reproduction called fission. The malaria protozoan reproduces sexually by forming eggs and sperm in the stomach of the mosquito. The egg and sperm unite and develop into new malarial organisms.

Protozoa are found everywhere— in water, in soil, in the air, and even as parasites living in other organisms. Biologists believe the flagellated group to be the ancestors of multicellular animals.

Some protozoa cause serious diseases in man and animals. Amoebic dysentery, sleeping sickness, and malaria are caused by protozoa of different types.

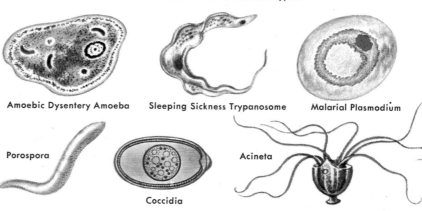

Amoebic Dysentery Amoeba   Sleeping Sickness Trypanosome   Malarial Plasmodium

Porospora   Coccidia   Acineta

Porospora and coccidia are parasites of animals. Podophyra resemble crystals and are immobile during adulthood. The foraminifera are covered by a protective shell.

Acineta catch other protozoa by means of tentacles and then ingest the protozoa. The elaborately shaped stentor and the paramecia are covered with hairlike cilia.

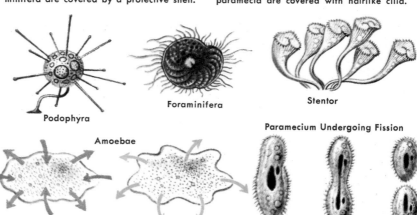

Podophyra   Foraminifera   Stentor

Amoebae   Paramecium Undergoing Fission

Brown Brothers

Marcel Proust, French novelist

PROUST, MARCEL (1871-1922), French novelist, born in Paris. Proust attended the Lycée Condorcet and later studied law and political science. However, a chronic asthmatic condition, first evident when Proust was nine years old, prevented him from entering a profession and to a great extent determined his career in literature. A semi-invalid from his childhood onward, Proust was indulged by his parents and was brought up in ease and luxury. Although of middle-class birth (his father was a physician and professor; his mother was of a well-to-do Jewish family), he gained admission to the fashionable salons of the Paris aristocracy through personal charm and ambitious curiosity. He soon acquired the reputation of being a hypersensitive, eccentric, and snobbish dilettante. A worsening of his physical condition, coupled with the deaths in rapid succession of his father and his mother, led to disillusionment and his withdrawal from society to the confines of his cork-lined Paris apartment. The last 20 years of his life, spent in semiseclusion, were devoted to the writing of his masterpiece, *Remembrance of Things Past*. During those years he rarely left his apartment, and then only at night, when his allergies would be least affected.

Proust's literary career had already commenced. In addition to his first published work, *Pleasures and Days*, which appeared in 1896, he contributed numerous articles to various publications and translated into French *The Bible of Amiens* and *Sesame and Lilies*, two works by John Ruskin, the British author. Proust's reputation as a novelist, however, rests almost entirely on *Remembrance of Things Past*, one of the great novels of the 20th century. Work was started on the novel in 1896. After the author's death his early sketches were edited and published as the novel *Jean Santeuil* (1951). Originally conceived as a three-volume work, the draft of the final version was tripled in length by the time it was published. The novel was published in seven individual installments. The first, *Swann's Way*, generally considered the best of the seven, was printed at Proust's own expense in 1913 and was received with indifference. The second, *Within a Budding Grove*, won the Goncourt prize in 1918 and brought international fame to the author. Remaining installments, the last three of which were published posthumously, were *The Guermantes Way*, *Cities of the Plain*, *The Captive*, *The Sweet Cheat Gone*, and *The Past Recaptured*. The authorized English translation, all but the final installment done by Charles K. M. Scott-Moncrieff, was published between 1922 and 1932. Essentially, *Remembrance of Things Past* describes the disintegration of the French aristocracy during the Third Republic and the rise of the wealthy middle class. In telling his story, actually an elaborate reconstruction of memories, Proust introduced as elements of fiction certain techniques of psychological analysis. Few works have had such a profound effect on literature.

PROVIDENCE, the capital of Rhode Island, is a commercial and industrial center. It is located on the Providence River in the northeastern part of the state. The city was once a great shipping port and still has important shipping in its improved harbor. Manufactures include jewelry, silverware, textile and electrical machinery, tools, textiles, and foundry products. In 1960 the city had a population of 207,498.

Providence has many points of interest, which include the John Carter Brown Library, the Capitol, and Roger Williams Park, with a museum and zoological gardens. Among the many 18th-century houses are the John Brown House (about 1786) and the Stephen Hopkins House (about 1743). Providence is the seat of Brown University and the Rhode Island School of Design.

In 1636 Roger Williams was exiled from Massachusetts and was granted by friendly Indians a tract of land on the site of the present Providence. Before the American Revolution the city was principally a seaport with a thriving foreign commerce. Industry was gradually developed, and metalworking and silverware manufacturing were begun in 1831. Providence became the state capital in 1900.

PRUSSIA, a former kingdom and a former state of Germany. It took the lead in the creation of the German Empire in 1871.

Prussia was ruthlessly conquered in the 13th century by the Teutonic Knights, who brought in colonists from Germany. By the 15th century the old Prussian customs and language had disappeared. In 1618, the first year of the Thirty Years' War, the duchy of Prussia was united to Brandenburg, which was ruled by the House of Hohenzollern. Frederick William, the Great Elector, obtained ducal Prussia as an independent sovereign possession of the House of Hohenzollern. He increased the power of the monarchy and provided Prussia's basic fiscal structure. His son, Elector Frederick III of Brandenburg, in return for giving aid in the War of the Spanish Succession, received from Holy Roman Emperor Leopold I permission to crown himself king of Prussia (1701).

Frederick William I, king of Prussia from 1713 until 1740, filled the treasury, strengthened the army, and added Stettin and much of Swedish Pomerania to his territories. His policy was continued by Frederick II, known as Frederick the Great, who was king from 1740 until 1786.

Prussia survived the Seven Years' War (1756-1763) through tenacity and good fortune, and Frederick— by discipline and strict economy— made Prussia the strongest of the German states and a rival of Austria. (See SEVEN YEARS' WAR.) The three Polish partitions (1772, 1793, and 1795) almost doubled the territory of Prussia, but they did not strengthen it.

Under Frederick William III (ruled from 1797 until 1840), Prussia collapsed at Jena and Auertstedt against Napoleon's armies. The revival of nationalism, the reforms of Heinrich vom Stein (who abolished

Above is a portrait of Frederick the Great, king of Prussia, patron of literature, and military genius, who, by diplomacy and war made Prussia the leading German state.

serfdom), and the military reorganization of Gerhard Scharnhorst made Prussia an important participant in the league that defeated Napoleon. The Congress of Vienna gave Prussia the rest of Swedish Pomerania, much of Saxony, Westphalia, and most of the Rhineland in return for much of its Polish territory gained in the partitions. The exchange of its agricultural and Slavic territory for potential industrial areas in Germany strengthened Prussia. However, Prussia played a secondary role in Europe after 1815 until the accession of William I to the throne in 1861.

William I's chief minister, Otto von Bismarck, by means of the successful war against Austria in 1866, made Prussia the master of Germany. Prussia gained Hanover, Hesse-Kassel, Hesse-Nassau, Frankfort, and the duchies of Schleswig-Holstein and Lauenburg. William I became emperor of a united Germany in 1871 following the defeat of France in the Franco-Prussian War. Prussia, with its tradition of militarism and discipline, exerted a profound influence on Germany. The Prussian city of Berlin became the capital of the new German Empire. See BISMARCK, PRINCE OTTO VON; FREDERICK THE GREAT; FRANCO-PRUSSIAN WAR; HOHENZOLLERN; ZOLLVEREIN.

PSITTACOSIS, or parrot fever, is a type of pneumonia caused by a virus and carried as an intestinal infection in certain birds. The principal carriers are the psittacines, a term that includes parrots, parakeets, macaws, lovebirds, and other parrot-like birds. However, poultry, pigeons, and canaries may also be affected by psittacosis.

The disease is contagious, and it may be communicated to man. It is possible for human beings to acquire the infection when they inhale the dust from the feathers of an infected bird or the contents of a cage occupied by a bird with the disease. In severe cases of psittacosis the mortality rate may be as high as 20 percent. Good results in treatment have been obtained with antibiotics. Control of the disease depends on restricting the importation of birds likely to be infected and on eradicating infected flocks of birds.

PSYCHIATRIST, a doctor of medicine (M.D.) who has specialized in the treatment of nervous and mental diseases. He deals with disorders of the anatomy of the brain, that is, organic diseases such as brain tumors and infections, and brain changes due to old age or disease of the body. He also deals with disorders of thinking, feeling, and acting which are primarily psychic in origin (functional or psychogenic disorders not due to alterations in brain struc-

ture or chemistry). His interest must extend to heredity, all diseases of the body, and all elements of the environment, especially the individual's relationship to his family and to others near to him. The psychiatrist must concern himself with any factor that could disturb normal mental attitudes and functioning.

The psychiatrist deals with the causes and treatment of part or all of the three great classes of mental illness: mental deficiency (feeblemindedness), personality or character disorders, and the psychoses (mental disorders with more extensive disorganization of the personality). His field of activity may include many legal procedures and the study of the causes and treatment of criminal behavior.

Psychiatry is a relatively new branch of medicine, but one index of its importance and of the need for more trained personnel may be seen in the figures that indicate that one-half of the hospital beds in the United States are occupied by nervous and mental patients. Psychiatry, in addition to treating the person who is mentally or socially sick, is concerned with improving the emotional and mental capabilities of well persons. The psychiatrist may join the psychologist in an effort to solve personnel problems in industry and government or to assist in educational programs.

The treatments used in psychi-

Philippe Pinel is often considered the father of psychiatry. In 1795 he ordered chains and fetters removed from insane women in La Sâlpétrière, a mental hospital in Paris. Thereafter Pinel replaced cruelty with understanding and therapy in treating mental illness.

Courtesy of and © 1960, Parke, Davis & Co.

PSYCHOLOGY

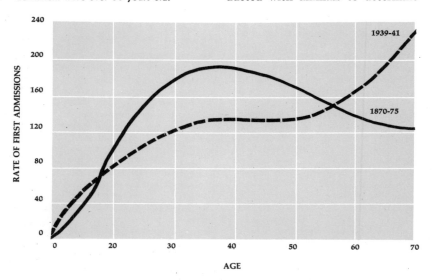

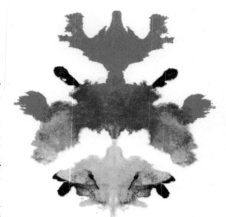

This design is of the same type as those actually used in the Rorschach ink-blot test.

PSYCHOLOGY is the study of consciousness and behavior in human beings and other animals, especially in relation to their total environments. Psychology grew out of ancient speculations concerning man's relationship to his environment, but as an experimental science it dates only from the late-19th century. In the 20th century psychology has developed through several major schools, or basic points of view, which have given rise to many different fields of psychology.

The beginnings of psychology can be traced from primitive concerns with "mind" and "soul" through the Greek philosophers, medieval religious philosophers, and Renaissance scientists. In particular, psychology followed from physiognomy —the supposed science of studying the mind through the outward appearance of the body—and phrenology—the study of the mind through contours of the brain surface as determined from the outer surface of the skull.

Scientific methods were introduced into psychological studies late in the 19th century. In 1879 a German, Wilhelm Wundt, opened a laboratory for psychological research, the psychological institute at the University of Leipzig. Wundt's laboratory was the training ground for many early psychologists. They carried his ideas back to England, America, and the other countries of Europe. Many went beyond Wundt, creating new research techniques and developing new theories. Through them, and others, each country came to develop its own psychology.

In England experiments were conducted with animals to determine how the brain and nervous system operate. There was new interest in the differences in behavior among individuals. In Germany, in addition to Wundt's work, experiments were being conducted on the function and structure of memory. In France psychiatry, the companion of psychology, was making advances toward understanding the mentally ill. In Russia Ivan Pavlov made a study of conditioned reflexes, discovered through research on the digestion of dogs. In Austria Sigmund Freud studied the mentally ill also and developed a theory of human personality and a method to help those whom he called neurotic.

By 1900, however, the center of psychological research was in the United States. Here, several schools of psychology had developed, each with its own theories and methods. Subsequently, a tendency developed among these schools to borrow ideas from each other and to look for similarities rather than to stress the differences.

FIVE MAJOR SCHOOLS

A school of psychology is a point of view with which a group of psychologists approach their subject matter. Among the major schools to develop in the 20th century are structuralism, functionalism, behaviorism, Gestalt, and psychoanalysis.

Structuralism is the name of the school derived directly from Wundt and founded by Edward Bradford Titchener. It used the method of introspection, or self-examination, to study the structure of the mind, or the way the mental processes occur.

Functionalism, the second great school to develop in the United States, took psychology beyond the structure of the mind. It studied

Wide World Photo

Carl Jung was a great Swiss psychiatrist.

atry include the control of the patient's environment and activities, the use of drugs and biological substances, the use of electricity, surgery, and other physical agents, and psychotherapy. This latter includes many methods, such as suggestion, reassurance, hypnosis, reeducation, ventilation or reliving of past experiences, and the recall of forgotten material. Psychotherapy may be used individually or in groups. The psychiatrist who, for the most part, confines his treatment to psychotherapy as outlined by the Freudian school or to similar schools of thought is known as a psychoanalyst.

The rise of psychiatry has caused significant changes in the treatment of mental illness. During the period 1870-1875 the bulk of first admissions to mental hospitals were severe psychotics from the 30-50 age group. In 1939-1941, because of an increased tendency to hospitalize the senile, most first admissions were over 60 years old.

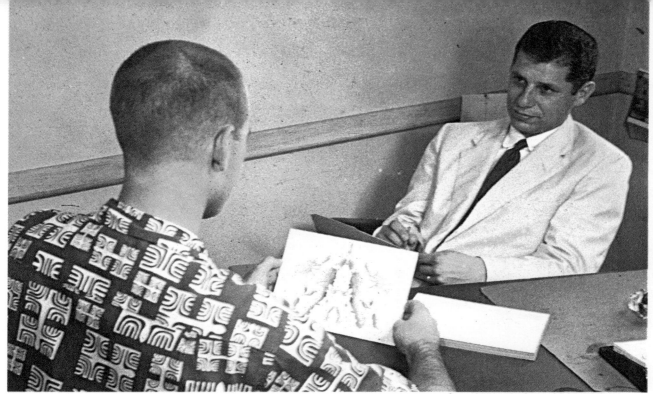

A psychologist uses the Rorschach ink-blot test to study a subject's personality. He notes the subject's responses in a code of letters.

human behavior in its natural setting to determine why it occurs and what are its consequences. This school opened the laboratory door and sent psychology out into the home, the school, the factory, and the clinic. One of the founders of functionalism was William James, who declared that mental life could not be broken down into parts but had to be understood in its totality. John Dewey, who wrote of the necessity of seeing behavior in its relation to society, was the major founder of functionalism.

This school led in turn to the development of behaviorism. Borrowing from the Soviet physiologist Pavlov, John Broadus Watson, in the early 1920's, developed a theory that all behavior could be described as a series of conditioned responses. He believed that human behavior could be so conditioned that individuals could be made to respond as was desired to any given stimulus. Conditioning is the process by which an animal is trained to make a specific response to a given stimulus. (See CONDITIONED REFLEX.) Watson's book *Psychological Care of Infant and Child*, which presented formulas for conditioning children, became a guide for pediatricians, nurses, and parents. It later became clear that Watson's ideas provided an oversimplified explanation of human behavior.

Gestalt psychology emphasized the viewing of individual behavior in its entire pattern rather than as a sum of separate parts, as behaviorism saw it. Gestaltists believe that individuals must be understood in terms of the goals they seek. This school was founded by three psychologists—Köhler, Koffka, and Wertheimer—in Germany in the first decade of the 20th century and was brought to the United States in the 1940's. Most of the work that has been done by this school has been in the fields of child psychology and social psychology.

The fifth great school was Sigmund Freud's school that used psychoanalysis, the name given to a method for analyzing the content and mechanisms of mental life. Although it was based on Freud's psychoanalytic method, the school has deviated considerably from Freud's original teachings. The theory on which this method is based, and which Freud developed during his years of research with emotionally disturbed patients, can be called the theory of motivation, or an explanation of why people act and feel as they do. Psychoanalysis was the first school of psychology that reached back into the history of personal motives to find the causes for present behavior in the past history of the person. It seriously considered daydreams, fantasies, nightmares, and other aspects of mental life as the proper study of psychologists. Freud called these aspects of life the content of the unconscious. It is this concept of the unconscious that changed the science of psychology more than any other in this century.

About the middle of the 20th century, although there were several schools of psychology with differences among them, the two major divisions were physiological psychology and psychoanalysis.

With its recent tremendous growth, as with the growth of all sciences, psychology has tended to spread out into many areas and to specialize in some of them. There are now more than a dozen specialized fields of psychology, the most important of which are discussed in the following section.

MAJOR FIELDS OF PSYCHOLOGY

Experimental psychology deals with that area that conducts laboratory research on the problems of sensation, perception, and behavior. This does not mean that experiments are not conducted in other fields, but only that this particular group is given this name. The majority of the experimentalists are behaviorists.

Learning psychology studies the processes and problems of how people learn. This term usually refers only to those behaviorists who study learning in the laboratory. Educational psychology, which also is concerned with problems of learning, deals with direct problems of school learning and other problems

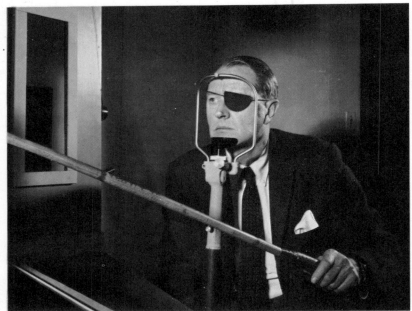

Educational Testing Service

Perception is one of the most important areas of interest in experimental psychology. Here a subject is taking part in an experiment to test his perception with only one eye.

attached to the educational process, while learning psychology deals with general learning problems.

Abnormal psychology is the one with which people are most familiar. It studies the various human emotional abnormalities and provides the theory for clinical psychology, which is the treatment of the abnormal. Clinical psychology applies the theories developed by those psychologists who are studying and experimenting with the various problems of abnormality. Clinicians also conduct their own research, in which they use patients as subjects. Much of their research is centered on ways of improving the methods of treatment.

Child psychology studies the growth and development of infants and children. This field, too, has become well known, particularly through the books of some of the major child psychologists, such as Arnold Gesell. Much of the material developed by the child psychologists has been adapted for articles and books of guidance for parents.

Physiological psychology studies the functions of the nervous system and other parts of the body involved in behavior.

The psychology of individual differences is concerned with the similarities and differences among individuals, particularly with respect to sex, nationality, age, environmental conditions, and race. Its main tools are tests devised to measure abilities, interests, aptitudes, intelligence, personality, attitudes, temperament, and achievement. The tests devised by this group of psychologists are used in several other fields as well. The educational pyschologist uses the intelligence, the aptitude, the abilities, and the personality test, as well as special achievement tests for reading, writing, and other skills. The clinician uses the personality test, particularly in the diagnosis of emotional illness. Child psychologists use all the tests to measure the growth and development of children. In addition, these fields have their own tests to measure the specific factors with which they are concerned.

Personnel and industrial psychology also uses the test to a great extent. This relatively new field studies the problems of personnel selection and training, on-the-job problems, management-labor relations, and other problems faced by industry and business. Closely akin to industrial psychology is vocational guidance, which attempts to assist individuals in job selection and preparation.

The industrial psychologist also makes frequent and wide use of the test. It is often necessary in applying for a job to take a variety of tests, intelligence or personality or aptitude. Research in industrial psy-

chology has showed that improper placement of workers in jobs often leads to low production, absenteeism, poor management-labor relations, and other problems. It is to avoid these problems that tests are given. It is the hope that the tests will indicate the best job for the person and the best working conditions and that they will also give other positive results.

Social psychology is the study of groups, the relations among individuals within groups, relations among groups, crowd behavior, the problems of war, and other problems in which more than one person is involved.

OCCUPATION: Psychologist

NATURE OF WORK: Studying the reactions and behavior of people and the reasons for them

PERSONAL FACTORS—ABILITIES, SKILLS, APTITUDES: An aptitude for the sciences and mathematics, emotional stability, interest in people, and social maturity are needed.

EDUCATION AND SPECIAL TRAINING: A master's degree is the usual basic requirement. A Ph.D. and at least one year of experience are needed for most advanced positions.

WORKING CONDITIONS:
  1. **INCOME:**
    COMPARED WITH OTHER CAREERS WITH EQUAL TRAINING: Average to high
    COMPARED WITH MOST OTHER CAREERS: Average to high
  2. **ENVIRONMENT:** Varies, from college classrooms to hospital wards, research laboratories, and business offices
  3. **OTHER:** Regular hours; industrial or institutional benefits; excellent opportunities for persons with advanced degrees

RELATED CAREERS: Occupational analyst, employment or personnel worker, counselor, occupational therapist, social worker

WHERE TO FIND MORE INFORMATION: American Psychological Association, 1333 16th Street NW, Washington 6, D.C.; National Institute of Mental Health, Bethesda, Md.; Chief, Division of Training, Office of Vocational Rehabilitation, U.S. Dept. of Health, Education, and Welfare, Washington 25, D.C.

PSYCHROMETER. See HYGROMETER.

PTARMIGAN. See GROUSE, PTARMIGANS, PRAIRIE CHICKENS.

PTERIDOPHYTE, a fern or another plant related to the ferns. Some botanists maintain that the pteridophytes, which include all ferns and the horsetails and club mosses, constitute an independent plant phylum. Others maintain that the pteridophytes should be classified in the same phylum as the spermatophytes, which comprise the gymnosperms and angiosperms.

The pteridophytes occupy a lower position in the evolutionary scale than do the gymnosperms and the angiosperms. Pteridophytes do not develop flowers, fruits, or seeds and do not reproduce by means of seeds. Instead, pteridophytes reproduce asexually by means of spores.

The spores of the pteridophytes are microscopic particles that, after developing on the leaves of pteridophytes, are discharged into the air and borne some distance away by the wind. If the spores alight in moist soil, they will grow. Since pteridophytes show alternation of generations, the spores will not grow into new pteridophytes but, instead, will produce the gametophyte generation, which in turn produces the spore-bearing plant.

Living ferns are of many types. Some tropical ferns attain the height and breadth of trees. Most ferns of the Temperate Zones generally grow in moist, shaded woods, resemble shrubs, and have long, bending, pinnately compound leaves, or fronds, with deeply indented leaflets. The forms of most fern fronds are intricate and graceful. The maidenhair fern, bracken fern, southern lady fern, sensitive fern, Christmas fern, and ostrich fern are native to North America.

Horsetails, which grow on the wet shores of lakes, have straight, dark-green, thick stalks that are topped by light-colored cones. Clubmosses, which resemble true mosses but are not related to them, are pteridophytes that grow in clumps in the moist shade of woods and on the rocky slopes of mountains.

Pteridophytes were a dominant form of vegetation during the Carboniferous period, between 230 and 290 million years ago. Ferns that resembled trees grew 30 or 40 feet high and formed extensive forests. Horsetails and clubmosses also were as large as trees. Much of our coal was formed from Carboniferous pteridophytes that died, fell into the marshy earth, and later were compressed by heavy layers of earth and rock. See CLUB MOSS; FERN.

PTEROSAUR. See FLYING DRAGON.

The ferns and horsetails are pteridophytes.

PTOLEMY (flourished in first half of 2d century A.D.), an ancient Greek astronomer, mathematician, and geographer, who elaborated what became known as the Ptolemaic system of the universe. According to this system, the earth is the center of the universe, and the sun, planets, and stars revolve around the earth. Ptolemy developed this system logically from the astronomical facts known to him. The Ptolemaic system was accepted as correct by most scientists and philosophers until it was superseded during the 16th and 17th centuries by the Copernican system, according to which the earth and the planets revolve around the sun.

Ptolemy was born at Alexandria, Egypt, which with its famous libraries and university was a center of Hellenistic culture and science. He lived and did much of his work in Alexandria. He developed spherical trigonometry as an astronomical tool from the basis established by another Greek astronomer. The principles of Ptoemy's trigonometry remain valid during modern times. He also developed a geography of the known world, in which cities and other places were located by mathematically determined latitudes and longitudes. His geography was more accurate and comprehensive than any of its predecessors.

PUBLIC HEALTH, a complex of enterprises having the aim of protecting the health of the population, including the prevention and treatment of disease. The content, forms, and extent of public health services vary in different countries according to the social structure and the level of science, culture, and technique. For example, in England the Ministry of Health is a major branch of the government. It supervises local public health services as well as a socialized medical service. In Norway public health is a part of the activities of the Department of Public Assistance. In Italy there are a large number of voluntary agencies that receive grants from the national government. In the Soviet Union the functions of the Ministry of Public Health include the organization of medical and prophylactic assistance to cities and towns, the superintendence of sanitation in living quarters and public establishments, the provision of supplies for all medical establishments and organizations for dispensing medicines, sanitary instruction, and medical education. In the Soviet Union all medical services are free.

A public-health program in Chicago offers free chest X-rays at such mobile units as this.
Tuberculosis Inst.

PUBLIC OPINION

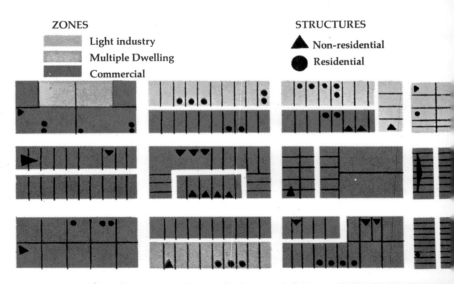

Tony Chapelle—Monkmeyer

Under Point Four, U.S. doctors administer public health programs in the Middle East.

The United States Public Health Service is under the supervision of the Department of Health, Education, and Welfare. It has five major divisions: Office of the Surgeon General, National Institutes of Health, the Bureau of Medical Services, the Bureau of State Services, and the National Library of Medicine. The Office of the Surgeon General has overall management of the organization; the Bureau of Medical Services is primarily concerned with the development of medical care and health-service programs; the Bureau of State Services is concerned with federal-state and interstate health programs; and the National Institutes of Health are concerned with the extension of basic knowledge in health problems. In addition, the United States has state public health departments that vary in organizational patterns. All of them include among their functions the enactment of sanitary regulations, the maintenance of laboratory services, the collection of vital statistics, and the control of waste disposal.

The most important public health activities on an international level are those of the World Health Organization, with headquarters in Geneva, Switzerland; and regional offices in Africa, the Americas, Southeast Asia, Europe, the eastern Mediterranean, and the western Pacific. The World Health Organization receives technical and financial assistance from the United Nations but is an independent organization with its own constitution. It directs and coordinates international health work; provides technical services, such as the standardization of drugs and assistance against epidemics; and provides direct help in the organization of public health services in individual countries.

PUBLIC OPINION, the judgment or attitude of a large part of a population toward any statement or issue. Public opinion includes both the majority view and the minority view. In most instances, a full consensus is not achieved.

Before there can be public opinion about an issue, it must be discussable. There are usually some beliefs held so strongly by the members of a society that they are never questioned. In such instances behavior is usually guided by tradition, rather than by an opinion that is achieved through active discussion.

Sociologists have found that the public contains several interest groups. Such groups try to influence the public on various issues. The emergent opinion about an issue is often determined by the neutral, disinterested group that listens to the information and propaganda put forward by the various interest groups.

When there is little information available, people listen to rumors. These transitory beliefs have a part in shaping public opinion, itself in a large part transitory.

In times of war, rumors have spread panic. Any distressing event shakes public confidence in official information and may leave the way open to rumor. When there was a great earthquake and fire in San Francisco, rumors spread that a great tidal wave had swept New York at the same time.

Clear information should reduce rumors. After President Franklin D. Roosevelt's fireside talk in February, 1942, people who were interviewed had more confidence in official information given about Pearl Harbor. Providing clear in-formation reduces the anxieties of the public and opens the way for a more rational public opinion.

Public opinion can be intelligent and thoughtful or it can be colored by censorship and propaganda. It is influenced by public discussion—on the radio, on television, in newspapers, or at meetings. Usually the discussion and conflict of ideas give it, in part, a rational character.

PUBLIC RELATIONS consists of all of those activities of an individual, organization, or institution that play a part in the development and maintenance of good rapport with the public at large or with such special groups as customers, employees, stockholders, constituents, or contributors. It is a management-level function that is as much involved in the formulation and execution of policy as in its interpretation.

The maintenance of good public relations requires honesty, integrity, ability to evaluate and adapt to a particular environment, and awareness of and regard for the public interest. There is nothing magic about public relations. Its power lies in the honest, effective presentation of the truth. Attempts to influence public opinion through misinformation, trickery, deception, or half-truth are alien to the concept of public relations. The firm providing an inferior product or service, the hospital affording its patients substandard care, the elected official catering to a special-interest group, or the welfare agency diverting an excessive proportion of contributions to administrative expenses cannot long deceive the public.

The range of activities within the profession is broad and involves a

The census tract below is a map of a 12-block city area. It is used by social scientists to draw samples for public opinion polls. For example, every tenth house might be polled.

ZONES

Light industry

Multiple Dwelling

Commercial

STRUCTURES

▲ Non-residential

● Residential

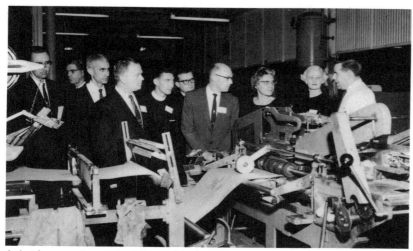

Industries promote good public relations by offering conducted tours of their factories.

wide variety of skills and techniques. There is, therefore, a tendency on the part of many public relations people to specialize—to confine their work to such areas as writing press releases, preparing speeches, plan-

ning special events, or maintaining liaison with editors or broadcasters. In the one-man agency or small department, however, one must be capable of performing varied tasks. A well-rounded program of public relations requires an individual or a group with facility in the use of the written word, the spoken word, and visual aids of all types, as well as the ability to counsel on matters of policy.

The achievement by public relations of the important place it now holds can be traced largely to developments of the past 60 years, and much of its dynamic growth has occurred since World War II. A great majority of the 300 leading companies in the United States now have public relations departments, as compared with only 1 out of 50 in 1936. Thirty years ago there were some 1,000 public relations people in the country. Today there are estimated to be 100,000. In addition to the many firms, government agencies, trade unions, and other organizations and institutions employing public relations personnel, there are more than 1,500 agencies providing counsel to clients in all fields.

Though public relations is a relatively young profession, it plays a key role in business, in government, in philanthropic endeavors, and in virtually all fields of activity. Informed public opinion is vital in dealing with the complexities of modern society. So long as this is true, the need will exist for public relations skills to guide individuals, organizations, and institutions in the effective presentation of factual information on their activities and their plans.

PUBLISHING, the business of producing and selling books and periodicals. From the time Gutenberg printed the first books in Europe (about 1450) until well into the 18th century all aspects of publishing, printing, and selling were usually handled by one firm. Thereafter, the three chief operations became independent. (See BOOK; JOURNALISM; NEWSPAPER; PRINTING.) Publishers began to contract for the composition, printing, and binding of their books and periodicals with independent printing and binding companies, and they began to sell their products to retailers. That is the pattern of the industry today.

The United States has hundreds of book-publishing firms, which annually publish somewhat more than 12,000 different titles. But only about 25 houses publish more than 100 titles each year. Broadly speaking, there are five types of publishing houses. Subscription-book houses publish reference works, anthologies, and so on, usually in sets, which are sold generally from door to door. The publishers usually have their own sales forces and thus bypass book retailers.

Reprint publishers deal in reprints of already published books, printing them in cheap paperbound editions. Reprint publishers also publish original works in cheap editions, but this practice is still the exception. Reprint publishers dispose of their books largely to wholesale jobbers.

General publishers print two types of books: trade books (those books of fiction and nonfiction of general interest that make up the large part of the stock of general bookstores) and technical and professional books of limited interest. Many general publishers print both types of books; others print only one type or specialize even further in particular types of fiction or nonfiction, mystery stories, juveniles, and so on.

Magazine publishers deal in weekly, monthly, or quarterly publications. Part of the writing is usually handled by the staff. Also, the publisher handles the marketing and circulation himself.

Newspaper publishers often own their own printing plants. Since they also employ the journalists and control the circulation, they still perform all the various operations of publication.

Essential, of course, to the publishing business is the author, but few writers actually work for publishing houses. Some houses have

A publishing project requires the coordination of three kinds of activities—layout, editorial, and art. The layout department (above, left) incorporates text and illustrations into attractive page designs. In the editorial department (left), copyreading, proofreading, and other processes necessary to prepare the text are carried out. Illustrations are prepared by the art department (above).

staff writers who prepare certain books, and others have contracts with writers, which give the house first options to publish their works. But by far the majority of writers work freelance, or independently, and try to find a publisher for their work after it is done.

A publisher, technically speaking, is the owner or director of a publishing house. The ideal publisher has good literary taste, a fair knowledge of the techniques of book production, and a lively sense of what makes a book sell as well as selling know-how. The publisher may have one or more assistants to supervise. From the many unsolicited manuscripts the book publisher receives, the reading staff selects the few that

show some promise of becoming successful books.

The responsibilities of the editorial department are varied. Some editors conceive ideas for, and stimulate and advise writers on, the writing of books. Copy editors correct and improve manuscripts. Newspaper editors cut and revise news stories and write the headlines. Magazine editors sometimes do everything from writing to pasteup and illustrative art. The latter is usually done by staff artists, who also design book covers. Typographers choose the style and size of type to be used and design the typographical layout.

The production department buys the necessary type, paper, and bind-

ing materials. It also makes contracts with typesetters, printers, and binders and supervises the various stages of printing. With the editorial department, it supervises proofreading and correction of proofs.

The sales and promotion department carries out the selling of the publication.

The legal department draws up a contract between the publisher and the author. It also handles matters of copyright and copyright infringement as well as contracts governing the sale of subsidiary rights.

PUCCINI, GIACOMO (1858-1924), was born in Lucca, Italy, a member of the fifth generation of a family of professional musicians. At Lucca he received what education he could and at the age of 19 was choir master and organist at a local church. In 1880 he entered the Milan Conservatory. His main teacher there was Amilcare Ponchielli, composer of *La Gioconda*. Ponchielli developed in his young pupil a love for the stage and directed his abilities toward the composing of operas.

Puccini's first opera, *Le Villi*, was written in 1884 and was entered in a contest for one-act operas being conducted by the music-publishing house of Sonzogno. The contest was won by Pietro Mascagni's *Cavalleria Rusticana*, but it did bring Puccini to the attention of Giulio Ricordi, who was the head of a powerful music firm.

With Ricordi's help Puccini composed the three-act opera *Edgar*, but this failed (the failure is usually attributed to a bad libretto). Four years later, in 1893, Puccini's first success, *Manon Lescaut*, was produced. This opera is based on Abbé Prévost's novel, the same source that Massenet used for his opera *Manon*.

In 1896 Puccini began the association with the librettists Guiseppe Giacosa and Luigi Illica that was to produce three of the most popular contemporary operas—*La Bohème*, *Tosca*, and *Madame Butterfly*. *La Bohème*, taken from Henri Murger's *Vie de Bohème*, is a charming story of student love in the Bohemian quarter of Paris. Its first performance, in Turin, Italy, in 1896, was conducted by Arturo Toscanini. *Tosca*, based upon the Victorien Sardou play, told of Italy in the time of Napoleon I. *Madame Butterfly* was next adapted from David Belasco's play of the same name. This opera was remarkable for its attempt to depict Japanese life.

With the death of Giacosa the trio of collaborators was broken up; Puccini now turned for source material to the works of David Belasco. The resulting opera was *The Girl of the Golden West*, which was produced in 1910. However, because of a bad libretto it never achieved the popularity of Puccini's three earlier works.

Puccini's next opera, *La Rondine*, was a failure; but his next work, *The Triptych* (three one-act operas) produced a masterpiece of comic opera, *Gianni Schicchi*. The two other operas of *The Triptych—Suor Angellica* and *Il Tabarro*—were also successful.

Puccini's last opera, *Turandot*, was taken from a play by Gasparo Gozzi. In this opera, his masterpiece, Puccini explored a newer and more complex mode of music than he had done previously. In its own way this work is as important as Verdi's last opera, *Falstaff*. Unfortunately Puccini died before finishing *Turandot*. It was completed by the composer Franco Alfano.

PUEBLO INDIANS, several tribes of North American Indians living in the American Southwest, so named by the Spanish because of the communal nature of their traditional dwelling places, which were built of masonry and adobe, were often five or six stories high, and sometimes had as many as 100 rooms to a story. (*Pueblo* is Spanish for "village.") The Pueblo group consists of six major tribes: Jemez (almost extinct), Keresan, Piro, Tewa, Hopi, and Zuñi. There are four distinct language stocks among the Pueblos, as well as many dialects.

Their culture, descended from that of the prehistoric Anasazi, dates from about 900. Unlike their ancestors the Pueblos became skilled farmers, pottery makers, and hunters. They also mastered the craft of weaving.

The first Indians the Spanish explorers of the 16th century encountered in North America were Pueblos. Spain claimed the area and established missions to convert the Indians to Christianity. Because of oppressive measures the Pueblos revolted against the Spanish in 1680. However, Spanish control was once again established in 1692. During the next 200 years the Pueblos were marauded by the Comanches, Apaches, Navahos, and Utes. Peace was restored when the U.S. government established a number of military outposts upon its occupation of the territory of New Mexico shortly before the Mexican War. Since that time relations between the Pueblos and the U.S. government have been generally peaceful. Today the Pueblos, greatly reduced in population, occupy traditional sites in New Mexico and Arizona. Tribal affairs are carried on by a tribal council in cooperation with the U.S. Department of the Interior.

Many elements of Pueblo culture —its religious ceremonies, its arts, and its crafts—have been preserved, although they have all been strongly influenced by American artists, who have encouraged the development of native arts and crafts. See CLIFF-DWELLER; FAMILY.

Here are a number of Pueblo Indian artifacts, with a view of the Taos pueblo, Taos, N.M. At the upper left are arrowheads; at upper center, baskets and a pottery bowl; and at upper right, stone tools. At left center a dancer is costumed for the Pueblo eagle dance. Pueblo jewelry is at right center. At the lower left is a katcina, a Pueblo ceremonial object.

Courtesy of the Puerto Rico News Service

A Puerto Rican farmer rests from his labors in a field of sugarcane.

PUERTO RICO

PUERTO RICO, a commonwealth of the United States, is the smallest and easternmost island of the Greater Antilles in the West Indies. It lies between the Atlantic Ocean on the north and the Caribbean Sea on the south. The Virgin Islands are to the east. Puerto Rico (which includes a few offshore dependent islands) is separated by the Mona Passage from the Dominican Republic. Covering 3,435 square miles, Puerto Rico is about 35 miles wide and 100 miles long. It is approximately 1,400 miles southeast of New York.

San Juan, the capital, is the trade, financial, and industrial center of Puerto Rico. It has a fine harbor and is a principal West Indies port. Other cities and communities include Río Piedras (now a part of San Juan and the seat of the University of Puerto Rico), Ponce, Mayagüez, and Caguas.

Mountain ranges run the length of the island. The narrow coastal plain reaches its greatest extent along the northern shore, where it is about 10 miles wide. The many rivers of Puerto Rico are used for irrigation and for power, but they are not navigable.

Puerto Rico has one of the highest population densities in the world. There are approximately 675 persons per square mile. With a population in 1960 of 2,353,297, the island is about 12 times as densely populated as is the United States.

Puerto Rico has a mild tropical climate. The northeast trade winds temper the climate, which has little seasonal change. Rainfall, varying with the topography, is generally heavier on the northern coast. The island is subject to occasional hurricanes. San Juan's average temperature in January is 75° F. and in July is 80° F.

Agriculture and industry are the mainstays of the Puerto Rican economy. Crop diversification and increased industrialization have helped to overcome the island's dependence on a one-crop (sugar) economy. In recent years industry has been more important to the economy than has agriculture. Operation Bootstrap, an economic-development program started in 1947, has been the backbone of this growth. There also has been a great development of hydroelectric power. Chief manufactures include food products (refined sugar), alcohol and rum (employing molasses), machinery and metals, chemicals, tobacco products, and stone, clay, and glass products. Approximately 90 percent

The flag and seal of Puerto Rico

of the island's trade is with the United States. Sugar is the chief export.

Christopher Columbus discovered Puerto Rico in 1493 and claimed it for Spain. Ponce de León was its first settler and governor. He founded San Juan in 1521. The island continued in Spanish posses-

A large sugarcane plantation occupies this fertile valley of Puerto Rico.

Courtesy of the Puerto Rico News Service

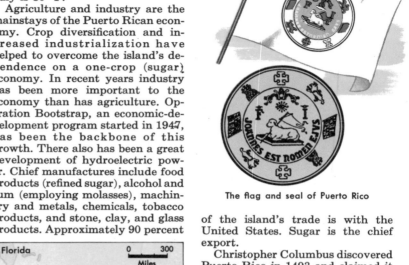

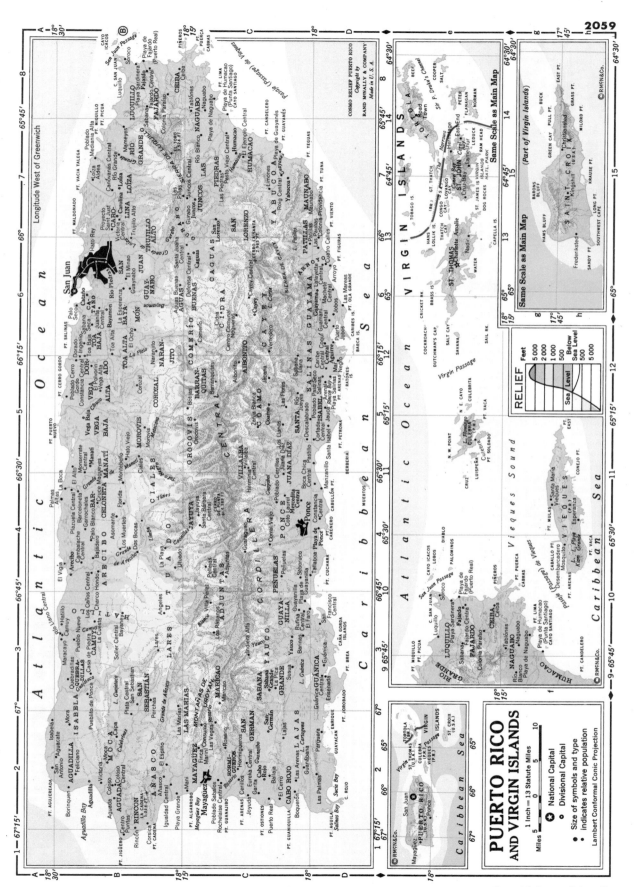

RELIEF

Feet	
5 000	
2 000	
1 000	
500	Sea Level
	Below Sea Level
	500
	5 000

CROSMO RELIEF PUERTO RICO

Copyright by
RAND McNALLY & COMPANY
Made in U.S.A.

PUERTO RICO
AND VIRGIN ISLANDS

1 Inch = 13 Statute Miles

Miles 5 0 5 10

★ National Capital
◉ Divisional Capital
Size of symbols and type
● indicates relative population

Lambert Conformal Conic Projection

sion until after the Spanish-American War in 1898, when it was turned over to the United States.

By the Jones Act of 1917 all Puerto Ricans became citizens of the United States. Since 1899, and particularly since the 1930's, great progress has been made in commerce, industry, agriculture, and social welfare. The island is also a popular winter-resort area.

Puerto Rico became a free commonwealth associated with the United States in 1952. A governor, elected by popular vote, is the chief executive. The island has two official languages, Spanish and English.

PUFFIN. See AUKS, MURRES, PUFFINS.

PUJO COMMITTEE, a subcommittee authorized in 1912 by the House of Representatives to look into the concentration of money power in the United States. The committee, a subcommittee of the House Committee on Banking and Currency, was headed by Representative Pujo of Louisiana. Samuel Untermyer of New York acted as counsel. At the hearings of the committee in 1913 J. P. Morgan, George F. Baker, and other well-known financiers presented testimony. As a result of the evidence it accumulated, the committee issued a majority report stating that the existing banking practices led to the concentration of money and credit in the hands of a few men. Indeed, J. P. Morgan and Company and associated companies controlled resources amounting to 22 billion dollars. The Democratic supporters of William Jennings Bryan called for a reserve system and government-controlled currency supply on the basis of the Pujo report. Conservative Democrats proposed a less centralized, privately-controlled reserve system. In an attempt to alleviate the conditions revealed by the Pujo committee, Representative Carter Glass of the House banking committee prepared a bill with the aid of President Woodrow Wilson. This bill, with modifications, was passed by the House and Senate as the Federal Reserve Bank Act. See FEDERAL RESERVE SYSTEM.

PULASKI, CASIMIR (1748?-1779), born in Podolia, Poland (now in the Ukranian S.S.R.), was a member of the Polish nobility. After several unsuccessful attempts to fight against the Russian domination of Poland Pulaski arrived penniless in Paris, where he was put into con-

tact with Benjamin Franklin. Franklin wrote him a letter of introduction to Washington, and in 1777 Pulaski sailed for the United States.

Pulaski fought in many battles of the Revolutionary War, including those at Brandywine and Germantown. In 1778, however, he resigned his commission because of disagreements with his superior officer, General Anthony Wayne.

An idle Pulaski petitioned Congress for a new command, and he was sent to Egg Harbor, N.J., to protect supplies. Later he fought at the siege of Savannah; here, bravely charging the enemy, he fell wounded and died.

St. Louis Post-Dispatch

Joseph Pulitzer, pioneer in U.S. journalism

PULITZER, JOSEPH (1847-1911), a journalist and newspaper publisher, was born in Mako, Hungary, and received his early education there. At the age of 17 he came to the United States, and he fought in the last year of the Civil War. In 1868 Pulitzer joined the staff of the *Westliche Post*, a St. Louis German-language newspaper, and there worked under its owner, Carl Schurz.

In St. Louis Pulitzer was politically active and was part of the convention that nominated Horace Greeley for president in 1872. When the Greeley movement failed, Pulitzer left the Republican party and became a Democrat; for the rest of his life he remained one.

Pulitzer bought the St. Louis *Dispatch* in 1878 and in that year merged it with the *Post* as the St. Louis *Post-Dispatch*. This paper was quite successful, and its success allowed Pulitzer to buy the New York *World* from Jay Gould in 1883. Pulitzer converted the *World* from the sensational sheet it had been into a distinguished daily. In 1885

Pulitzer was elected to Congress, but he resigned after a few months. His eyesight began to fail in 1887, and by 1889 he was totally blind.

Pulitzer is remembered today not only as a great journalist but also as a man who made many endowments, including one for the journalism school at Columbia and the prizes awarded there that bear his name.

PULLEY, a grooved or flat-surfaced wheel used with a rope, belt, or chain to gain a mechanical advantage or to change a force's direction. The two general types are movable and fixed pulleys, which may be combined into a pulley system.

A movable pulley is attached to a weight. Each end of a rope running through the groove of the sheave (pulley wheel) supports, and exerts a pull equal to, one-half of an attached weight. If the weight is lifted, it moves only one-half as far as the rope end to which force is applied. Since work equals force times distance, the work of lifting a 2-pound weight a distance of 1 foot equals a force of 1 pound exerted on the rope for a distance of 2 feet. A mechanical advantage (the ratio of the force acting on the pulley to the force exerted by it) of two is gained because the weight lifted is twice the force necessary to lift it.

A fixed pulley is attached to a nonmoving support with a rope running through the sheave's groove. A weight on one end of the rope must have an equal force on the other end in order to raise the weight. No mechanical advantage is gained because force and weight are equal.

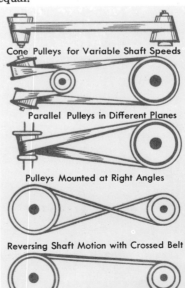

Cone Pulleys for Variable Shaft Speeds

Parallel Pulleys in Different Planes

Pulleys Mounted at Right Angles

Reversing Shaft Motion with Crossed Belt

Open Belt Arrangement

The puma can climb mountains by leaping from one rocky ledge to another.

A pulley system can be any combination of fixed and moving pulleys. Using four sheaves with one groove each as an example, the rope is attached to the fixed pulleys and is run through all four grooves. The weight attached to the movable pulleys is then supported by four strands of rope. The force required for lifting an object is one-fourth the weight, and the mechanical advantage is four.

The principle of the pulley has many common applications, such as the water pump-generator drive system on an automobile. There are also many belt-driven, flat-surfaced pulleys that are used in operating factory machines.

PULLMAN STRIKE, a strike that broke out in Chicago in 1894 over the reduction in wages paid to the workers of the Pullman Palace Car Company. Its immediate cause was the company's refusal to arbitrate the matter.

The American Railway Union forbade its members to operate or service pullman cars, and the strike spread to 27 states. Governor John Altgeld of Illinois refused to call out the militia because no violence was involved. President Grover Cleveland, on the grounds that the strike interfered with the U. S. mails, ordered government troops to Chicago. On July 2 a federal court issued an injunction against interference with the mails or interstate commerce.

Eugene Victor Debs, who was the head of the union, was jailed for defying the injunction. Deprived of leadership, the men were forced to give up the strike. Although public opinion in general was against the strikers, most people eventually agreed that the federal government should not use force in the form of troops to settle labor disputes. Debs and some of the other leaders were later tried for contempt of court and were convicted.

PULSE is a regular throbbing in the arteries, caused by ejection of blood into them with the contraction of the ventricles of the heart. (See HEART.) The arteries are already full before each contraction, and the additional blood causes a distention of their elastic walls. The pulse wave travels much faster than the blood itself, usually 10 to 15 times faster. The normal pulse rate per minute varies from 70 to 72 in men and from 78 to 82 in women. The human pulse rate is usually observed in the radial artery of the wrist.

PUMA, or cougar, a tawny feline found in both North America and South America. It is also known as a panther or a mountain lion. It is one of the large members of the feline family, exceeded in size in America only by the jaguar. The cougar's head is small, and the general color of the body is yellowish brown. It preys on wild sheep, goats, and deer and has been known to attack domestic cattle. It ranges from Canada to Patagonia and is especially numerous in the forest districts of Central America.

A small sample of pumice is shown above.

PUMICE, a frothy, porous glass of volcanic origin. It forms the upper crust of acidic lava flows and is produced by the explosion of high-temperature water vapor through the relief of pressure in the lava in the vent of the volcano or in the top portion of a flow. This is a process somewhat similar to that which produces foam when a bottle of beer is opened. The chemical composition of pumice is the same as that of obsidian or granite, but it differs from them in texture and mode of occurrence. Pumice is generally white or light colored. The pores in pumice are glass-sealed air bubbles, which make the rock lighter than water. Pieces of pumice ejected by volcanoes near the sea may be carried to distant places by ocean currents. The rock is used as an abrasive for polishing and for toilet purposes. Most commercial pumice comes from the Lipari Islands, north of Sicily, in the Mediterranean Sea.

PUMP, a machine or device for moving fluids from one location to another, for compressing gases, or for producing a vacuum.

The lift pump operates by producing a partial vacuum in a pipe; atmospheric pressure then forces the water or other liquid up the pipe into the pump. Such a lift pump can raise water only about 34 feet. If the pump is placed within the well, so that it need not lift the water far by atmospheric pressure, water above the piston can be raised much higher. Lift pumps are often com-

pletely submerged in the liquid that they are to lift. In oil wells, lift pumps raise oil several thousand feet to the surface; force pumps then drive the oil long distances through pipelines.

If a piston pump is used to pump gases, the same pump may produce both vacuum and high pressure. When the piston is moved toward one end of the cylinder, the gas on that side of the piston is reduced in volume (compressed), while the gas on the other side has its volume increased (its pressure decreased). The compressed gas will flow through the valve, out of the pump, and into a pressure chamber; gas will flow into the reduced-pressure end of the cylinder from the vessel in which a vacuum is desired.

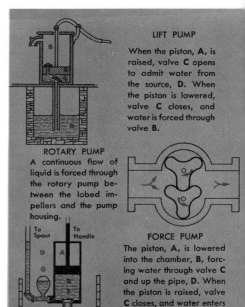

LIFT PUMP
When the piston, A, is raised, valve C opens to admit water from the source, D. When the piston is lowered, valve C closes, and water is forced through valve B.

ROTARY PUMP
A continuous flow of liquid is forced through the rotary pump between the lobed impellers and the pump housing.

FORCE PUMP
The piston, A, is lowered into the chamber, B, forcing water through valve C and up the pipe, D. When the piston is raised, valve C closes, and water enters the chamber through the valve E from the water source, F. The air chamber, G, maintains pressure in the pipe.

There are other types of pumps as well as piston, or reciprocating, pumps. A centrifugal pump consists of a circular housing, inside which an impeller spins rapidly, driving the liquid by centrifugal force to the outer rim, where it leaves the pump; more liquid enters the housing near the shaft at the center. Centrifugal pumps usually move large amounts of liquid at low pressures; other rotary pumps can operate at high pressures. A jet of steam or water can be used to lift or move a column of water in a pipe. Muddy water or sand in water is often pumped by a pulsometer, which has no piston. It uses steam to force the water into a pipe; then the steam condenses, leaving a vacuum into which more water is forced by atmospheric pressure. In irrigation Archimedean screws are used to lift very large volumes of water only a few feet. There are many other types of pumps for special purposes. See AIR PUMP; VACUUM PUMP.

PUMPKIN, a large vegetable that grows on a creeping vine. It belongs to the same genus as the squashes and gourds. The pumpkin, which is an annual, creeps along the ground and bears dark-green leaves and large yellow flowers. The pumpkin, which is actually the fruit of the vine, is shaped like a globe that is flattened at both ends. Its diameter ranges to 2 feet or more, and its color is yellow, orange, or brown.

The word *pumpkin* is derived from the old French word *pompion*, which means "melon." Probably native to Mexico and the southwestern United States, the pumpkin was being cultivated by the Indians in their cornfields when America was discovered. It is thought to have been cultivated by them as early as 1500 B.C.

Although pumpkins are most frequently made into pies, they are sometimes boiled or baked and are eaten as a vegetable. Pumpkins are also often grown as a field crop and used to feed livestock.

Pumpkins grow best in the hottest weather.

PUN, a humorous play on words. The humor of a pun may depend on the substitution of one word for another with a similar sound but a different meaning (for example, "They went and told the sexton and the sexton tolled the bell") or on the use of a word that has several meanings (for example, when one speaks of an automobile driver as "the nut that holds the wheel"). "There is a hare in the brush" is an example of a pun the humor of which depends both on the use of words that sound alike (*hare* and *hair*) but have different meanings and on a word with different meanings (*brush* meaning a shrub or a similar form of vegetation and a device for brushing hair). Punning is considered by many to be one of the lowest forms of wit.

Puns can be serious as well as ludicrous. Shakespeare often used puns to heighten the tragedy of certain events in his plays; for example, in *Romeo and Juliet*, Mercutio puns after he has been mortally wounded, "Ask for me tomorrow and you shall find me a grave man."

PUNCH AND JUDY are the chief characters in a comic puppet show of Italian origin. Until its decline at the end of the 19th century, the Punch and Judy show had frequent presentations. The story has Judy leaving her husband, Punch, to mind the baby while she goes shopping. Almost immediately the baby cries. Punch tries to soothe it but is unsuccessful. He then scolds the child, but it only cries louder. Desperate, Punch finally throws the baby out the window.

Judy returns and berates Punch and hits him with her stick. Punch takes the stick from his wife and beats her to death. He then encounters various characters, most of whom he kills. Punch is captured and is about to be hanged, but he persuades the hangman, Jack Ketch, to put his own head into the noose. Ketch does this, and Punch quickly pulls the rope. Only the ghost of Judy and the Devil, who comes to take him off, frighten Punch. But he wins here, too, by killing the Devil after a tremendous fight and hoisting his head on a stick.

This entertainment, which originated in the Italian *commedia dell' arte*, is limited by usually having only one man to manipulate the puppets. Since the man has only two hands, only two characters can appear on stage at the same time. See COMMEDIA DELL'ARTE.

PUNCTUATION, the use of certain marks for the purpose of facilitating the reading and comprehension of written discourse.

The chief terminal markings, that is, punctuation marks placed at the end of sentences, are the period, the question mark, and the exclamation point. A period (.) is used at the end of a declarative sentence: "John went to the store." An imperative sentence also ends in a period: "John, pick up the book." The period is also used after indirect questions: "John asked me how to make the map." A period is also used with most abbreviations: "John Jones, Jr.," *Mr., Dr., Calif.,* and so on. Three consecutive periods (. . .) constitute an ellipsis, which indicates hesitation, emotional excitement, unfinished statements in fictional dialogue, or omission of words or sentences from a quoted passage.

The question mark, or interrogation point (?), indicates that a sentence is a direct question requiring an answer: "Where are you going, John?" When a question mark is placed in parentheses after a fact, it means there is some uncertainty regarding that fact: "He was born in 1350(?) and died in 1410."

The exclamation point (!) indicates an expression of strong feeling: "Run for your life!" No more than one such mark should be used at a time after a sentence. Interjections such as "Oh!" and "Ah!" are also punctuated by the use of exclamation points.

Important internal punctuation marks that indicate grammatical units within the structure of a sentence are the comma, the colon, the semicolon, the dash, and parentheses. Of all the marks of punctuation the comma (,) has the greatest variety of uses. The following are three of the commonest uses. A comma or commas set off nonrestrictive modifiers: "He hired Mr. Jones, who had experience in that type of work. Mr. Brown, who had less training, was not hired." Commas separate words or elements in a series: "He bought a ball, a bat, and a pair of shoes." A comma separates coordinate clauses joined by a conjunction: "I knew he was hurt, but there was nothing I could do."

The semicolon (;) is a stop weaker than a period but stronger than a comma. It joins coordinate clauses that are not joined by conjunctions, especially those clauses of a compound sentence that are long and contain other punctuation.

The colon (:) indicates that what is to follow constitutes an explanation, example, or restatement of something preceding the colon, and what follows may be a simple list or enumeration of particulars: "He purchased everything he needed for the job: paint, brushes and sponges."

The dash (—) indicates a sudden interruption or break in the thought or grammatical structure of a sentence: "He asked me—maybe I shouldn't be telling you this." "This song—not many people know the words any more—was very popular 30 years ago."

Parentheses ( ) appear in pairs, and they enclose independent statements that are supplementary to what is expressed in the sentence proper: "John (even though he knew it was wiser to ignore it) answered Jim's angry challenge."

Other marks of punctuation include the apostrophe, brackets, and quotation marks. The apostrophe (') indicates the possessive of a noun ("John's hat") and the omission of numbers and letters (*don't*, "the spirit of '76"). It also forms the plural of figures and letters used as words. "They were at 6's and 7's." "Watch your p's and q's." Brackets [ ] are primarily used for editorial purposes to enclose corrections and information interpolated to clarify quoted material. Double quotation marks (" . . . ") are used to set off the exact words of some speaker. Single quotation marks (' . . . ') enclose quotations within quotations. For example, Bill stated, "The teacher said to me, 'All right, you are excused from class tomorrow.' " Commas and periods are placed inside quotation marks except when they precede the quotation: "I believe," he said, "that you are right." Question marks, semicolons, and exclamation points go outside the quotation marks unless they belong to the quoted words: He shouted "Ahoy!"; but the boat did not change course.

PUNIC WARS, three great wars between the Romans and the Carthaginians. At the beginning of the first war Rome ruled Italy and was seeking to expand, while Carthage controlled the northwestern part of Africa, the Mediterranean islands, and the general trade of the West. The close of the Punic Wars marked the complete destruction and annihilation of Carthage.

The First Punic War (268-241 B.C.) originated in Sicily in a dispute between Messana and Syracuse. The Messanians asked both Rome

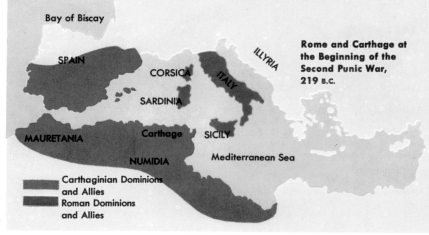

Rome and Carthage at the Beginning of the Second Punic War, 219 B.C.

Bay of Biscay
SPAIN
CORSICA
ILLYRIA
ITALY
SARDINIA
MAURETANIA
Carthage
SICILY
NUMIDIA
Mediterranean Sea

Carthaginian Dominions and Allies
Roman Dominions and Allies

and Carthage for help, and armies were sent by both powers. The Punic (Carthaginian) army arrived first and arranged peace between Syracuse and Messana, but this peace was set aside by the Roman army, and the two great powers then began a struggle for Sicily. The island was taken with little difficulty by the Romans, but their invasion of Africa failed. A great sea battle at the Aegates (now the Egadi Islands) in 241 B.C. ended in victory for the Romans and led to negotiations for peace. Carthage had to pay a large indemnity and ceded western Sicily and the Lipari Islands to Rome.

The Second Punic War was begun in 219 B.C. when Hannibal, the famous Carthaginian general, captured Saguntum, a Roman ally. This led to a terrific struggle, in which Hannibal gained a number of victories in Italy, but the ultimate result was victory for Rome in 201 B.C.

In the Third Punic War (149-146 B.C.) Rome was the aggressor. Carthage held out against a Roman siege for three years, but the city was finally conquered and razed to the ground, the site plowed over, and the inhabitants massacred or sold into slavery.

PUNISHMENT, a penalty for crime. Punishment has many purposes. These include vengeance, prevention of other crimes, expiation, and reformation. The original idea of punishment was that it should be painful enough to deter prospective criminals.

Primitive punishment was done for retribution: "An eye for an eye." For that reason the death penalty was frequent and took a variety of forms. Retribution was also the aim of duels and blood feuds. Such blood fueds as that of the Hatfields and the McCoys sometimes last for many generations. They are often more disastrous than the original crime, which is often forgotten after a few generations.

Expiation was the motive behind many forms of punishment in the Middle Ages. The criminal had sinned, and punishment was the means of cleansing his soul. Banishment took the place of the death penalty in Rome. It was also common in Europe through the Middle Ages and until the 19th century. The French banished criminals to Devil's Island, where many died. Russian offenders were sent to Siberia. Great Britain transported offenders to Australia. In colonial America the idea behind many punishments was disgrace. Offenders were placed in stocks and pillories, scolding wives were placed on the ducking stool, and major offenders were flogged or branded. Such punishments are no longer commonly used. The Eighth Amendment to the Constitution forbids any "cruel or unusual punishment."

In Europe during the 18th-century Enlightenment the idea arose that imprisonment was the best punishment. It would remove the criminal from society and allow a process of reformation. This was a step forward from the times when even minor crimes were punishable by death. The men of the Enlightenment also doubted the value of punishment as a deterrent to crime. At first, the prisons were very bad, but at the end of the 19th century reform movements began. The prisoners were studied, and modern penology developed. The major purpose of punishment in modern society is (aside from the protection of society) the reformation of the offender so he can return to normal society. During the past 100 years the death penalty has been abolished by more than 30 nations, by a number of states of the United States, by the Commonwealth of Puerto Rico, and by the Virgin Islands, with no consequent increase in crime rates. It is thought by some that the greatest deterrent to crime is scientific criminology. See CRIMINOLOGY; PAROLE; PENOLOGY.

The symmetrical pupa of a green-bottle fly

The gold pupa (above) of a comma butterfly

This capsular pupa—that of a moth—is enclosed in the cocoon shown above it. The pupal stage of some moths lasts from autumn to spring. Cocoons protect pupae from injury and shelter them from the weather.

PUPA, the name applied to a metamorphosing insect while it is in a quiescent stage and undergoing transformation from its larval form to its adult form. Only insects that undergo a complete metamorphosis pass through a pupal stage. In a complete metamorphosis the final adult form is totally different from the larval form. Some of the insects that undergo a complete metamorphosis and hence pass through a pupal stage are butterflies, moths, flies, beetles, and mosquitoes. During their larval stage all of these insects are wormlike: Butterflies and moths are called caterpillars; flies are called maggots; beetles are called grubs; and mosquitoes are called wigglers. However, these insects emerge from the pupal stage in their adult form.

After a larva of any of these insects has been active for a while and has grown to a certain size, it ceases all activity and enters the pupal stage. The pupa remains quiet and motionless. It is usually enclosed in a case, which is customarily affixed to a tree branch, to a leaf, or to the ground. This case shelters the pupa from the weather and protects it from injury. The case of a butterfly pupa, which is called a chrysalis, becomes hardened and brown. Most moth pupae rest in silken cocoons, which they spin around themselves before entering the pupal stage. The pupal stage of many butterflies and moths may begin in early autumn and last throughout the winter. The pupal stage of other insects may last from one to three or four weeks.

Pupae of butterflies, moths, flies, beetles, and mosquitoes undergo a complete transformation of both their external form and their internal organs. The wormlike larvae that entered the pupal stage emerge as adult insects. These adult insects do not resemble the larvae in any detail. See LARVA; METAMORPHOSIS.

PUPIL. See EYE.

PUPPET AND MARIONETTE, small doll-like figures, made to perform in a sort of miniature theater. Puppets are moved with the fingers or by means of rods; marionettes are manipulated with strings and wires. The figures may be made of wood, animal skins, papier-mâché, cloth, and other miscellaneous, lightweight materials.

The earliest use of puppet shows seems to have been in religious drama. In Greece such performances were put on to familiarize the common people with their native religious myths. In India and the Far East incidents in the life of Buddha were presented. Puppet showmen of Burma, Java, and Bali still put on these miniature religious dramas. During the Middle Ages itinerant puppet theaters brought biblical

The puppets shown in the theater below are supported and manipulated from beneath the stage by long rods. The marionettes of the famous American puppeteers Bill and Cora Baird are controlled with strings and wires.

UPI

UPI

stories to the European peasantry, traveling even to remote villages. They were a regular feature of entertainment at the medieval country fair.

In the hands of the ingenious Italian puppetmasters Fantoccini marionettes were designed to attract attention of another kind. Audiences marveled at the quick, realistic motions of the dolls. They were elaborately constructed and very skillfully manipulated. See PUNCH AND JUDY.

In the 18th century it became fashionable for the aristocracy of Europe to go to these entertainments. In some cities puppetmasters even put on miniature operas to amuse the audience. As a popular art puppetry continued to be a lively and rather crude form of amusement, but before more sophisticated audiences the art became subtler and more charming. Social and political satires were presented with especial skill. In Italy some of these performances were so effective that the puppet theaters were closed in the middle of the 19th century. In France the puppet show was frequently put on at literary salons.

At the turn of the century there was a resurgence of interest in puppetry as a popular art, especially for children. United States schools have encouraged the handicraft of puppet making as well as puppet theaters for children.

PURCELL, HENRY (1658?-1695), an English composer, showed, as Mozart did, his musical genius from an early age. Although little is known of his early life, records show that he became a chorister at the Chapel Royal when quite young. In 1680 he succeeded John Blow, his teacher, as organist at Westminster Abbey, and in 1682 he became an organist at the Chapel Royal. Purcell held both appointments until his death.

A set of sonatas, published in 1683, was his first published work. He continued writing instrumental works throughout his life, but he was chiefly known for the incidental music he wrote for the plays of such contemporaries as John Dryden and Aphra Behn and for the plays of Shakespeare. His one opera, *Dido and Aeneas*, is considered a masterpiece. The libretto for this was written by Nahum Tate and was based on Virgil's *Aeneid*. It was performed in 1689. Other stage works include *The Indian Queen* and *King Arthur*. Purcell is buried in Westminster Abbey.

PURE FOOD AND DRUG LAWS, laws passed to protect customers from adulterated or misrepresented foods or drugs. The clamor for a pure-food-and-drug law in the United States began during the Spanish-American War, when the soldiers claimed that the canned meat issued to them was Civil War stock. Upton Sinclair's *The Jungle* was written to show how bad were working and sanitary conditions in the U.S. packing industry. President Theodore Roosevelt decided to rectify these conditions.

In 1906 he obtained the passage of the Meat Inspection Act. The Pure Food and Drug Act was passed in the same year. The Pure Food and Drug Act applied to all goods moving in interstate commerce. By the act, the adulteration of foods or drugs was prohibited. Thus, candies with poisonous ingredients were banned from interstate commerce. Foods containing animal matter or unhealthful ingredients were considered adulterated. Medicines had to be labeled to show the contents. Manufacturers guilty of infractions of the laws could be prosecuted by the federal government.

The Pure Food and Drug Act was amended a number of times. The amendments prevented false claims about the ability of drugs to cure diseases and provided that the weight of packaged goods be stamped on the package. The growth of advertising resulted in the Wheeler-Lea Act of 1938, which made false advertising claims subject to federal prosecution, provided they were broadcast or distributed over state boundaries. The Federal Trade Commission prosecutes those guilty of misleading advertising, while the Food and Drug Administration deals with cases of misbranding. Either agency can move into the other's area in the conduct of a particular case.

For England and Wales the Food and Drugs Act of 1955 consolidated laws pertaining to the purity, description, and hygiene of food. Scotland is protected by a similar act passed in 1956.

In 1887 Germany forbade the use of picric acid and other poisonous coloring agents in foods. A list of acceptable food-coloring agents was distributed. All food-coloring agents were forbidden for meat, coffee, and chocolate. A number of separate food laws regulate the preparation of foods, forbid the preparation of foods injurious to health, and prevent false advertising. Such laws also exist in many other countries.

PURGE, a term used to describe the mass execution of political opponents or rivals. Purges are carried out by persons in authority, especially dictators.

The Nazi purge of June 30, 1934, is one of the most extreme examples in history. On that day all persons whom Hitler considered rivals or leaders of potential opposition were summarily executed. Included in the slaughter were Storm Troop officers, Roman Catholic leaders, high Nazi-party officials, and individuals against whom the dictator had old grudges. No one knows the exact number who were slain in that 24-hour period, but estimates range as high as 922.

Such purges have also been a recurrent feature of the Communist regime of the U.S.S.R.; often they have followed a change in the party line or party leadership. In an effort to eliminate all opposition to Stalin's leadership about one-third (one million) of the members of the Soviet Communist party were expelled in 1933. Between January, 1935, and March, 1938, many of the most prominent of the older Bolsheviks, as well as high-ranking officials in the administration and the army, were tried and liquidated. Among them were Rykov, Zinoviev, Kamenev, Pyatakov, Radek, Bukharin, and Tukhachevski. They were charged with such varied offenses as planning to restore bourgeois capitalism, engaging in treasonable conspiracy with the exiled Leon Trotsky, and plotting with Germany and Japan against the regime. In a series of spectacular "show trials" many of them "confessed" their guilt. In the atmosphere of fear and confusion created by the trials thousands of others, many of them friends or associates of the accused, were arrested. Some were hastily executed on flimsy evidence. Others were imprisoned or deported to Siberia. More recent purges occurred after Stalin's death (in 1953) and again in 1957. These, however, were limited to the party leaders and avoided the widespread bloodletting of the past.

PURIM, a Jewish festival celebrated on the 14th of Adar, the sixth month of the Jewish year. The 14th of Adar falls in either February or March. The basis for the festival is related in the Book of Esther in the Bible. Haman, vizier to King Ahasuerus, had appointed by lot the 13th of Adar on which to destroy the Jews of Persia. The plan was foiled by Mordecai and his foster-daughter and cousin Esther. The Jews triumphed over their enemies instead, and Mordecai and Esther decreed the annual observance of Purim.

The historicity of the Book of Esther is doubtful. Some biblical scholars trace the origin of Purim back to a Babylonian New Year's festival. In any case, Purim developed, as decreed in the Bible, into a joyous folk festival. It adds a leaven of merrymaking to the serious religious commitment of Judaism.

On Purim, children masquerade (perhaps an influence of the Italian carnival), beg for refreshments at Jewish homes, and sometimes present burlesque mummers' plays. Gifts are exchanged. Even the reading of the Book of Esther at the synagogue on the eve of Purim has an air of merriment, and the reading of the name of the wicked Haman and his sons is drowned out by noisemakers.

PURITANS included members of the Church of England and Separatists during the 16th and 17th centuries who criticized the church and English morals. The Puritans were persecuted by James I and Charles I of England. Some of the Puritans immigrated to America and established the Plymouth and Massachusetts Bay colonies. The majority remained in England and achieved some of their desires by means of the English Civil War.

The Puritans carried on one of the basic ideas of Protestantism—that man should communicate directly with God. Therefore they objected to the authority of the higher clergy of the church and to certain church ritual as interfering with direct communication. The belief that man needed no intermediary between himself and God implied the worth of each individual and his right to decide many things for himself. Thus the Puritans opposed not only the authority of bishops but James I's doctrine of the divine right of the king to rule without restriction. The Puritans' faith in the individual also led them to oppose contemporary restrictions on trade and industry, particularly the king's habit of granting monopolies in certain types of trade. The restrictions were particularly harmful to the Puritans because many of them were merchants. Much of the opposition was carried on in Parliament, which had many Puritan members.

The average Puritan wanted to live a life modeled on the teachings of the Bible. He condemned luxury and idleness and the favorite popular entertainments, gambling and the theater. Puritans often thought that financial success, if achieved by honesty and hard work, was the mark of a virtuous person and that poverty was the mark of a sinful person. Above all, the Puritans wished to do the will of God; they often appointed special lecturers to interpret the Bible to them and met in one another's houses to hear these lecturers and discuss religion.

Those Puritans who came to America tried to make their settlements holy communities. Only members of their church could be citizens, and dissenters, such as Roger Williams and Anne Hutchinson, were expelled. Church attendance was required by law, and liars and other sinners were fastened in the stocks, whipped, or tied to the ducking stool and repeatedly plunged into a nearby pond or river. Puritanism began to die out in Massachusetts at the end of the 17th century when people were no longer required to be church members to vote.

PUSHKIN, ALEXANDER (1799-1837), Russian poet, was born in Moscow into one of the oldest and most distinguished families of the Russian nobility. He was educated at the newly opened military lyceum at Tsarskoye Selo (now Pushkin, Russian S.F.S.R.), and while there he wrote his first verse. In 1820 he won immediate fame with his first published work, the narrative poem *Ruslan and Ludmila*. The same year he was transferred from St. Petersburg (now Leningrad, Russian S.F.S.R.), where he had held a position in the foreign office, to a government post in a remote part of southern Russia; the purpose of the transfer was to remove him from the capital, where the liberal political ideals of his clandestinely circulated poems were not appreciated by the tyrannical Russian government. Four years later he was removed from office and forced to spend two years in exile on his mother's country estate. In 1826 he was allowed to return to St. Petersburg, but only on the condition that he submit all his writings to the personal censorship of the czar. In 1831 he married a beautiful girl of 18, whose extravagances brought him financial and emotional problems. In 1837 his wife's flirtations involved him in a duel in which he was fatally wounded.

Pushkin is regarded by many of his countrymen as the greatest figure in the history of Russian literature. In addition to lyric poetry, Pushkin wrote plays, the best of which is the historical tragedy *Boris Godunov*; fiction, including *The Captain's Daughter* and *The Queen of Spades*, that set a new standard for Russian prose; and the long narrative poem *Eugene Onegin*, which is generally regarded as his greatest work.

Chicago Hist. Soc.

Colorful American patriot Israel Putnam

PUTNAM, ISRAEL (1718-1790), American Revolutionary War general, was born at Danvers, in Connecticut. He received little education, but in his youth and young manhood he developed striking qualities of courage and self-reliance. After his marriage in 1739 he moved to Pomfret, in Connecticut.

At the outbreak of the French and Indian War Putnam volunteered for service in the Connecticut forces and was commissioned a second lieutenant. He was active with Robert Rogers' Rangers throughout the war. In 1762 he sailed in an unsuccessful expedition to capture Havana, Cuba. In 1764, then a lieutenant colonel, he participated in Pontiac's War, after which he returned to his farm in Connecticut. See PONTIAC'S CONSPIRACY.

In the years preceding the American Revolution Putnam was an active patriot in the colonial cause. In 1773 he participated in an exploring expedition to the West Indies, the Gulf of Mexico, and the lower Mississippi River. In 1775, upon hearing of the skirmish at Lexington, Putnam joined the Continental forces and was commissioned a major general. He participated with distinction in the Battle of Bunker Hill, commanded for a brief period the forces at New York, supervised the retreat from New York, and for a time commanded the forces at Philadelphia. However, his refusal on several occasions to obey Washington's orders brought him before a court of inquiry. Putnam was exonerated and later placed in charge of army recruiting in Connecticut. A paralytic stroke ended his military career in 1779.

PUZZLE, one of the oldest forms of entertainment, depending for its enjoyment on the exercise of mental agility. Puzzles may be divided into three main types: mathematical, mechanical, and word puzzles. Chinese puzzles, mainly of the mechanical type, have been known for thousands of years. Word puzzles and mathematical puzzles were popular among the ancient Greeks.

Numbers have always had a special fascination. The solution of number puzzles is a pleasant test of one's reasoning power. The following is an old example of such a puzzle:

A farmer must move a fox, a goose, and a basket of corn across a river. He finds that the boat will carry only himself and one of the articles. If he leaves the fox and the goose alone, the fox will eat the goose. If he leaves the goose with the corn, the goose will eat the corn. How can he take them all safely across the river? Answer: He takes the goose across, returns, and takes the fox across. Bringing the goose back with him, he leaves it and takes the corn across. Finally he returns and gets the goose.

The following puzzle is perfectly possible of solution although it appears to be quite the opposite:

If you take 9 from 6, and from 9 you take 10; and if 50 from 40 be taken; there will just half a dozen remain. The answer:

From SIX	From IX	From XL
take IX	take X	take L
S	I	X

Mechanical puzzles include those requiring the drawing of figures or lines, those that consist of wire or wooden links to be put together or taken apart, ones involving shapes to be cut out and fitted together, and others. The ancient Chinese tangram is an example of the type requiring cutting and fitting together of paper shapes to form a variety of figures. Napoleon, during his exile on St. Helena, occupied himself for many hours with this type of puzzle.

Word puzzles have always been popular. The formation of anagrams can be quite challenging. An anagram is a word or group of words formed by transposing the letters of another word or group of words. For example, the letters in the word *astronomer* can be transposed to form the words *moon starer*. Another type of word puzzle is the palindrome, a word or group of words that can be read both forward and backward. For instance, Adam was supposed to have said to Eve: "Madam, I'm Adam." Similar to the palindrome is the word square, a pattern of words that can be read down as well as across. For example:

C A T
A R E
T E A

The acrostic and the crossword are puzzles that are closely related to the word square. The pun and the riddle are types of word puzzles that are based primarily on word sense rather than on the pattern of letters or words.

PYLE, HOWARD (1853-1911), a U.S. author and illustrator, was born in Wilmington, Del., and studied at the Friends School there. His mother was influential in interesting him in literature and art.

After his studies, first in Philadelphia and later at the New York Art Student's League, Pyle began his work as an illustrator.

In 1883 he began writing and was the author of a long series of books for young people. His books, for which he did the illustrations, include *The Merry Adventures of Robin Hood, Pepper and Salt, Men of Iron,* and *The Garden Behind the Moon.*

PYRAMID, the name given to each structure in a group of buildings erected as mausoleums (tombs) by the ancient Egyptians in the Old Kingdom (from before 3000 B.C. to about 2000 B.C.). They were constructed of rough stone blocks laid in horizontal rows in a pyramidal shape. No one knows just why the pyramid shape was chosen. Some were as high as 750 feet. The massive pyramids, although destroyed in part by robbers, invaders, and weathering, still rise out of the desert just south of Cairo.

Most of the large Egyptian pyramids were built by six Pharaohs of the Old Kingdom. They were considered sacred shrines. The body of only one man, the king, occupied them. In later years, other pyramids were erected, but they were poor imitations of the original.

No written records of how the pyramids were built exist. Archaeologists, however, are fairly certain of some of the details of construction. The pyramid was always built on the west side of the Nile River, for that was the side of the setting sun. The river was also important

1. Remove two matches so that you leave two squares.

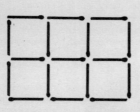

2. Remove four matches so that you leave only three squares.

3. Remove five matches so that you leave only five squares.

4. Remove four matches so that you leave only five triangles.

Puzzle answers given on page 2068.

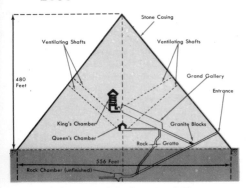

A section of the Pyramid of Cheops

as a means of shipping rock from the quarries. The workers began by leveling the rock base on which the pyramid was to be built. The site was then surveyed to be sure that the base of the pyramid would be a perfect square oriented toward the north. As the rocks were removed from the quarry, the workmen placed the name of their work gang on the block. Vigorous Gang and The Craftsmen Gang are two names that occur on blocks in the pyramids. Excellent wedges and copper saws and chisels were the tools used in limestone quarrying. No one knows how granite was quarried. The blocks, some of them weighing 200 tons, were hauled overland by sledges. Men drew the huge stones on sledges over a path paved with timbers and moistened with water to cut the friction. According to Herodotus, the Greek historian, the blocks were raised from step to step by means of machines made of wooden beams. Archaeologists doubt this statement. They think that the ancient Egyptians hauled the stones up long brick ramps built up against the pyramid-to-be at the proper level. When the apex stone was fitted in place, the workmen dressed the pyramid so that the sides would be smooth. Herodotus said that the Great Pyramid of Khufu took 20 years to build. Archaeologists estimate that 100,000 men must have worked on it each year. See EGYPT, ANCIENT; MUMMY.

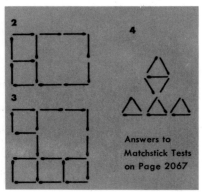

Answers to Matchstick Tests on Page 2067

PYRAMID OF KHUFU. See SEVEN WONDERS OF THE ANCIENT WORLD.

PYRENEES, a large mountain range in southwestern Europe, dividing France from Spain. It stretches in an east-west line from Cape Higuer on the Bay of Biscay to Cape Creuse on the Mediterranean Sea. The length is about 270 miles, and the width is 50 to 80 miles. Smaller ranges under various names branch from the Pyrenees into French territory on the north and into Spanish territory on the south. On the southern face of the range the slopes are very steep and are broken by a series of rugged chasms, high cliffs, and huge masses of bare rock. On the French side, where there has been greater erosion, the slopes are generally gradual. The average height of the range is 4,000 feet, and the snow line is at 9,200 feet. The principal peaks are Monte Perdido (10,997 feet), the Pico del Medio (11,004 feet), and the Pico de Aneto (11,168 feet). The principal rivers rising in the Pyrenees are the Adour, Garonne, and Aude, flowing north, and the Aragon, Gállego, Cinca, and Segre, flowing south.

PYRITE, also known as fool's gold or iron pyrites, is a common mineral. It is a compound of iron and sulfur, FeS_2. It is a very hard metal, brass yellow in color. It has often been mistaken for gold by inexperienced seekers; hence it is sometimes called fool's gold. It occurs in veins and masses in rocks and also in beautiful crystallized forms, such as cubes, octahedrons, and pyritohedrons. Pyrite is used commercially to make sulfuric acid, iron sulfate, and sulfur. It used to be called marcasite, and in the 17th century in Europe it was used to make ornaments. Nowadays the term *marcasite* is used for another mineral, also FeS_2 but with different crystal structure from pyrite and

Samples of iron pyrite are shown below. On the left are two common crystal forms: the cube (top) and the pyritohedron (bottom). Faces of pyrite cubes are commonly striated.

of a somewhat lighter color and weight; marcasite disintegrates more easily than pyrite. An important variety of copper ore that looks something like pyrite but is more brassy yellow is known as copper pyrite, or chalcopyrite. Arsenical pyrites, or arsenopyrite, is a compound of sulfur, iron, and arsenic.

PYROMETER, a device for measuring high temperatures. The three types of pyrometers commonly used are the thermoelectric pyrometer, the optical pyrometer, and the radiation pyrometer.

The thermoelectric pyrometer contains one or more thermocouples. (See THERMOELECTRICITY.) One end of a thermocouple is placed where the temperature is to be measured; the other is kept at a constant reference temperature. When the two ends are at different temperatures, an electrical potential, or voltage, is set up between them. The greater the temperature difference, the greater the voltage. The pyrometer has a voltage-measuring instrument connected to the thermocouple. The measuring instrument can be calibrated to indicate temperature differences between the two ends of the thermocouple. The thermocouple end subjected to high temperatures is often protected by a metal or ceramic tube.

An optical pyrometer measures temperature by determining the brightness of a glowing heated object. The higher the temperature of a heated object, the greater its brightness. An optical pyrometer is a telescope with an electric lamp mounted in the focal plane of the telescope. The lamp is connected to a battery, a current-measuring device, and a variable resistance. To measure the temperature of a glowing object the operator points the telescope at the object, looks through the eyepiece, and allows current to flow through the filament of the lamp. The current heats the filament, and the filament gives off light. The operator adjusts the amount of current flowing through the filament, by varying the resistance, until the filament is exactly as bright as the heated object. The amount of current in the filament is measured. It indicates the temperature of the glowing object. To make the visual comparison of the brightness of the heated object and the filament easier and more accurate, the telescope contains filters. The filters allow light waves of only a narrow range of frequencies to reach the observer's eye.

Radiation pyrometers usually employ a group of thermocouples connected in series and called a thermopile. Half of the junctions of the thermopile are exposed to the heat source; the other half are exposed to room temperature. A voltage is generated. Measurement of the voltage provides a temperature reading. Some radiation pyrometers use photoelectric cells and judge temperature by the color of the light radiated.

PYROXENE, a group of related minerals containing silica, oxygen, and one or more other elements. The pyroxenes have cleavage angles of 87 degrees and 93 degrees; the cleavage directions are parallel to the prism form. Their other physical properties and their occurrence are varied. In addition to silica and oxygen one or more of the following elements are present in pyroxenes: calcium, magnesium, iron, sodium, aluminum, and lithium.

The pyroxenes have a prismatic form and a vitreous (glasslike) or pearly luster. Some are translucent, and a few have a degree of transparency. Pyroxenes are various shades of green, black, white, gray, brown, pink, or yellow. On the mineral hardness scale they vary from 5 to 7, being in the penknife steel to file-steel range. Their spe-

The top pyroxene mineral is diopside, a calcium magnesium silicate. Enstatite, in crystal and massive form, is in the middle. It is a magnesium silicate. Augite, bottom, has a complicated range of compositions.

cific gravity (a body's density in relation to water) varies from 3.15 to 3.9.

The commonest pyroxenes, augite and the enstatites (enstatite and hypersthene), are found in igneous rocks, such as basalts and gabbros. Augite is especially associated with rocks high in iron, calcium, and magnesium; enstatite and hypersthene are common in very dark, heavy, igneous rocks. The diopsides occur in metamorphosed limestone and in some other metamorphic rocks. The diopsides are used as gem stones, as is jadeite, from which jade ornaments are made. Jadeite occurs in large masses in serpentine. Spodumene, a lithium source, is comparatively rare and is found in crystals in pegmatites. Aegirite is also rare and is found especially in rocks high in soda and poor in silica, such as phonolite and nepheline syenite.

PYTHAGORAS (flourished 6th century B.C.), a Greek philosopher and the discoverer, according to tradition, of the Pythagorean theorem concerning right triangles. Pythagoras was born on Samos, an island in the Aegean Sea. His father was said to have been a well-to-do citizen named Mnesarchus. Samos was governed by the tyrant Polycrates, whose rule Pythagoras grew to dislike. Pythagoras left Samos and may have journeyed to Egypt, where he is said to have learned certain mathematical truths. He finally settled in Crotona, a colony in southern Italy. In this place Pythagoras founded a religious association that aimed toward the moral regeneration of society. The group taught that the soul must be purified so that the individual could escape the "wheel of birth," a doctrine very similar to Hinduism. The citizenry opposed the Pythagoreans, however, and Pythagoras was forced to move to Metapontum, which was also in southern Italy. He died in that city. After his death, legends about him began to circulate. He was said to have had magical powers. His most lasting contribution was his reduction of mathematics to a demonstrative and deductive argument.

The Pythagoreans continued to be influential after the death of their founder. The order extended its political rule over a section of Magna Graecia (southern Italy), but it was overthrown and suppressed in the middle of the 5th century B.C.

Pythagoras' speculations on numbers and astronomy are important

in the history of science. Copernicus admitted his debt to the Pythagorean ideas about the planetary movement of the earth. Pythagoras believed that "all things are numbers," meaning that all things were explainable by mathematics as he understood it. He was said to have discovered the underlying harmonic interval of musical sounds. He is also credited with the discovery of the theorem that bears his name. The Pythagorean theorem states that the sum of the squares of the sides adjoining the right angle of a right triangle is equal to the square of the third side, the hypotenuse. The combination of mathematics with philosophical speculation was another influence that was handed down from Pythagoras and continued to intrigue philosophers and theologians down to modern times.

PYTHIAS. See DAMON AND PYTHIAS.

PYTHON, a large tropical snake that kills its prey by coiling around and squeezing it until it suffocates. Because it thus kills its prey, the python is classified as one of the giant constrictors that are related to the boa constrictor. Pythons are of several species. Except for a single small species native to Mexico, they are native only to tropical regions of Asia, Africa, and Australia. Pythons lack poisonous fangs.

The reticulated python of the Malay Peninsula and the Philippine Islands attains a length of 28 feet and a weight of 200 pounds. This python's prey consists chiefly of fowl and small mammals that seldom weigh more than 100 pounds. Dogs, cats, small hogs, and ducks are included in its diet. It rarely attacks, kills, or devours human beings.

Certain bones of the skeletons of pythons and boa constrictors are actually vestigial hind limbs. These vestiges indicate that these snakes have evolved from reptilian ancestors that possessed functional hind limbs.

QUADRILLE, a gay and spirited French dance in five parts—the first in two-four or six-eight time, the third in six-eight time, and the others in two-four time. The sections, or parts, are called: (1) the *pantalon* or *chaîne française*, (2) the *été* or *en avant-deux*, (3) the *poule*, (4) the *pastourelle*, and (5) the *boulangère*. Originally the quadrille was a country dance. When it was introduced to the French ballet in the 18th century, it was performed by four, eight, or twelve dancers. After it became popular in fashionable circles under Napoleon, it was danced by two or four couples; however, it remained close to the original country style. Around 1816 the quadrille was introduced to England, where it became very popular in ballroom dancing.

In America the quadrille was danced to French music, but the five parts varied from the original French pattern. As in the square dance, four couples formed a square, and the steps were done in couples.

QUAIL. See PHEASANTS, PARTRIDGES, QUAILS.

QUAKER. See SOCIETY OF FRIENDS.

QUANTRILL, WILLIAM CLARKE (1837-1865), American Confederate guerrilla chieftain, was born at Canal Dover (now Dover), Ohio. After teaching school in Ohio, Illinois, and Kansas, Quantrill settled at Lawrence, Kan., in 1859. Forced to flee because of a horse-stealing charge in 1860, he began to fight irregularly against the abolitionist cause. In 1861 he organized a band of guerrillas and with himself as chief pillaged towns and stagecoaches in Missouri and Kansas. In 1862 the band was mustered into the Confederate army, and Quantrill was made its captain. On Aug. 21, 1863, Quantrill and a band of over 450 men attacked Lawrence, Kan., massacring about 150 townspeople. Although they were pursued by federal troops, the raiders managed to reach Confederate Missouri and safety. As dissension grew in the troop, it broke into smaller groups, and with only 33 men Quantrill moved to Kentucky, where he continued his pillaging and killing. In May, 1865, the guerrillas were attacked by a federal force, and Quantrill was fatally wounded.

Chicago Hist. Soc.
William Quantrill led a band of guerrillas.

QUANTUM THEORY, a theory proposed in 1900 by Max Planck, a German physicist. It states that radiant energy is absorbed or emitted only in discrete quantities. Energy is not continuously absorbed or emitted. The only unit of energy a body can absorb or emit at a particular wavelength is a quantum. Whenever a body emits or absorbs radiant energy of a particular wavelength, the amount of energy is a whole-number multiple of the particular quantum.

Physicists in the late 1800's discovered that such radiant energy as light, infrared, and ultraviolet had wave properties. (See ELECTROMAGNETIC SPECTRUM; RADIATION.) Such radiation could be measured in terms of wavelength. Soon experiments were made to determine the amounts of energy radiated from a body at various wavelengths and temperatures. It was discovered that at each different temperature there is radiation of one wavelength that carries more energy than the radiations of other wavelengths. It was also determined that the cooler a body is, the longer is the wavelength of the maximum-energy radiation.

Explanations that regarded the radiations as emitted or absorbed in infinitely varying amounts were unsuccessful in accounting for the phenomena observed. Planck's quantum theory enabled him to derive an expression that showed how the quantities of energy radiated varied with the wavelength.

All electromagnetic radiations have the same velocity in vacuum or air, which is the velocity of light, C. But the frequency, γ, and the wavelength, λ, are different in each radiation. The general relation between these values is $C = \gamma\lambda$. The velocity of a radiation equals the frequency times the wavelength. The greater the frequency, the shorter the wavelength.

According to Planck the quantum, E, the unit of energy for a particular radiation, is given by the expression
$$E = h\, v$$
The h stands for a universal constant of nature known as the Planck constant. Since $v = \dfrac{C}{\lambda}$ (from $C = v\lambda$), the quantum of energy for a radiation is also given by
$$E = h\, \frac{C}{\lambda}$$
Since both h and C are constants, the size of a quantum is inversely proportional to the wavelength. The longer the wavelength, the smaller are the units of energy, the quanta, emitted.

Suppose there is a body capable of giving off radiations of all wavelengths. If the body is cold, a rather limited amount of energy is available to be given off. According to the laws of probability, it is not as likely that a few large quanta (short wavelength radiations) will be emitted as that a great number of small quanta (long wavelength radiations) will be emitted. So, in cold bodies most of the emitted energy is carried by long wavelengths. If the body is very hot, and large amounts of energy are available, the body will radiate most of its energy in large quanta.

The quantum theory has resolved many former problems and is widely applied in modern physics. Matter, generally regarded as composed of particles, can display wave properties, while electromagnetic radiation can display particle properties. The quantum theory combines both the wave concept and the particle concept in a satisfactory manner.

QUARANTINE is the restriction placed on the entrance to and exit from a place where a case of communicable disease exists. In the Middle Ages quarantines were first employed in Italy, consisting chiefly of restrictions placed on maritime enterprises during the course of any epidemic. The word itself originated in the Italian word *quarantenaria*, which referred to a 40-day period adopted by one Italian port. Today quarantine is similar. It includes the fumigation and surveillance of ships suspected of harboring infectious organisms or coming from infected ports. During quarantine no passenger or member of the crew of the vessel may leave the ship, and no one other than a government official may board it.

By analogy, the term *quarantine* has been used in international affairs to refer to the application of sanctions against an aggressor nation. In a speech in Chicago in 1937 President Franklin D. Roosevelt referred to Japan's attack on China and suggested that aggressor nations should be quarantined. Such a quarantine envisaged the application of sanctions, such as those provided for by Article XVI of the Covenant of the League of Nations (severance of all trade and financial relations with the aggressor nation). Sanctions, or quarantine measures, are the subject of Article 41 of the UN Charter, which provides for "complete or partial interruption of economic relations and of rail, sea, air, postal, telegraphic, radio, and other means of communication, and the severance of diplomatic relations."

QUARRYING, the excavation of stone from open pits. Stone is detached from the surrounding rock by drilling, blasting, cutting, or wedging.

Common types of quarried stone are granite, sandstone, limestone, marble, basalt, and slate. These occur in deposits from which the overburden of soil and loose rock is removed by washing or by digging with a power shovel. The method by which the stone is removed from the rock deposit depends on whether it is to be used for roadways and concrete work (crushed rock) or for building blocks and ornamental facing (dimension stone).

The commercially more important crushed rock is obtained mostly (75 percent) from limestone. Drilling and blasting are used to break the rock from the quarry face. Drills held by supports, such as bar or tripod drills, bore spaced holes of $1\frac{1}{2}$ to $2\frac{1}{2}$ inches in diameter and often 10 feet deep. Ammonia or gelatin dynamite is placed in the holes and detonated, thereby breaking the rock loose. The broken rock, destined for the crushing mill, is handled by such machines as crawler cranes and 300-horsepower tractors that pull side-delivery trailers having a 40-ton capacity.

Dimension stone is cut out of the rock face in blocks. In the softer limestone and sandstone cutting is done with channeling machines or wire saws. Channeling machines run on a track and, by a chopping action, cut a groove 6 inches or less in width and several feet deep. A wire saw consists of a wire that runs, like an endless belt, between pulleys. The wire cuts by being placed against the rock face and having an abrasive, such as sand or aluminum oxide, poured on it as it runs. In harder stone, such as granite, blocks are removed by light blasting with black powder or by drilling closely spaced holes and then knocking out the remaining sections (broaching).

Wedges are used to subdivide large blocks and to break loose the bottom of the key block (first block to be cut out of a rock face) after it has been channeled.

QUARTZ, composed of silicon and oxygen, is one of the commonest minerals in the earth's crust. It is found in many igneous, sedimentary, and metamorphic rocks in all parts of the world. Three distinct types of quartz exist: the coarsely crystalline type that occurs in distinct crystals or in large masses without external crystal form and is transparent or translucent; the granular cryptocrystalline type that occurs in masses that have a dull, opaque appearance like unglazed porcelain; and the fibrous cryptocrystalline type that has a waxy appearance and is translucent. Cryptocrystalline quartz is made up of crystals so small they cannot be identified, even though a microscope is used.

Crystals of coarsely crystalline quartz are commonly in the form of six-sided prisms. The ends of the prisms may consist of a variety of crystal faces. The prism faces may be marked by fine horizontal indentations. Quartz crystals are commonly long and narrow with tapering ends. Some quartz crystals are several feet in diameter. Other crystals are so small they can be seen only through a microscope.

All quartz is hard: It cannot be scratched by a steel file, and it can easily scratch window glass. Quartz breaks, like glass, into smooth, curved surfaces. Pure quartz, SiO_2, is white or colorless, but many specimens of quartz are colored by various impurities.

Many varieties of coarsely crystalline quartz exist. Rock crystal is a colorless, clear quartz in distinct crystals. Milky quartz is white and almost opaque. Its whiteness is caused by minute inclusions of fluids in the solid quartz. Smoky quartz is a yellow, brown, or nearly black transparent or semitransparent variety. Its smoky appearance may be the result of exposure to radiation from radioactive materials in rocks. Rose quartz commonly occurs in large masses without external crystal form. The rose or pink color is caused by small amounts of titanium in the mineral. Amethyst is purple or violet quartz and is often found in distinct crystals. The impurity causing the purplish color is ferric iron. Citrine is yellow transparent quartz.

Fibrous cryptocrystalline quartz also occurs in many varieties. A general name for the different varieties is chalcedony. Chalcedony is translucent, has a waxy appearance, and is often found filling or lining rock cavities. Carnelian is red chal-

Limestone to be used as dimension stone is being lifted from a quarry in southern Indiana.

cedony. Sard is reddish-brown chalcedony. Chrysoprase is light green; heliotrope, or bloodstone, is green with red spots. Agate and onyx are banded forms of chalcedony. See AGATE; ONYX.

Granular cryptocrystalline varieties of quartz include flint, chert, and jasper. Flint is a tough, dark material that can be broken into sharp-edged pieces. (See FLINT.) Chert is similar to flint but generally has a lighter color. Jasper is a granular cryptocrystalline quartz colored red, yellow, or brown from an included iron oxide. See JASPER.

Quartz occurs in nearly all light-colored igneous rocks and in some darker igneous rocks. Mineral veins and pegmatites commonly contain quartz. Quartz is a constituent of many metamorphic rocks, such as schists and gneisses. Quartzite, a metamorphic rock, is nearly pure quartz. Many sedimentary rocks contain quartz: most sandstones consist chiefly of quartz grains; some limestones contain flint and chert nodules. Quartz is found in most soils and is present in large amounts in most sands.

Quartz has many uses. Some varieties of coarsely crystalline quartz and fibrous cryptocrystalline quartz are used as gem stones. Examples are rock crystal, amethyst, citrine, agate, onyx, and carnelian. Quartz sand is used in mortar and cement. Pure quartz sand is used in large quantities in manufacturing ordinary glass. Ground or powdered quartz is used as an abrasive and as an ingredient in ceramic bodies, glazes, and enamels. Quartz is used as a flux in smelting certain ores. Silica firebrick, made from quartz, is used as a refractory substance. Quartzite and sandstone are used as building stones. Pure quartz crystals are made into lenses and prisms for optical equipment. Small plates cut from flawless quartz crystals are used to control the frequency of electrical impulses in some radio oscillators. Because the supply of natural quartz crystals that can be cut into oscillator plates is limited, synthetic quartz crystals are grown in laboratories.

QUEBEC is Canada's largest province in area and second in population and in the economic field. It is also the home of French Canada, preserving much of the atmosphere of old France. Quebec, the capital, is one of the oldest cities on the continent and a stronghold of French Canadian cultural life. Montreal is the largest city in Canada and the country's industrial center. Other important cities in Quebec include Trois Rivières, Sherbrooke, Granby, Hull, and Chicoutimi. Quebec has a population of over 4,750,000.

The province is located in eastern Canada. It covers a vast area of nearly 600,000 square miles. A large part of Quebec is in the Laurentian Plateau, an area that is very rocky and not good for agriculture but rich in minerals. Another region of Quebec is the lowland area in the St. Lawrence Valley. The highlands of the Appalachian Mountains are in the east. The highest summits are in the Shickshock Mountains of the Gaspé Peninsula.

Many lakes and rivers are found in Quebec. The lakes include Mistassini, Minto, and part of Abitibi. In addition to the St. Lawrence, the principal rivers include the Ottawa, Gatineau, Mistassini, St. Maurice, Saguenay, and Richelieu. Quebec leads all provinces in the production of electric power. This cheap power is one of the reasons for the province's industrial growth.

Farming, mining, lumbering, and industry provide occupations for the majority of the population. The southern part of Quebec has many fine agricultural regions. Grains, fruits and vegetables, and tobacco are important products. Dairying is carried on in many areas. Many persons are employed in the fishing industry along the St. Lawrence River. Fur farming is gaining in importance.

Quebec ranks next to Ontario in manufacturing. The leading manufactures include paper and pulp, cotton products, chemicals, and food and tobacco products. Metal smelting and refining are important.

Quebec is a land of vivid contrast and historic memories. Villagers in the St. Lawrence Valley still maintain many of their old French customs. French is still spoken in many parts of the province. French is the language of instruction at Laval University in Quebec and at the University of Montreal.

Jacques Cartier explored the Quebec region in 1534. Later in 1608 Samuel de Champlain made the first settlement in the region at the site of the city of Quebec. The settlement at Quebec was for many years the population and trading center of the area. The French and the British fought for supremacy of the area. In 1763, by the Treaty of Paris, Great Britain obtained the territory. In 1774 the Quebec Act provided a form of government for the province, extended its boundaries, and allowed the use of French civil law (which still is in effect). Known as Lower Canada before the confederation was formed, Quebec was established in 1867 as one of the original provinces.

Several varieties of quartz are shown below: 1, jasper, colored red by hematite inclusions; 2, carnelian; 3, rose quartz; 4, citrine quartz; 5, agate; 6, amethyst quartz; 7, smoky quartz; and 8, rock crystal, colorless quartz on a crust of small quartz crystals.

Quebec Province—Photo Driscoll

This well-kept farm is on the Isle of Orleans in Quebec. The lowland region of the St. Lawrence Valley is an excellent farming area.

QUEBEC

Shield: Three horizontal sections containing two fleurs-de-lis at top, British lion in middle, three maple leaves at bottom

Flag: White cross with four fleurs-de-lis on blue field

Flower: Iris

Capital: Quebec

Largest city: Montreal

Area: 594,860 sq. mi. (including 71,000 sq. mi. inland waters)

Rank in area: 2d (including territories)

Population: 4,750,000

Chief universities: McGill University, University of Montreal, Laval University

Chief river: St. Lawrence (with tributaries St. Francis, St. Maurice, Gatineau, Ottawa, Chaudière)

Chief lakes: Mistassini, Minto, Clearwater

Average temperature: Montreal (south), 15° F. (Jan.), 70° F. (July)—Fort McKenzie (north), −12° F. (Jan.), 54° F. (July)

Average annual rainfall: 35 to 40 inches in south, decreasing to 15 inches in north

Chief economic activities: Manufacturing, mining, lumbering, agriculture (including dairying)

One of the first signs of spring in Quebec is the gathering of sap from the maple trees.
Can. Govt. Trav. Bur.

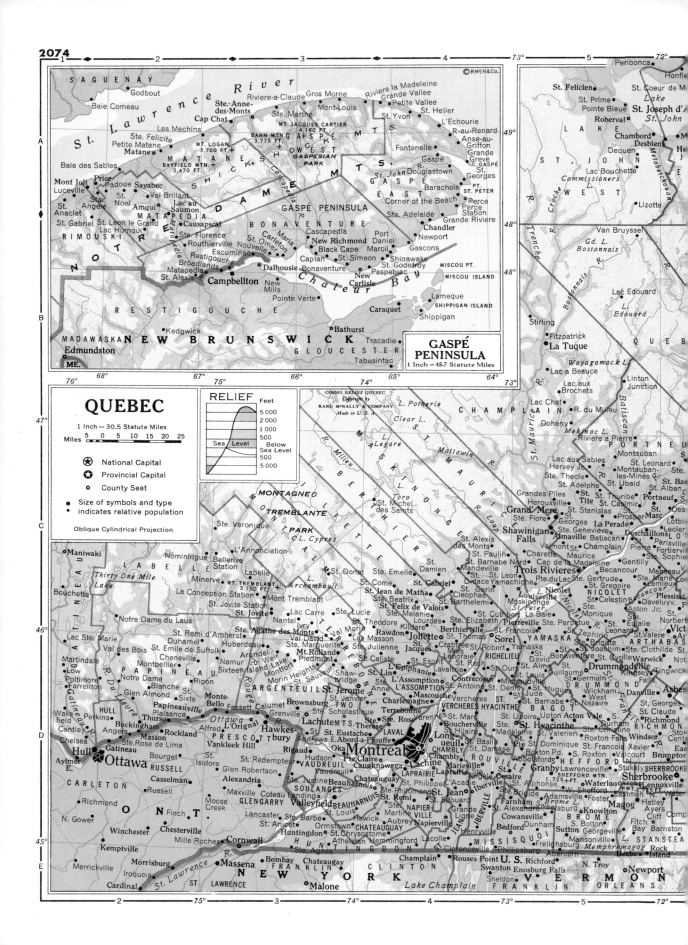

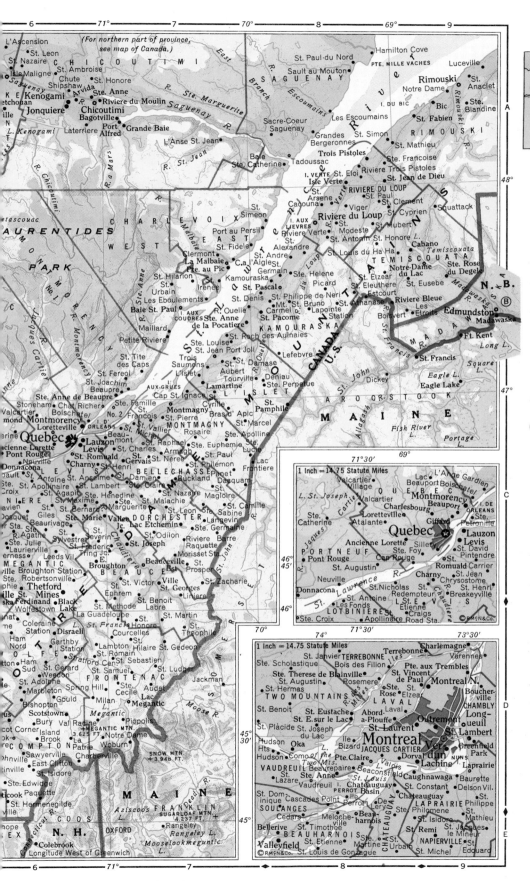

Location map

The principal cities and towns of Quebec are clustered in the regions along the St. Lawrence River. Here the first French settlers established their homes and churches, the foundation of the earliest Christian civilization in the north of the American continent. Montreal, the metropolis of Quebec, is the second largest French city in the world.

Above is the iris, the floral emblem of the Canadian province of Quebec.

A 550-mile highway skirts the shoreline of the beautiful Gaspé Peninsula, one of the great tourist regions in Canada. At Sainte Anne de Beaupré, on the north shore of the St. Lawrence, is one of the most famous Christian shrines in the New World. It receives thousands of pilgrims each year.

The Quebec shield combines the fleur-de-lis of France with the maple leaf.

Photo, N.F.B.

The majestic Château Frontenac overlooks the historic city of Quebec. The Upper Town, surrounded by a wall on top of a rocky bluff, rises above the picturesque Lower Town.

Chief crops: Hay, grains, vegetables, fruit

Chief minerals: Iron ore, asbestos, copper, gold, zinc

Chief manufactures: Pulp and paper, smelted metals, clothing, food products, machinery

Notable attractions: Laurentides, Mont Tremblant, and Gaspesian provincial parks—Gatineau Park —Fort Chambly and Fort Lennox national historic parks—Mt. Royal, Montreal—Lower Town in city of Quebec

Important historical dates:

1534 Landing of Jacques Cartier on Quebec's Gaspé Peninsula

1608 City of Quebec founded by Champlain

1763 Treaty granting New France (Canada) to Great Britain

1791 Canada divided into Upper Canada (Ontario) and Lower Canada (Quebec)

1867 Membership of province in federation

QUEBEC is the capital of the Canadian province of Quebec and is an important industrial city. However, its major roles are political, religious, and intellectual. It is the seat of the Roman Catholic archbishop of Canada and the site of Laval University. The city is situated in a picturesque and commanding position on a promontory 200 to 350 feet high. The city is located at the confluence of the St. Lawrence and St. Charles rivers, in the southern part of the province. The city has a population of approximately 200,000.

The Montmorency Falls and the Shawinigan Falls furnish waterpower for factories. Woodpulp, paper, cigars, cigarettes, leather goods, and textiles are manufactured. Situated in an advantageous position, Quebec is also important commercially. It has steamship connections with European ports and with other U.S. and Canadian ports along the St. Lawrence Seaway.

The city is the French Canadian cultural center. Quebec contains the magnificent Parliament Buildings. Other attractions include many historic churches, such as the Basilica of Notre Dame, originally constructed in 1647; old homes of the 17th century; and one of the oldest hospitals in North America, Hôtel-Dieu de Précieux-Sang, founded in 1639.

The city was settled by Samuel de Champlain in 1608. In 1663 it became the capital of New France, having grown as a trading center. In 1759 British forces commanded by Wolfe captured Quebec by defeating Montcalm on the nearby Plains of Abraham. Shortly thereafter the whole territory was ceded to Great Britain, and the city became the seat of the government. Quebec was the capital of Canada for two short periods after the union of Upper and Lower Canada.

QUEBEC ACT, an act of the British Parliament passed in 1774 providing for the permanent government of the province of Quebec. The boundaries of the province extended from the French settlements along the St. Lawrence River and the Great Lakes, east to Labrador and included the area north of the Ohio River bounded by Pennsylvania on the east and the Mississippi River on the west. By this extension the 13 American colonies, already on the verge of revolution and claiming the regions lying west of them, were limited.

The act also established French law in civil cases, although British law was maintained in criminal cases. An appointed council exercised authority. The Roman Catholic Church was granted a privileged status, which included freedom of public worship.

The act proved to be unworkable and was superseded by the Constitutional Act of 1791, which divided the province into Upper Canada and Lower Canada.

QUEEN ANNE'S WAR, in American history, that part of the War of the Spanish Succession that took place in America. Spain and France were allied against England. It began in 1702 with a successful expedition from South Carolina against the Spaniards in Florida. The entire frontier of New England was exposed to attacks by the French and Indians from 1702 to 1713. New York was saved because of an agreement with the Iroquois Indians. The British captured Port Royal (now Annapolis Royal), Nova Scotia, in 1710 after two unsuccessful attempts, but failed to conquer Canada. By the Treaty of Utrecht, in 1713, the War of the Spanish Succession was brought to a close. The French gave up the territory around Hudson Bay, and ceded Acadia and Newfoundland, retaining the privilege of drying fish on the west coast. They kept Cape Breton, which they were allowed to fortify, and the islands of the St. Lawrence.

The quetzal is a tropical American bird.

QUETZAL, a beautiful Central American bird, the emblem of Guatemala. It was worshiped by the Aztecs and Mayas as the god of the air and was related to the worship of the Aztec god Quetzalcoatl, who was represented as a conventionalized quetzal.

This colorful bird, one of the trogon family, lives in virgin forests in the mountains of Central America. The crested male, iridescent green and crimson, is almost 4 feet long, including his 2-foot tail coverts. The flight feathers are covered by long, curled wing coverts. The female is colorful but less ornamented.

The quetzal perches with its feet almost covered by the body plumage and with its tail coverts straight down or angled forward. Each note of the bird's call is accompanied by a movement of the tail. Quetzals fly weakly, freeze briefly when they land, and usually sit very quietly among the foliage. The nest, in a natural cavity, contains from three to five whitish eggs. The male, gorgeous though he is, helps his mate with the nest duties.

QUICKSAND, an area of sand so saturated with water that it is unable to bear weight. Quicksand is formed when water under pressure, as from a spring, is forced upward through a sandbed. When the water pressure equals the sand's weight, quicksand is formed. The sand grains are slightly separated, each surrounded by water.

Quicksand is generally confined to small areas that can occur separately or as a part of larger, less-saturated sandbeds. These areas are found where the water pressure is maintained because the water is not drained away quickly, such as spots having impervious bottoms and small slope. Quicksand is uncommon in flat country, where the gradient is not sufficient to produce water under pressure, and in mountainous territory where drainage is too fast in canyons and gorges for the building up of underground water pressure. Most commonly, quicksand occurs in hilly terrain, especially in limestone, where channels containing water under pressure are easily formed. It is found along streams and also on seashores. The location can be above the water level, under the water, or in apparently dry streambeds.

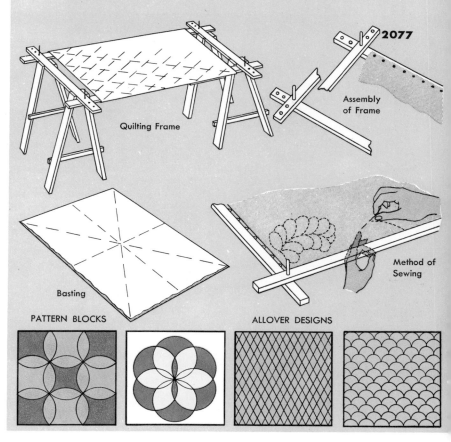

2077

Quilting Frame

Assembly of Frame

Basting

Method of Sewing

PATTERN BLOCKS

ALLOVER DESIGNS

Quilting is done on a frame. The quilt lining is attached to strips of material anchored to the frame (top). Filler is basted to the lining, and the quilt top is placed over the filler and similarly basted (center, left). The design is then worked into the quilt top (center, right). Below are two patterns for quilt blocks and two allover quilting patterns.

Visual detection of quicksand is difficult, especially if the top is dry and crusted. Thrusting a pole into the suspected sand area is the most practical means of determining its reliability. If a person is trapped in quicksand, release is secured in several ways. Some methods are distribution of the weight by lying on the back or across a pole, moving toward solid ground by a rolling action, and pulling on a tree branch or a rope.

QUILTING, making coverlets and other articles by sewing together two layers of material with a filler of cotton, flannel, wool, or the like in between. Designs for quilts are of endless variety. They may be formed by stitches of different colored threads against a plain background, or they may be pieced from patches. A coverlet of this type is known as a patchwork quilt. The patches themselves are small squares, triangles, or diamonds of different fabrics and colors.

Quilts are made in sections called blocks. This procedure simplifies work by directing the sewer's attention to a limited area. After the required number of blocks have been made they are sewed together to form the top. Blocks may be of patches or they may merely be the areas marked out on a continuous surface. Appliqué quilts have a plain background with colorful and variously shaped pieces sewed on the surface to form a design. The comforter, which is different from both patchwork and applique quilts, is made entirely of a single color. However, the comforter may be stitched in a variety of designs.

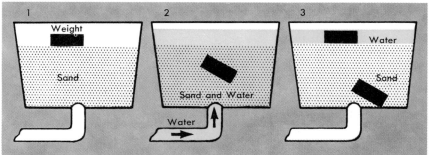

Dry sand, **1,** will support a heavy weight. If water is pumped into the sand under pressure, **2,** the water will separate the grains of sand, producing a semifluid mixture called quicksand. The object will then sink, provided it is denser than the quicksand. If the pressure is removed, **3,** the sand will settle to the bottom and again support a heavy weight.

Two Frenchmen, Pelletier and Caventou, first extracted quinine from cinchona bark in 1820.

Courtesy of and © 1954, Parke, Davis & Co.

The quilting stitch, or running stitch, is used to hold the thicknesses of material and the lining together. It is also used to ornament a plain background, as in the comforter, or to vary a basic pattern with contrasting movements of straight or curved lines. The hemming stitch is used in quilting to sew borders or to do appliqué work. Occasionally the buttonhole stitch is used in its stead to elaborate part of an appliqué pattern.

Like so many of our sewing crafts, quilting is of ancient origin; it seems to have flourished earliest in India or the Middle East. During the Holy Wars of the 11th and 12th centuries the Crusaders brought quilted garments home with them and stimulated interest in the art. Europeans were attracted as much by the warmth of quilted articles as by their striking, colorful designs. Even before the craft was at its height on the Continent (in the 16th century), rich materials were used in quiltmaking—silk, damask, velvet, brocade, satin, fine cotton, and linen. Women of the court in France, Spain, Italy, and England became skilled in the art.

With the colonization of America quilting was revived and given new impetus. It was an important homecraft in all regions of the early states. In many communities the quilting bee was a most welcome pretext for social gatherings. But by the end of the 19th century the general interest in making things by hand had been so discouraged by the machine production of goods that quilting has since survived only as an art.

QUININE, a medicine that formerly was used to combat malaria. Quinine is extracted from the bark of the cinchona tree, which is native to the tropical forests of Java and South America. It is a white crystalline alkaloid with a bitter taste.

The quinine compound used to combat malaria is quinine dihydrochloride. This can either be taken orally in the form of pills, or an aqueous solution of it can be injected into the bloodstream. Quinine dihydrochloride combats malaria by preventing the multiplication of the parasitic protozoans that infest the bloodstream and cause the disease. It also reduces the high fever that accompanies malaria.

Quinine can now be synthesized, or made from chemicals in the laboratory. However, the cinchona bark is still the commercial source of quinine. Quinine has been replaced in the treatment of malaria by synthetic drugs that are more effective.

QUINTUPLETS are a group of five children born in the same labor. Quintuple births occur only once in 57 million confinements. There are fewer than 100 authenticated births of quintuplets reported in medical literature. Only in a few instances have all five lived beyond a short period. The most famous set of quintuplets were five daughters born to Oliva and Elzire Dionne, of Callander, Ontario, Canada, on May 28, 1934. The attending physician was Allan R. Dafoe. They were named Cécile, Emilie, Marie, Yvonne, and Annette. Their total weight one week after birth was only 13 pounds, 6 ounces.

QUOITS, a game played with a flat ring of iron, 8½ inches in diameter with a 4-inch hole in the middle. It is convex on the upper side and flat on the underside. The convex side is held uppermost in throwing.

The game is played in the following manner: Two pins, called hobs, are driven into the ground from 20 to 30 feet apart and extending 1 inch above the surface. The players, usually two or four, stand beside one hob and in regular succession throw their quoits (of which each player has two) as near the other hob as they can. The player or partnership counts one point for each quoit nearer the hob than any of those of the opposing player or partnership. If the quoit is thrown over the hob (a ringer), it counts three points; a hobber (a quoit leaning against the hob) counts two points. A game is usually 21 points.

QUOTATION, the words of others, either spoken or in print. A quotation that consists of a repetition of the actual words is usually written within quotation marks.

Proper credit should always be given to the originator of the quotation. If a person attempts to pass quotations off as his own inventions, he is committing plagiarism. The publication of plagiarisms of copyrighted works is unlawful. Even when it is not against the law, plagiarism is a contemptible dishonesty.

Plagiarism in a written assignment is serious enough to justify a failing course grade. Quotations are sometimes called for in school essays, but either in the text of the paper or in the footnote the student must indicate the author, book, and page of the passage quoted or any other source the citation may have. Standard forms for citing references to quotations are valuable for every writer.

So-called familiar quotations are those that have gained general usage because of particular aptness of diction or image. They may be from the Bible, from Shakespeare, from a speech of a famous person, or from less obvious sources. Sometimes, as with many proverbs, it is impossible to trace the originator. It is not always necessary to mention the source of a familiar quotation, since it is usually well known and can be found in reference works that list famous quotations. However, it usually appears within quotation marks. The use of many well-known quotations in speech or writing can lead to triteness and pompousness. See PUNCTUATION.

R is the 18th letter of the English alphabet. Lowercase italic R (r) stands for radius in mathematics. Capital italic R (R) stands for the gas constant in physics and chemistry. In electricity italic R (R or r) also stands for *resistance*. The radical sign ($\sqrt{}$) in mathematics is a modification of r, for the Latin word *radix*, meaning "root."

RABBIT FEVER. See TULAREMIA.

RABBITS AND HARES, which belong to the mammalian order Lagomorpha, are characterized by long ears and by long, muscular hindlegs for rapid, agile leaping. The teeth of rabbits and hares, like those of rodents, are adapted to an exclusively vegetarian diet. Their incisors are shaped like chisels to facilitate the cutting and gnawing of vegetation. They have no canine teeth for seizing prey and tearing meat. Rabbits and hares belong to the same family. Rabbits differ from hares in having shorter ears, smaller heads, and shorter hindlegs.

A main defense of rabbits and hares against their many predatory enemies is their ability to run rapidly and to twist, turn, and leap nimbly. Rare is the man who has ever laid hands on a live wild rabbit or hare, and only the swiftest, most skilled dogs can catch one. The long ears of rabbits and hares enable them to hear with exceptional acuity, and their eyesight also is very keen.

Most species of rabbit and hare breed rapidly and give birth to several litters of young each year. If it were not for their many predatory enemies, rabbits and hares would multiply rapidly enough to cover entire continents. In fact, rabbits did overrun the continent of Australia after they were introduced there during the 19th century. They seriously damaged crops and pastures until a united effort was made to exterminate them. Various species of rabbit or hare are native to every continent except Australia.

For many centuries rabbits and hares have been domesticated for their fur and meat. They also make interesting pets. The wild ancestors of most domesticated varieties were certain European species. Many different domesticated varieties have been developed.

Winter Coat

European Hare

Varying Hare or Snowshoe Rabbit
Autumn Coat

European Rabbit

Spring Coat

Dutch Rabbit

Desert Cottontail

Brush Rabbit

Swamp Rabbit

Eastern Cottontail

Antelope Jack Rabbit

Black-Tailed Jack Rabbit

RABELAIS, FRANÇOIS (1494?-1553?), French writer and humanist, born near Chinon, in Touraine. Virtually nothing is known of his life until 1520. According to tradition he lived near Angers from 1515 to 1518 and studied at a nearby Franciscan monastery. In 1520 Rabelais became a monk in the Franciscan monastery at Founteny-le-Comte, in Poitou. There he began the study of Greek. Since Greek was at that time held in disrepute by the Franciscans, Rabelais moved to a Benedictine monastery in the same area and there continued his humanistic studies. Toward the end of 1527 Rabelais quit the monastery and, as a secular priest, turned to the study of medicine, which he pursued at the universities of Paris and Montpellier. From the latter institution he received the degree of bachelor of medicine in 1530. By this time he had acquired a reputation as a classical scholar and as a student of law, botany, and archaeology as well. Although he did not receive his doctorate until 1537, Rabelais practiced medicine in Lyon as early as 1532. In 1534 Rabelais acquired the patronage of the bishop of Paris and as his physician traveled throughout France and Italy. Rabelais served as physician to the governor of Piedmont until the governor's death in 1543. After spending some time in Rome, Rabelais returned to France to assume the curacy of Meudon. He resigned his position in 1552 and, according to tradition, spent his last months in Paris.

Rabelais is remembered as the author of *Gargantua and Pantagruel*, regarded as one of the masterpieces of world literature. The work consists of five books, published between 1532 and 1564. At once a satire, a fantasy, and a burlesque, *Gargantua and Pantagruel* is a mixture of popular lore, serious philosophy, mock erudition, obscene buffoonery, and gross realism. Not insignificant is the extravagant and racy nature of the prose itself. For many years the standard translation was that made by Thomas Urquhart and Pierre Motteux. It was completed in 1708.

RABIES, also called hydrophobia, is a virus disease of the central nervous system and is usually transmitted to man by the contaminated saliva in the bite of a rabid dog. All warmblooded animals are susceptible. The only method of transmission of the virus is by inoculation with the infected saliva through the skin. It is not transmitted if the skin is unbroken. The incubation period is 10 to an average of 50 or 60 days.

Symptoms of rabies in dogs may take the form of either violent agitation or unusually quiet behavior with excessive flow of saliva followed by paralysis. Similar symptoms or irritability and other signs of nervous-system involvement occur in man, the most specific symptom being difficulty in swallowing. Once the disease begins, it is invariably fatal in man, usually within three to five days. For persons exposed to a potentially rabid animal, antirabic vaccine is indicated. An animal suspected of being rabid should be kept alive under close observation for up to ten days and should not be killed before rabies can be either proved or disproved.

RACCOON, a carnivorous, fur-bearing mammal that is about as large as a small dog or a fox. The raccoon is usually about 33 inches long, including the 10-inch tail. Its long, straight, shaggy fur is yellowish gray with black-tipped hairs. The bushy tail is ringed and tipped with brownish black. Raccoons range from southern Canada through Central America to Paraguay; however, they are not native to any other continent.

The raccoon lives in unfrequented, thickly wooded swamps and in forests that border on lakes or streams. The raccoon usually sleeps in hollow trees or on shaded boughs during bright, sunny days, but it is not entirely nocturnal and sometimes visits cornfields and poultry yards in the daytime. It is an excellent climber and is very fond of birds' eggs and of young birds. After detecting the odor of turtle eggs buried in the sand, the raccoon digs up the eggs and eats them. It seizes young ducks as they come to the water, catches frogs and shellfish, and is extremely fond of ripe, juicy corn. The raccoon frequently dips its food in water before eating it, thereby falsely giving the impression of washing it.

The raccoon generally builds a nest in a hollow tree. Between four and six young are raised in the nest each year. In northern regions the raccoon sleeps in its nest during the coldest part of the winter. However, this sleep is not a true hibernation.

Raccoon hunting—especially at night with trained dogs—is a favorite sport in many regions of the United States, especially in the south. The pelt is sold to hatters or

These raccoons are hunting frogs in a pond.

furriers, and the flesh, which is tender and juicy, with the flavor of pork, is eaten. Many raccoons are also caught in traps. The colloquial name for the raccoon is coon.

RACE, a population having a combination of physical characteristics, inherited through biological descent, that distinguishes it from other populations. A race is isolated to some extent, either socially or geographically or in both ways. Human racial distinctions, although different at the extremes, shade into one another and become lost, both through geographic overlapping and through interbreeding. Groups differ from one another, but individuals in each group may also differ from each other so much that the overlap is wide. So we can speak only of average racial differences between groups. Criteria frequently used in the classification of race are shape of nose, head, eye, or mouth; body height; and color of eye, hair, or skin.

The segregation of the people of India into castes has caused, through inbreeding, differences in physical type. The members of a caste can marry only members of their own caste. They usually live in their own sections. The traits that were distributed in a small group of people are passed on from generation to generation, and no new traits come in from the outside. In these inbred groups characteristic sets of traits develop. Sometimes these differences between groups are great enough for certain scientists to call the groups races.

Since there are always individuals with characteristics different from those by which their race is defined, race is a statistical concept. Thus you may say that in population A 30 percent of the members have certain traits, while 90 percent of the members of population B have the same traits.

Scientists have discovered that many of the traits used in measuring races are affected by the environment and therefore are not reliable measures. For example, the head form changes with diet because chewing habits affect muscles that change the pattern of the jaw and of other bones. The children of immigrants to the United States are on the whole taller than those who stay in the country of origin. Thus, there has been a search for traits that are known to be inherited and that are not affected by the environment.

The principal traits known to be inherited are the blood groups. A, B, AB, and O are four blood types. (See BLOOD TRANSFUSION.) Everybody in the world fits into one of these categories. No matter what his race, any person may give a transfusion to any other person with the appropriate blood type.

Scientists have classified races according to blood type. The American Indians came from Asia thousands of years ago. Being isolated from the home of their ancestors and marrying strictly among themselves (they were the first people in the New World) their population has had a high proportion of the O blood type—over 90 percent. Some people consider the American Indians—often classified as part of the Mongoloid race—to be a separate race.

This type of classification, using statistical counts of inherited features, enables scientists to trace historical relationships of populations. Hungarian gypsies and certain populations of western India have a similar pattern of blood types. In this way, scientists have confirmed the origin of the Hungarian gypsies in western India.

There are always people who cannot be classified. There are no pure races.

The three major racial stocks are considered to be Negroid, Mongoloid, and Caucasoid, with the primitive-appearing Australoid as a fourth, but minor, stock. The areas in which the major stocks are most markedly seen are western Africa, eastern Asia, and northern Europe, respectively.

Races that have lived in a particular locality for a long time seem well adapted to their environment. Dark-skinned people, with pigment in their skin that filters out the rays of the sun, are found in sunny areas. It is believed that those who were well adapted increased in number, in each area, because such people had more children or because they were more likely to live until childbearing age.

In more recent times, human beings have been able to change their environment, making it more comfortable. Thus, increasingly, anybody can live almost anywhere in the world.

There is no evidence for inheritance of any mental trait. As far as tests show, no race has a premium on intelligence. Race has nothing to do with a person's language or culture. A child of Chinese parents, of the Mongoloid race, born in England and living with British people, will grow up speaking English, wearing British clothing, and learning British ways.

Race is simply a distinction between populations. This distinction is determined by known genetic processes and serves as a tool to fill in the story of man.

Children of different races who grow up in the same cultural environment will have a common language and a common cultural heritage.

Rus Arnold

RACHMANINOV, SERGEI (1873-1943), Russian composer and pianist, was born in Novgorod into a noble family. His talent was manifest as early as his fourth year, and he began lessons early in life. He attended both the St. Petersburg and the Moscow conservatories. An early influence on Rachmaninov was the composer Tchaikovsky, who unfortunately died in 1893, the year Rachmaninov was graduated from the Moscow Conservatory. In this same year Rachmaninov composed a student symphony and the one-act opera *Aleko*. When he was only 20 years old he also composed his Prelude in C Sharp Minor.

From 1897 to 1906 Rachmaninov was director first of a private opera in Moscow and later of the Imperial Theater. Rachmaninov's second piano concerto was written in 1901 and the tone poem *Isle of the Dead* in 1907. In 1909 he toured the United States, as both a conductor and a pianist. In 1917 he left Russia and never returned. He lived thereafter in Switzerland and the United States.

RACINE, JEAN BAPTISTE (1639-1699), French neoclassic dramatist, born at La Ferté-Milon near Soissons. His parents died when he was quite young, and he was raised by his grandparents at Port-Royal. In 17th-century France Port-Royal was the stronghold of Jansenism, that belief, condemned by the pope as heresy, which viewed man as totally depraved and a creature governed by predestination. Jansenism and a thorough education in classical literature were the forces that conditioned Racine both as a man and as a dramatist.

In 1658 Racine went to Paris and studied there at the University of Paris. He became friendly with three of the chief representatives of the Age of Louis XIV, Jean de La Fontaine, Nicolas Boileau, and Molière. *La Thébaïde*, Racine's first play, was produced by Molière, with moderate success, in 1664. In 1665 Racine's second play, *Alexandre le Grand*, appeared in Molière's theater first and later at the Hôtel de Bourgogne. (Racine's transferring of his play to another theater caused a quarrel with Molière that was never healed).

Racine's first great success, *Andromaque*, appeared in 1667. In 1668 his one comedy, *Les Plaideurs*, was produced. In the following years Racine produced his great tragedies, which, with the works of Corneille and Molière, are the great dramatic

heritage of the French theater. These plays include *Britannicus, Bérénice, Bajazet, Mithridate, Iphigénie,* and *Phèdre*. What characterizes these plays, aside from their classical and oriental subject matter, is a concentration of effects and an observance of the unities of time, place, and action. After writing *Phèdre*, Racine gave up the theater for some years. With Boileau, he was given a court post as historiographer to the king. In 1689 Racine returned to the theater and wrote his great play *Esther* (based on the Book of Esther in the Bible) for performance at a girl's school. His last play, *Athalie*, also derived from a biblical source, was not produced until after the author's death.

RADAR, an electronic device used to detect and locate objects by sending and receiving electromagnetic waves. The name was derived from the first letters of the phrase "*radio detecting and ranging*." Radar equipment operates in the electromagnetic wave spectrum at wavelengths of a few centimeters to several meters. Wavelengths of about 10 centimeters are now much used. The short wavelengths permit the use of radar antennae of a few feet in width that will form directional beams of transmitted energy.

The principle upon which radar operates is the transmitting of a short, high-energy pulse of electromagnetic waves. These can be considered radio waves of short wavelength. These waves travel in directions and strengths determined by the geometry of the radar antenna. When this short pulse of radio waves reaches another object, the object itself is excited by the radio waves, and it becomes a sort of parasite antenna. The object then reradiates radio waves in a pattern depending upon its geometry. In this way some of the radio waves are reflected back to the radar antenna. The radar set itself has both a transmitter and a receiver. It ordinarily uses the same antenna for both transmission and reception and has a device to protect the very sensitive receiver from the powerful outgoing pulse. The common type of receiver in radar

equipment is a superheterodyne receiver. The receiver amplifies the energy from reflected radio waves and changes the energy to signals that can be fed into the display or indicator. The indicator visually presents the information gathered by other parts of the radar system. Nearly all indicators make use of a cathode-ray tube, the same type of device used in TV picture tubes. Indications of reflected radio waves are seen in the indicator as a change of direction in a bright line or as a bright spot or spots. Some indicators show only the range of the reflecting object. Others show the range and bearing, the bearing and elevation, or the range and elevation. A type of indicator (used with a rotating antenna) that shows a map of the surrounding area is called a plan position indicator (PPI).

In a single pulse of operation of a radar set the following takes place: The power supply produces a high voltage in a large condenser, as well as the other lower voltages needed to operate the vacuum tubes and other parts. The keyer, or modulator, circuit starts and stops the transmitted pulse in a few millionths of a second (microseconds). This pulse is largely supplied by the energy stored in the large condenser. The transmitted pulse is coupled to the antenna and prevented from entering the receiver. The antenna directs the pulse, from which it travels outward at the speed of light—186,000 miles per second. As it travels outward, it excites all objects in its path, the degree of excitation depending upon the energy remaining in the pulse. Rainstorms, snow, and hurricanes, as well as ships, airplanes, and objects ashore, will reradiate, or reflect, some of the energy of the pulse, which returns at the speed of light to the radar antenna. The receiver is now open; the large condenser is being charged by the power supply; and the timer circuits in the display are charging the voltages and currents in the controls of the cathode-ray tube. When the returning pulse enters the receiver, it is amplified, and a signal is sent to the cathode-

Radar is used in weather prediction. On the radar screen, left, a storm is seen approaching. As it passes over the observer's head, it appears in the center of the screen, right.

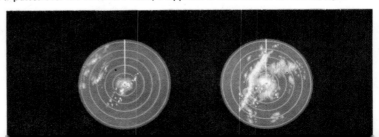

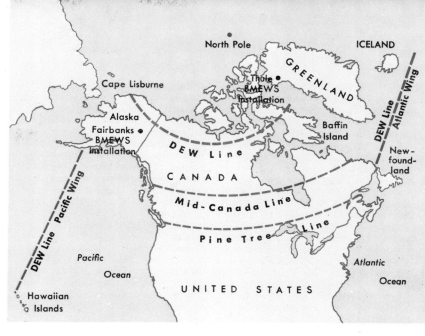

ray tube, which brightens a spot on the tube face. Any other returning energy will likewise brighten the tube face, depending upon the strength of the returning pulse. At the end of the silent period, which is controlled to permit objects at the maximum range to return a pulse, another pulse is transmitted. Pulses vary in length from .25 to 50 microseconds. Pulse frequency averages about 1,500 per second. Suppose, for example, that a pulse of radio waves is transmitted toward a distant object. Each 6.2 microseconds the waves travel 1 nautical mile. (For radar applications, distances are commonly measured in nautical miles.) If the reflected waves come back in 310 microseconds, they have traveled a total of 50 miles out and back. The reflecting object is thus 25 miles from the radar set.

If accurate location of an object is required, as in gunfire or control of aircraft, it may be located by two thin-beamed radars to measure azimuth and elevation or by one radar with a conic, or pencil, beam. The timing, or ranging, circuits would be made with great accuracy.

Some radar sets are fitted to measure the frequency of the returning pulses to assist in obtaining the speed of the object. Others are fitted with special electronic or mechanical (rotating or oscillating) devices to increase accuracy in azimuth or elevation or to permit the radar to "lock on" a moving object and give continuous information of its location.

In 1922 in the United States Albert M. Taylor observed that an object, such as a ship, passing between a radio transmitter and a radio receiver reflected some radio waves back toward the transmitter. During the 1920's experiments and tests proved that ships hidden by fog, darkness, or smoke could be detected by radio waves. It was also discovered that aircraft could be detected. The first radar set was developed in Britain by Robert Watson Watt and was demonstrated in 1935. By the beginning of World War II Britain had a series of radar stations for the detection of enemy aircraft. The United States also had produced and installed radar equipment. Early in the war the British began using airborne radar, which led to the development of high-frequency radar sets.

Radar is now used to navigate ships in darkness and bad weather by locating buoys, lighthouses, islands, and so forth. Radar is extensively used in air navigation and at airports in air traffic control-and-landing systems. Radar can be used to operate altimeters in airplanes, and it can be used for aerial mapping. Radar can be used to track storms and to study cloud formations. See LORAN; RADAR-WARNING NETWORK.

RADAR-WARNING NETWORK, a chain of many radar stations designed to detect hostile aircraft or missiles and to signal the detection. Both northern North America and much of Communist Asia and Europe are surrounded by radar networks. The North American networks are controlled by the North American Air Defense Command and are operated by Canadian and U.S. civilian and military personnel.

Four ground radar networks span North America from east to west. The networks have elaborate communications systems. The radar stations of one chain are linked by dial telephone, teletype, and radio. Main radar stations in each chain can communicate directly with the headquarters of the North American Air Defense Command. The data from the main radar stations are fed into the computers of the SAGE system of the North American Air Defense Command. Flying objects are identified, if possible. Unidentified objects are tracked, and interceptor aircraft or missiles are guided to the objects.

The BMEWS (ballistic missile early warning system) ground-radar network is the newest of the North American networks. The BMEWS Line, stretching from northwestern Alaska to Greenland, has radars that are designed to detect ballistic missiles. The BMEWS radars send continuous waves and collect continuous echoes. The echoes are electronically analyzed to obtain the speed, distance, and direction of an object. The BMEWS radars can detect ballistic missiles 3,000 miles distant.

The DEW Line (Distant Early Warning Line) extends from the east coast of Baffin Island, Canada, to western Alaska. Two types of radars are used in the line. The rotating surveillance radars give information on the altitude, direction, and distance of objects they spot. The stationary radars provide low-altitude detection and are aimed at areas that are poorly covered by the rotating radars. The DEW Line is manned by civilians under the supervision of Air Force officers.

The DEW Line employs a special type of high-frequency radio called forward propagation tropospheric scatter.

The Mid-Canada Line, built by Canada, extends across that nation from near the southern tip of Alaska to the northern tip of Newfoundland. The radar stations employ the Doppler principle and can give data to supplement the information received from the two radar lines farther to the north. See DOPPLER'S PRINCIPLE.

The Pine Tree Line extends from the west coast to the east coast of Canada, just above the northern border of the United States. The radars of the Pine Tree Line can provide information on the height, speed, and direction of movement of an object they spot.

Seagoing warning networks are formed by lines of ships with special radar and communication equipment. Airborne warning networks are provided by patrolling, radar-equipped aircraft.

RADIATION, the giving off of energy in the form of electromagnetic waves. Sunlight is the product of radiation by the heated and ionized gases of the sun. Radio waves are electromagnetic waves carrying energy given off by electric charges.

Electromagnetic waves of all varieties have the same velocity in the same medium. They all have the velocity of light, 186,000 miles per second in vacuum or air. Electromagnetic waves can be refracted, reflected, diffracted, and polarized. They have no mass and are not electrically charged. Electromagnetic waves differ from each other in their wavelengths and frequencies (number of waves per unit of time). The longer the wavelength of a particular wave, the less is its frequency; the shorter the wavelength, the greater the frequency. The waves of greatest frequency carry the most energy. The waves are called electromagnetic because they are produced by oscillations of electric and magnetic fields. In all electromagnetic waves an electric field oscillates at right angles to an oscillating magnetic field. An electromagnetic wave travels at right angles to both oscillating fields. See ELECTROMAGNETIC SPECTRUM.

An example of waves of great frequency and short wavelength is gamma radiation. Gamma radiation is given off by an atomic nucleus when the nucleus undergoes a change of energy. Gamma rays are one of the products of nuclear disintegration. They can penetrate matter.

X-rays are very similar to gamma rays, but they have less energy and less penetrating power. See X-RAY.

Ultraviolet rays are radiated from very hot bodies and from ionized gases. They have shorter wavelengths and greater frequencies than visible light. Light is radiated in the same manner as ultraviolet rays. Light is simply a range of frequencies of electromagnetic radiation that affect human and animal eyes. Infrared rays, heat waves, are radiated by heated bodies and have lower frequencies than light. See CONDUCTION, CONVECTION, RADIATION.

Radio waves are propagated by high-frequency alternating electric current. The frequencies are from 10^{12} to about 10^2 cycles per second. Radio waves are long electromagnetic waves.

The term radiation is often used as a name for particles, such as electrons and helium ions, that are emitted by radioactive substances. See RADIOACTIVITY.

RADIO is a method of communication between distant points by signals carried by electromagnetic radiation. This kind of communication is called radio because it makes use of radiation. The electromagnetic radiations used are called radio waves. A radio transmitting station and a radio receiving set are not connected by electrical wires or by any other direct means. (When the first radio sending and receiving sets were made, they were called wireless sets. Radio still is called wireless in Britain.) A radio transmitting station manufactures signal-carrying electromagnetic waves that it sends off in all directions. The radio waves travel with the velocity of light through air, space, or the earth. A radio receiving set has parts that are affected by passing radio waves and that can interpret the signals carried by the radio waves.

HISTORY

Guglielmo Marconi, who is usually credited with the invention of the radio, produced the first practical radio apparatus for sending and receiving messages. In 1896 Marconi succeeded in sending messages over distances of 9 miles. The messages were not spoken but were in code. In 1897 Marconi was granted a patent on his radio apparatus by Great Britain. In 1901 the first radio message was sent across the Atlantic by Marconi.

Ships were among the first users of radio. The advantages to a ship of a type of communication that does not depend on direct wires or connections is obvious. Shortly after 1900 most large ships installed radio sending and receiving equipment. In 1910 the United States passed its first federal radio legislation, which stated that any United States ship carrying more than 50 people had to have radio sending and receiving equipment capable of communication over a hundred miles. Early ship radios, like all other early radios, were wireless telegraphs. They sent and received code messages.

The first broadcast of voice and music by radio telephony was made in 1906 from Brant Rock, Mass., as an experiment. It was heard by radio operators on ships hundreds of miles at sea.

Not until after World War I were sufficient advances made in radio technology to make regular broadcasting practical. In 1920 a broadcasting station at East Pittsburgh, Pa., was built. The station acquired

Westinghouse Elec. Corp.

This hand-built radio apparatus was used before 1920. Continual refinements in design have eliminated many parts in modern radios.

a government license and began broadcasting programs for the entertainment of amateur radio operators. Other broadcasting stations began operation at about the same time.

The first radio sending and receiving sets, made by Marconi, utilized several people's theories and inventions. The behavior of electromagnetic radiation had been explained by James Clerk Maxwell, a Scottish physicist. To prove Maxwell's explanation, Heinrich Hertz, a German physicist, conducted experiments in which the first radio waves were sent and received. Marconi's original radio apparatus was an adaptation of the experimental equipment used by Hertz. Marconi's radio sets contained many parts that had been developed by other people.

The first radio transmitters were spark transmitters. An intermittent oscillatory discharge of electric current between two electrodes produced separated trains of radio waves that traveled in all directions. The first radio receivers consisted of an antenna for picking up passing radio waves, a source of electric current, a coherer that allowed electric current to pass through a circuit when radio waves passed the antenna, and a sounder or a set of earphones. Later receivers contained crystals instead of coherers. (See CRYSTAL SET.) When a radio operator tuned his set to receive signals from a spark transmitter, he heard the dots and dashes of code through his earphones. The dots and dashes were all the same pitch. The pitch was determined by the frequency at which the diaphragm of the earphone was vibrated; this frequency was the same as that at which the trains of radio waves were produced in the transmitter.

Radio broadcasts today are sent and received with very different equipment than the spark transmitter and the crystal set. Modern radio communication was made possible by invention of the vacuum tube. An early tube, a type of diode, was the Fleming valve, invented by Ambrose Fleming, a British scientist. The diode is used in radios as a detector—it separates the fluctuations of the audio signal from the radio waves carrying the signal. Lee De Forest invented a different kind of vacuum tube, which was called the audion. It was a triode tube. This vacuum tube acted as a detector and as an amplifier. Vacuum tubes help perform nearly all the essential functions of modern radio transmitters and receivers. See VACUUM TUBE.

RADIO TRANSMISSION

When you turn on a radio in your home, you are turning on a mechanism for receiving and interpreting the signals carried by radio waves. A broadcasting station makes radio waves and sends them into space.

Radio waves are a form of electromagnetic radiation. They travel with the speed of light through space, through air, and, under suitable conditions, through ground. In many ways they behave like light, another form of electromagnetic radiation. Radio waves have longer wavelengths and lower frequencies than light. Radio waves used in ordinary broadcasting have wavelengths from 650 to 1,960 feet long. The frequencies used range from 550,000 to 1,600,000 cycles per second. These numbers are often expressed in kilocycles or megacycles. One kilocycle is 1,000 cycles; one megacycle is 1,000,000 cycles. The frequencies mentioned above can also be written as 550 kilocycles and 1,600 kilocycles, or as 0.55 megacycle and 1.6 megacycles. The abbreviation for kilocycles is kc; the abbreviation for megacycles is mc.

Radio Telephony. A number of steps must be gone through before music, speech, and other sounds can be transmitted by radio waves from a broadcasting studio to your radio receiving set.

The first step of all is to translate the air vibrations produced by music or speech, which affect human beings as sound, into electrical vibrations. Microphones accomplish this task. The electrical vibrations, an alternating current, produced by a microphone, vary in step with the variations of the air vibrations, or sound waves. The electrical vibrations are the electrical equivalent of sound.

In the transmitter system of a radiotelephone sending station the electrical signals from the microphone, called the audiofrequency, are amplified. The transmitter also contains an oscillator, which produces radiofrequency signals. One or more amplifiers boost the strength of the radiofrequency, or carrier, signals. The modulator is a part of the transmitter that combines the amplified audiofrequency signal and the carrier signal to produce a modulated signal. Several methods of modulation exist.

Amplifiers designed to increase the strength of electrical signals of about 15 to 15,000 cycles per second are called audiofrequency amplifiers. They amplify signals from a microphone. Radiofrequency amplifiers strengthen alternating currents of frequencies above 15 kilocycles per second. The audio-amplification section of most transmitting stations consists of several amplifiers. Each amplifier is a vacuum tube (a triode or a more complex tube) and its related circuit. The output of one amplifier may be fed into another until the audiofrequency signals are strong enough to modify the radiofrequency signal. The radiofrequency amplifiers increase the strength of the alternating current that comes from the oscillator. See AMPLIFIER.

Any one of many types of oscillators may be used in a transmitting system. Commercial broadcasting stations and other stations needing to have a frequency (number of cycles per second) that does not vary commonly use crystal-controlled oscillators. These oscillators contain a specially cut piece of quartz crystal that controls the frequency. See OSCILLATOR.

The audiofrequency signals, no matter to what strength they may be amplified, cannot travel far in space if fed to an antenna from the transmitter. The radiofrequency, or carrier, signals can be radiated from the antenna to travel great distances through space. But unless the carrier signal is modified in some way, it carries no message. The section of the transmitter system that modifies the carrier signal so that it carries a message is called the modulator.

Amplitude modulation (AM), the commonest system of modulation, is accomplished by making the amplitude of the carrier frequency vary as the amplitude of the audio signals vary. The amplified audio signals are fed into the final, or next to final, radiofrequency amplifier. The commonest method of amplitude modulation is plate modulation. The varying signal from the final audiofrequency amplifier is fed to the plate of the vacuum tube in the final radiofrequency amplifier. This causes the radiofrequency signal leaving the vacuum tube to vary in amplitude. The varying radiofrequency signal causes the power fed into the antenna of the transmitting system to vary with the audiofrequency signal. A modulated radio wave is radiated from the antenna.

When the alternating electric currents of audiofrequency and radiofrequency are combined, the resulting alternating current has at least four frequencies. Two of the frequencies are the audiofrequency and

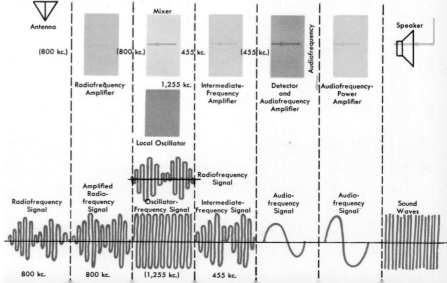

Below is a block diagram of a typical superheterodyne radio receiver. A superheterodyne receiver converts any received frequency to a certain fixed lower frequency, which is amplified by special tuned circuits. Such receivers have superior sensitivity and selectivity.

DIAGRAM OF AM RADIOTELEPHONE TRANSMITTER

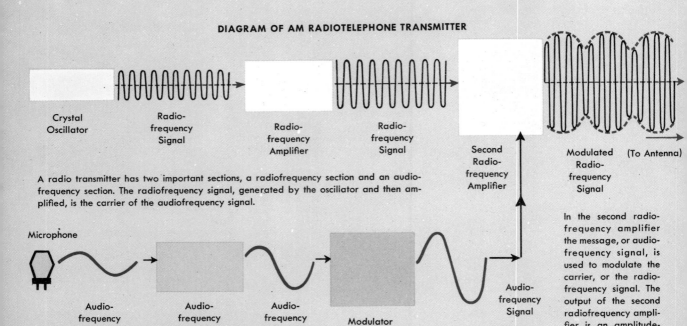

Crystal Oscillator | Radio-frequency Signal | Radio-frequency Amplifier | Radio-frequency Signal | Second Radio-frequency Amplifier | Modulated Radio-frequency Signal　(To Antenna)

A radio transmitter has two important sections, a radiofrequency section and an audiofrequency section. The radiofrequency signal, generated by the oscillator and then amplified, is the carrier of the audiofrequency signal.

Microphone

Audio-frequency Signal | Audio-frequency Amplifier | Audio-frequency Signal | Modulator | Audio-frequency Signal

In the second radiofrequency amplifier the message, or audiofrequency signal, is used to modulate the carrier, or the radiofrequency signal. The output of the second radiofrequency amplifier is an amplitude-modulated signal.

MODULATION OF RADIOFREQUENCY SIGNALS

Some radiofrequency signals used in radiotelephony are shown in these diagrams. Diagram 1 shows a continuous, unmodulated radio signal. If such a signal has its amplitude modulated, it acquires a waveform like that shown in diagram 2. A continuous wave that has had its frequency modulated by an audio signal is shown in diagram 3. Notice that the frequency-modulated waveform has a constant amplitude but a varying frequency.

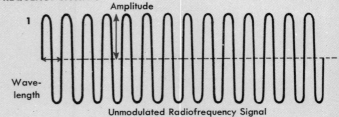

1

Amplitude

Wave-length

Unmodulated Radiofrequency Signal

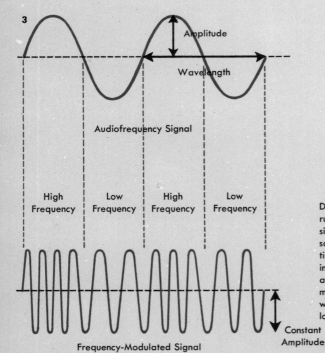

3

Amplitude

Wavelength

Audiofrequency Signal

High Frequency | Low Frequency | High Frequency | Low Frequency

Frequency-Modulated Signal

Constant Amplitude

2

Amplitude-Modulated Radiofrequency Signal

Diagram 4 shows an interrupted continuous-frequency signal used to convey a message in radiotelegraphy. The timing of the transmission and interruption of signals forms a code. The first radio communication was by continuous wave. It is still much used for long-distance messages.

4

Dot　　Dot　　　　Dash

Interrupted Continuous-Frequency Signal

the radiofrequency. The two other frequencies are the difference frequency, a frequency that is equal to the difference between the audiofrequency and the radiofrequency, and the sum frequency, which is equal to the sum of the audiofrequency and the radiofrequency. The process of combining two radiofrequency signals is called heterodyning. The sum-and-difference frequencies are called sidebands or sideband frequencies. Suppose a radiofrequency current of 1,000,000 cycles per second is being modulated by audiofrequency currents that range up to 5,000 cycles per second. Two bands of side frequencies would be produced. One band would have frequencies between 1,005,000 and 1,000,000 cycles per second; the other band would have frequencies between 1,000,000 and 995,000 cycles per second. Thus, a modulated radio signal occupies a group of frequencies, or a channel, rather than a single frequency.

The modulated radiofrequency, or carrier, signal leaves the transmitter system as an alternating electric current. It travels to the antenna through a transmission line, which may be a wire centered inside a tubular conductor (a coaxial cable) or two wires side by side.

A transmitting antenna is a device for radiating radio waves into space. The antenna used for broadcasting radio programs is vertical, with one end attached to the ground. As alternating electric current is fed into the antenna from the transmission line, electric and magnetic fields are set up around and through the antenna. Each time the direction of current in the antenna changes, some portion of the electric and magnetic fields and the energy they carry is radiated into space from the antenna. The traveling electric and magnetic fields are radio waves.

When a radio wave leaves the transmitting antenna, it spreads out in all directions. One portion travels along the surface of the earth. It is called the groundwave. Another portion travels away from the earth and is called the skywave. The groundwaves are the ones picked up by radio receiving sets during the day. The groundwaves become weaker and weaker as they move away from the antenna, but groundwaves from a powerful AM broadcasting station may be picked up by receiving sets 200 miles from the antenna. Most of the skywaves emitted from an AM broadcasting station during the day travel into

space and are lost. Some, however, are reflected back to earth from layers of ionized, rarefied air in the earth's upper atmosphere. The part of the earth's atmosphere where these ionized layers are found is called the ionosphere. At night more skywaves are reflected from the ionosphere than during the day. A skywave may be reflected several times between the earth and the ionized layers of the ionosphere and may travel many hundreds, or even thousands, of miles. That is why a greater number of distant broadcasting stations can be received at night than during the day.

In recent years a new system of modulation and broadcasting has come into use. It is called frequency modulation (FM). The frequencies used (88 to 108 megacycles) are much higher than the frequencies used in AM broadcasting (550 to 1,600 kilocycles). Instead of making the amplitude of the radiofrequency signal vary, as in amplitude modulation, the frequency of the radiofrequency signal is made to vary as the audiofrequency signals change. The greater the amplitude of the audiofrequency signal (the louder the sound that affects the microphone), the greater the variation, or deviation, of the radiofrequency. The audiofrequency determines the number of frequency variations per second of the carrier signal.

Modern FM transmitters operate with a band width of about 150 kilocycles—that is, the transmitted frequency may deviate 75 kilocycles from the unmodulated carrier frequency. High frequencies are employed in FM transmission so the necessary wide-band widths can be used without one station interfering with another. Because such high frequencies are used, the radio waves sent out from FM stations behave differently from the radio waves sent from AM broadcasting stations. High-frequency waves lose their energy so rapidly traveling along the earth's surface that the groundwave does not exist. High-frequency skywaves penetrate the ionosphere layers instead of being reflected and are lost. The only waves that reach an FM receiving set are those that travel to the set in a straight line from the transmitting antenna. The distance FM radio waves can be transmitted is limited by the curvature of the earth.

Radio Telegraphy. The transmission of messages by code rather than by voice or music is known as radio telegraphy. Continuous-wave transmitters are used in radio telegraphy.

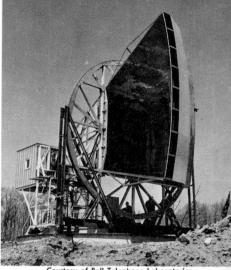

Courtesy of Bell Telephone Laboratories

The horn antenna is used to receive faint microwave radio communication signals.

A continuous-wave transmitter consists of an oscillator and other suitable equipment that produces radiofrequency alternating current. A device called a key is used to interrupt or start the radiofrequency current. When the key allows the current to flow to the transmitting antenna, a train of radio waves is sent into space. The current can be allowed to flow for shorter or longer periods of time. The shorter and longer trains of radio waves given off from the antenna are signals in a code. An example of such a code is the continental Morse code.

RADIO RECEPTION

A radio receiver consists of an antenna, a transmission line, a detector, and a reproducer. The receiver antenna intercepts the signals carried by radio waves. When radio waves pass by an antenna, the changing electric and magnetic fields of which the radio waves consist induce in the antenna an alternating electric current that is like the current sent to the transmitting antenna, except that the current in the receiving antenna is very weak. The transmission line of a radio receiver functions like the transmission line of a transmitter. The detector separates the message from the carrier signal. The reproducing section of the receiver delivers the message as sound if the message is an audio signal. The superheterodyne is the common AM receiver.

All the alternating currents induced in the antenna of a superheterodyne receiver are fed into a radiofrequency amplifier tuned circuit. The circuit is variable and can be tuned to different frequencies. Suppose the receiver is tuned to a radiofrequency of 800 kilocycles. An alternating current of 800 kilocycles per second is amplified, but all other frequencies of current are rejected.

All superheterodyne receivers contain a tube and circuit, an oscillator, that produces an alternating current of higher frequency than the current selected by the radiofrequency amplifier. The oscillator is also a variable circuit that can be tuned to different frequencies. The circuits are arranged so that the frequency of the oscillator is always a set number of cycles above the frequency accepted by the radiofrequency amplifier. Suppose the oscillator always produces alternating currents of 455 kilocycles higher frequency than the currents accepted by a radiofrequency amplifier. Then, if the radiofrequency amplifier accepts current of 800 kilocycles per second, the oscillator produces current of 1,255 kilocycles per second.

In some receivers the oscillator current and the current from the radiofrequency amplifier are both fed into a tube and circuit called a mixer. In other receivers the oscillator and mixer stages are combined and are called a converter stage. In either arrangement the two frequencies combine to produce two new frequencies, one of which is the difference between the two original frequencies. The process of combining frequencies and producing a new frequency is called heterodyning. If the oscillator frequency is always 455 kilocycles above the carrier-signal frequency, the difference frequency is always 455 kilocycles per second.

The difference frequency, or intermediate frequency, is accepted by the next stage of the receiver, called the intermediate-frequency amplifier. This amplifier is tuned to accept only the difference frequency. One of the advantages of a superheterodyne receiver is that amplification by a fixed tuned circuit, such as the intermediate-frequency amplifier, is more successful than amplification by variable tuned circuits.

The next stage of the receiver, the detector, separates the audio signal from the intermediate-frequency signal. Though the frequency of the carrier current has been changed, its modulation has not been affected. The detector circuit rectifies the alternating current —changes it into pulsing direct current. The direct current pulses at intermediate frequency with audiofrequency modulation. Next, this stage of the receiver filters out the intermediate frequency and passes on only a current pulsing at audiofrequency. Audiofrequency ampli-

fiers increase the strength of the audio-signal current until it can be used to power a loudspeaker.

The FM receiver is similar to the AM superheterodyne receiver except for one stage. A discriminator stage takes the place of the detector of the AM receiver. The discriminator separates the audiofrequency signal from the carrier signal as the carrier signal changes frequency at an audio rate. An FM receiver may also contain a limiter, which removes any amplitude modulation that may be present in the signal before it reaches the discriminator. The limiter is commonly the final intermediate-frequency amplifier of the receiver. The limiter suppresses static in the FM receiver because most static is amplitude modulated. Some FM receivers use a ratio detector instead of a discriminator. The ratio detector performs the functions of both the discriminator and the limiter.

RADIO FREQUENCY SPECTRUM

The Federal Communications Commission of the United States has divided the radio-wave spectrum into categories for easy identification. Each category includes certain frequencies.

Frequency kc	mc	Name	Abbreviation
10-30		Very Low	VLF
30-300		Low	LF
300-3,000		Medium	MF
3,000-30,000	3-30	High	HF
	30-300	Very High	VHF
	300-3,000	Ultra High	UHF
	3,000-30,000	Super High	SHF

The Federal Communications Commission has also allocated certain frequencies to particular uses in the United States.

Frequency Band	Uses
20-550 kc	government, commercial, maritime, ship-to-shore, aircraft, point-to-point, transoceanic
550-1,600 kc	commercial broadcast
1,600 kc-50 mc	ship-to-shore, aircraft, police, government, experimental, point-to-point, shortwave communication, international broadcasting
50-88 mc	television
88-108 mc	FM broadcasting
106-400 mc	television, police, aircraft, government, radar
400 mc and up	experimental

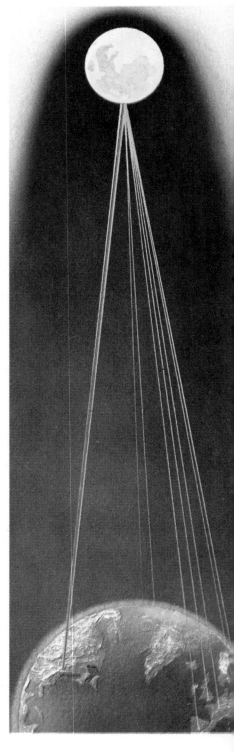

High-frequency radio can be used to communicate with other points on the globe by bouncing the radio signal off the moon. This method is superior to low-frequency radio broadcasting through the atmosphere because static and distortion caused by atmospheric disturbance are minimized.

RADIOACTIVE DATING is a group of methods for determining the age of a substance. The ratio of a naturally radioactive isotope to its disintegration product or to a nonradioactive isotope of the same element is measured in the substance to be dated. Each radioactive isotope disintegrates at a certain definite rate and to a definite product. See ISOTOPE; RADIOACTIVITY.

The first radioactive dating method was dating by the uranium/lead ratio. All minerals that contain uranium or thorium also contain helium and lead. The helium and lead are disintegration products of uranium and thorium. Because the rates of disintegration of thorium and uranium have been experimentally determined, the ratio of uranium or thorium to the disintegration products can be used to calculate the age of a uranium-bearing or thorium-bearing mineral. The actual calculations necessary are rather complex. For the simplest calculations the assumption must be made that the mineral originally contained no lead and has had no lead added or subtracted since its formation. Further to complicate matters, two isotopes of uranium and an isotope of thorium, all radioactive, are found in many uranium-bearing minerals. Each radioactive isotope disintegrates at a different rate to a different isotope of lead. Commonly, two or three separate ratios, one for each of the radioactive isotopes, are determined for one mineral sample. The many isotopes make the ratios difficult to find accurately.

A related method is dating by the lead/alpha-particle ratio in zircon. Zircon, a mineral often present in small amounts in igneous rocks, may contain some uranium or thorium. Some of the uranium or thorium has disintegrated to lead. If the relative content of lead in the zircon sample is determined, and if the present rate at which alpha particles are emitted by the remaining thorium and uranium is measured, the age of the zircon sample can be calculated.

The ratio of a radioactive potassium isotope to an isotope of argon can be used in the age determination of rocks. The argon isotope is a disintegration product of radioactive potassium. The radioactive potassium isotope is found in mica, a common mineral in igneous rocks.

The last common method for dating rocks is based on the rubidium/strontium ratio. Rubidium-87, a radioactive isotope, disintegrates to strontium-87. The minerals commonly used in this type of dating are lepidolite and biotite micas.

The uranium/lead, lead/alpha-particle, potassium/argon, and rubidium/strontium ratios cannot be used to date rocks or minerals less than 10 to 15 million years old.

The ratio of carbon-14, a radioactive isotope, to normal carbon, carbon-12, can be used to determine the age of organic substances that are 50,000 years old or younger. This method is called radiocarbon dating and was developed by W. F. Libby of the United States. Radiocarbon is formed in the outer atmosphere when nitrogen is bombarded by neutrons from cosmic rays. Radiocarbon combines with oxygen to form a special carbon dioxide, CO^2, and mixes with normal atmospheric CO^2. Carbon dioxide is used by plants in building tissues. Animals eat plants and assimilate carbon into their bodies. Live animal and plant tissues have the same ratio of carbon isotopes (radioactive to normal) as exists in the atmosphere. This ratio is constant. After an animal or a plant dies, the ratio of carbon-14 to carbon-12 in its body gradually changes as the radioactive carbon-14 disintegrates. The longer the plant or animal has been dead, the smaller the ratio of carbon-14 to carbon-12. Carbon-14 ratios are not easy to measure accurately in objects older than about 30,000 years. Radiocarbon dating is an important technique in dating organic objects from the late Pleistocene and the Recent epochs.

RADIOACTIVE FALLOUT. See FALLOUT.

Arizona State Museum

This carbonized corn will be tested for carbon-14 content to determine its age.

RADIOACTIVE ISOTOPE is an isotope that undergoes spontaneous disintegration and emits radiation. During its disintegration the isotope may emit beta particles (electrons or positrons), alpha particles (helium nuclei), or gamma rays, or it may capture electrons. See ISOTOPE; RADIOACTIVITY.

Radioisotopes that occur in nature are called natural; those produced by man are termed artificial. More than 50 radioactive isotopes occur in nature, but more than 700 radioactive isotopes have been produced artificially. Three methods are used to produce them: the bombardment of selected targets in nuclear reactors; the fission of nuclear fuels; and the bombardment of targets in particle accelerators.

The greatest quantity of artificial radioisotopes is manufactured by neutron bombardment of targets in nuclear reactors. Radioisotopes may be produced by an activation nuclear reaction or by a transmutation nuclear reaction. In an activation nuclear reaction, an element captures a neutron and becomes a radioactive isotope of the original element. A typical activation reaction is cobalt-59 + neutron→cobalt-60 + gamma rays

The atomic number (the number of protons) is not changed by the reaction. The atomic weight is increased by one unit—a neutron has been added. In a transmutation reaction an element captures a neutron and becomes a radioactive isotope of a different element. An

Radioactive isotopes are used by agronomists to study plant growth, nutrition, and structure.

example of a transmutation reaction is

nitrogen-14 + neutron→carbon-14 + proton

The atomic number is changed because a proton is given off during the reaction. The atomic weight remains the same because the captured neutron is compensated for by the emission of a proton.

The nuclear fissions that take place in a nuclear reactor result in the formation of a variety of elements. Some of the elements are in the form of intensely radioactive isotopes.

In particle accelerators the target material may be bombarded by protons, beta particles, alpha particles, or other charged atomic particles. Radioactive isotopes are formed by several types of reactions.

Radioactive isotopes have many uses in medicine, agriculture, industry, and research. New uses for radioisotopes are constantly being discovered and perfected.

Short-lived radioisotopes, such as iodine-131, phosphorus-32, and gold-198, are used by medical institutions and private physicians for a variety of diagnostic and therapeutic purposes. Large amounts of cobalt-60 are used in teletherapy units for the treatment of cancer.

The most extensive use of radioisotopes in industry is in radiography. Pictures of the internal structures of objects are taken by using gamma rays and film sensitive to

gamma rays. Many radioisotopes emit gamma rays. The object to be recorded is placed between the radioactive isotopes and the film. The amount of radiation that penetrates the object and is recorded on the film varies with the thickness or density of the object. Flaws or breaks in the object allow more radiation to pass than do other parts of the object, and the flaws or breaks are clearly shown on the film.

The next most extensive industrial use of radioisotopes is in thickness, density, level, and composition gauges. The material to be measured is placed between the radioactive-isotope mass and a radioactivity measuring device. The proportion of emitted particles or radiation that passes through the material is an indication of the thickness, density, level, or composition.

One of the newer applications of radioisotopes is the generation of electricity. Several types of small batteries containing radioisotopes have been designed and marketed. Some radioisotope batteries are used in military equipment.

RADIOACTIVITY is the spontaneous change of atomic nuclei, during which particles and radiations are emitted. Radioactivity can be either natural or artificial. Naturally radioactive elements are found in certain minerals. Artificial radioactivity is produced when the nuclei of atoms are bombarded with atomic or subatomic particles. See ATOM.

The discoverer of radioactivity was a French scientist, Henri Becquerel, who found, in 1896, that uranium spontaneously emitted radiation similar to X-rays. Later Pierre and Marie Curie isolated radium and polonium. More than 40 naturally radioactive isotopes have now been found. Two English scientists, Ernest Rutherford and Frederick Soddy, proposed the theory of radioactive disintegration, which states that radioactivity is caused by changes in the nuclei of atoms. The changes involve the

After drinking water containing the radioactive isotope iodine-131, a patient has his thyroid gland examined with a Geiger counter. The thyroid gland is now slightly radioactive.

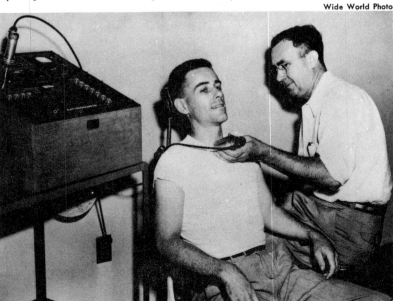

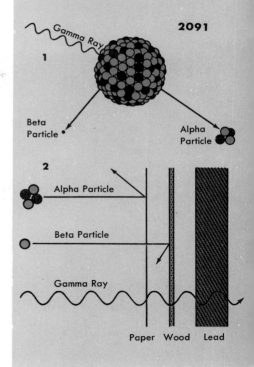

emission of particles and energy and the transformation of atoms from one element to another.

NATURAL RADIOACTIVITY

When a nucleus spontaneously changes, it gives off alpha or beta particles, or both, and may at the same time give off electromagnetic energy.

An alpha particle has an atomic weight of 4 and a charge twice as great as the charge on an electron but opposite in sign. It is the nucleus of a helium atom, and it contains two protons and two neutrons. Its symbol is either α or $_2He^4$. Alpha particles, ejected from nuclei at high-speeds, travel about 10,000 miles per second.

The other kind of particle has the same charge as an electron and the same mass. These particles are called beta particles and are electrons. The symbol for a beta particle is either β^- or $_{-1}e^\circ$. Electrons are emitted from nuclei at a number of velocities; some travel with almost the speed of light.

The electromagnetic energy emitted by a radioactive nucleus is called gamma radiation (γ). The γ rays are electromagnetic waves of high frequency. See ELECTROMAGNETIC SPECTRUM.

To describe the nuclear transformations in radioactive elements, we must first describe the nucleus of an atom. A simple method of describing a nucleus of the element X is to give the atomic number, n, and the mass number, a. The symbol describing the nucleus of an

element is then $_nX^a$. The nucleus of helium, atomic number 2 and mass number 4, is written as $_2He^4$. The atomic number is equal to the number of protons in the nucleus of an atom. The mass number is equal to the total number of protons and neutrons in the nucleus of an atom. A helium atom has two neutrons in its nucleus.

The radioactive element radium, Ra, decays into a daughter element called radon, Rn. During the transformation, or decay, radium emits alpha particles. The transformation is written in the form of a nuclear equation.

$$_{88}Ra^{226} \rightarrow {_{86}Rn^{222}} + {_2He^4} + energy$$

When an element emits alpha particles, the element is changed to another element of four less units of mass, and the atomic number of the new element is two less than the atomic number of the original element. The nuclei of the new element have two less protons and two less neutrons than the nuclei of the original element. The energy given off does not affect the mass and atomic number. Notice that the totals of the atomic numbers and of the mass numbers are the same on both sides of the equation.

The nucleus of a radioisotope of lead, Pb, decays to a radioisotope of bismuth, Bi, by emitting a beta particle. The equation is

$$_{82}Pb^{214} \rightarrow {_{83}Bi^{214}} + {_{-1}e^\circ} + energy.$$

The mass of the beta particle, an electron, is ignored because it is very small compared to the masses of the nuclei involved. But the electrical charge of the beta particle

is significant. When the original nucleus, Pb, loses a negative charge, it gains a positive charge. It now has one more proton than it had originally. The instant the nucleus changes charge, it acquires the properties of a different element. Lead is transformed to bismuth. Again, the algebraic sums of the mass numbers and the atomic numbers are the same on both sides of the equation.

Nuclear transformation, or radioactive decay, is often accompanied by the emission of gamma radiation, a form of energy. When one radioelement decays to a second radioelement, the second element, since it is radioactive, decays to a third element, which may also be radioactive. Thus, a radioelement may go through a series of transformations until it finally decays to a stable, or nonradioactive, isotope. Such series are found in nature and are called radioactive series or disintegration series.

One well-known series is the series of decay products of the heavy isotope of uranium, $_{92}U^{238}$. All the members of the series, except the end product, $_{82}Pb^{206}$, a stable isotope of lead, are radioactive. The gamma radiation that accompanies many of the disintegration steps is not included. The symbol U stands for uranium; Pa, for protactinium; Th, for thorium; Ra, for radium; Rn, for radon; Po, for polonium; Pb, for lead; and Bi, for bismuth.

Suppose you have a mineral mass that contains a certain number of

Below is the scheme of the uranium series, one of the radioactive, or disintegration, series.

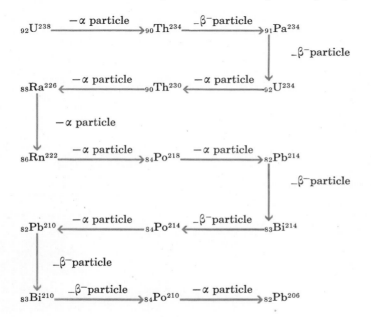

Operated by Union Carbide Corporation for the U.S. Atomic Energy Commission, Oak Ridge National Laboratory

Radioactive isotopes are being processed at the Fission Products Pilot Plant, Oak Ridge National Laboratory. Technicians operate master-slave manipulators from outside the cells that contain the radioactive isotopes. The thick wall and plate-glass windows are necessary to protect the technicians from the intense radioactivity inside the cells.

uranium atoms. All the uranium atoms are of the same isotope. During each minute a few of the uranium atoms decay. The number of atoms that will probably decay each minute is proportional to the total number of uranium atoms present. At the end of each minute the total number of uranium atoms that have been changed to atoms of other elements is greater, and the total number of uranium atoms is less. Therefore it is probable that fewer and fewer uranium atoms decay each succeeding minute.

After some period of time half of the original uranium atoms in the mineral mass have changed to atoms of other elements. The time it takes to change half the uranium atoms is called the half life of the uranium isotope. For example, the half life of uranium-234 is about 269,000 years. If your mineral mass contains uranium-234 atoms, half of them will have decayed to other atoms at the end of 269,000 years. After another 269,000 years half of the remaining atoms would have decayed.

Some radioactive isotopes have very long half lives. Uranium-238 has a half life of 4,500,000,000 years. Thorium-232 has a half life of about 14,000,000,000 years. Other isotopes have moderately long half lives. Radium-226 has a half life of about 1,600 years. Many radioactive materials have half lives that are measured in days, minutes, or even seconds. Polonium-216 has a half life of a fraction of a second.

All the naturally radioactive atoms are not members of a disintegration series like the uranium series. Some atoms, like potassium-40 and bismuth-40, are not formed by the decay of other atoms. They disintegrate, without intermediate steps, to stable atoms. Such radioactive isotopes have very long half lives.

ARTIFICIAL RADIOACTIVITY

The first artificial nuclear transformation was accomplished by Rutherford in 1919. The first artificial radioactivity was produced in 1934 as the result of an artificial nuclear transformation. Irène Joliot-Curie, the daughter of Marie and Pierre Curie, and F. Joliot-Curie

bombarded aluminum with alpha particles. They found that one product, an isotope of phosphorus, was radioactive. The phosphorus isotope had a half life of less than 3 minutes, emitted positrons, and decayed to a stable isotope of silicon.

Soon many scientists were experimenting by bombarding elements with various particles. In five years about 500 new radioactive isotopes had been discovered. More have been found since. This type of experimentation eventually led to the discovery of nuclear fission—the process that takes place in an atomic pile or in the explosion of an atomic bomb.

A number of atomic and subatomic particles are used to bombard elements. The most commonly used are the alpha particle, $_2He^4$ or α, the beta particle or electron, $_{-1}e^\circ$ or β^-, the neutron, $_0n^1$ or n, the proton, $_1H^1$ or p, and the deuteron, $_1H^2$ or $_1D^2$ or d. The neutron has no charge but does have one unit of atomic mass. The proton has the mass as a neutron and has a positive electrical charge. The proton's amount of charge is the same as that of an electron, but it is opposite in sign. A proton can be thought of as the nucleus of a simple hydrogen atom. The deuteron has the same charge as a proton but has twice as much mass. The deuteron can be thought of as the nucleus of a deuterium atom, a heavy isotope of hydrogen, which contains one proton and one neutron.

A type of particle emitted in the decay of some artificially radioactive isotopes is the positron. A positron is just like an electron except that it has a positive rather than a negative charge. Its symbol is $_{+1}e^\circ$ or β^+.

Bombardment is a process during which particles are made to strike atomic nuclei and combine with them to form new nuclei. To bombard atomic nuclei with positively charged particles, such as protons, deuterons, or alpha particles, it is necessary to give the particles a very high energy. Otherwise, they would be repelled or deflected by the positively charged atomic nuclei and not be able to combine with them. Charged particles are given a high energy by being given a high velocity by devices called particle accelerators. (See PARTICLE ACCELERATOR.) Beta particles, which have a negative charge, are also accelerated. Alpha particles, when they were first used in bombardment, were not artificially accelerated. When alpha particles are ejected from radioactive substances, they have rather high energies.

The formation of artificially radioactive nuclei by bombardment takes place in two steps. First, the bombarding particles strike and combine with atomic nuclei. Second, either the combined nuclei break up into two parts or they do not break up. If the nuclei do break up, which happens in most reactions, each combined nucleus turns into a new nucleus and ejects a particle. The nuclear reaction discovered by the Joliot-Curies is an example of a breaking-up reaction.

$$_{13}Al^{27} +_2He^4 \rightarrow_{15}P^{30} +_0n^1$$

The alpha particle is the bombarding particle. The radioactive phosphorus is the new nucleus, and the neutron is the ejected particle. Another breaking-up reaction is the result of bombarding nitrogen with neutrons.

The young man in the picture is testing for radioactivity with a Geiger-Muller counter. Radioactive ground is an indication that a valuable deposit of uranium or thorium minerals may be concealed underground nearby.
Wilson & MacPherson Hole

$$_7N^{14} +_0n^1 \rightarrow_6C^{14} +_1H^1$$

Nitrogen is transformed into radioactive carbon-14 and a proton is ejected.

If a combined nucleus does not break up, it gives off gamma radiation at the moment it absorbs the bombarding particle. The formation of cobalt-60 in atomic piles, or nuclear reactors, is an example of this type of reaction. Cobalt-60 is a radioisotope much used in medical therapy. The symbol Co stands for cobalt.

$$_{27}Co^{59} +_0n^1 \rightarrow_{27}Co^{60}$$
$$+ \text{gamma radiation}$$

DETECTION AND MEASUREMENT OF RADIOACTIVITY

Particles and waves emitted by radioactive substances have a very important property. They ionize gases. When an alpha particle, for example, travels rapidly through air, it pulls loose electrons from atoms and molecules of the air. The atoms and molecules that lose electrons become positively charged ions. The loose electrons either act as negative ions themselves or combine with atoms or molecules to form negative ions. One particle, as it travels through a gas, produces many positive and negative ions. Gamma radiation ionizes a gas indirectly by ejecting electrons from molecules and atoms. The ejected electrons, which have high velocities, produce the actual ionization.

When gases are ionized, they are electrical conductors; when not ionized, nonconductors. Suppose a chamber or tube encloses a gas and has two electrodes. Suppose, also, that a potential difference, or voltage, is maintained between the electrodes. As long as the air is not ionized, no electrical charges travel through the tube or chamber to either electrode. Nothing happens. Now, if a single particle or wave enters the chamber, it causes some ionization. The negative ions, or electrons, travel to one electrode; the positively charged ions, to the other electrode. Charges collect on the electrodes, and the device indicates a pulse of current.

Several instruments for detecting and counting particles make use of gas-filled tubes and chambers and electrodes. The instruments do not operate identically because they have different voltages between the electrodes and different electronic devices for counting the pulses of current. The earliest instrument of this type was the ionization chamber. Another instrument is the proportional counter, which can distinguish easily between ionization caused by alpha particles and ionization caused by beta particles and gamma radiation. The Geiger-Müller counter is an ionization instrument in common use. See GEIGER COUNTER.

Entirely different methods of measuring and detecting radioactivity are employed in scintillation counters. When gamma radiation or alpha or beta particles fall on certain substances, tiny flashes of light, or scintillations, are produced. The intensity of the radioactive source emitting particles and rays can be determined by counting the light flashes in a scintillating substance. Each flash means a particle or ray has struck the substance. Scintillations in most materials are very feeble; to be counted easily, they must be amplified. Modern scintillation counters use a photomultiplier tube to amplify light flashes. The light of one scintillation falls on the cathode of the photomultiplier tube. The light dislodges electrons, which travel along the tube and pick up other electrons. Soon, enough electrons have been collected to produce a pulse of current that can be counted. Each current pulse corresponds to one scintillation. Scintillation counters, particularly used to detect and count gamma radiation, are capable of very rapid counting. They can detect around a million particles or rays each second.

A third type of detector is the crystal conducting counter. Crystal counters may be used to detect any type of emission from radioactive substances, but they are most often used to detect gamma radiations.

RADIO ASTRONOMY, a branch of astronomy in which radio waves are the source of information instead of visible light. Radio telescopes gather radio waves for the astronomer in much the same way that optical telescopes collect visible light. The universe contains electromagnetic radiation that varies in wavelength from the ultralong wavelengths of radio waves to the ultrashort wavelengths of gamma rays. Of this broad range only two types of radiation penetrate the earth's atmosphere; these types are radio waves and visible light. Virtually all the rest is screened out by the atmosphere. Until recently man's knowledge of the astronomical universe was based almost entirely upon the narrow band of radiation called visible light. By using another "window" through the atmosphere radio astronomy has increased and altered our understanding of the universe.

Radio astronomy had its origin in 1931, when the American engineer Karl G. Jansky, associated with the Bell Telephone Laboratories, discovered radio waves from outer space. His discovery was corroborated in 1936 by Grote Reber, who built a crude radio telescope with a 31-foot bowl-shaped antenna and plotted a radio map of a section of the Milky Way. Radio astronomy profited greatly as a result of advances made in electronics during World War II. Radar in particular was adapted to astronomical purposes. It has been used to record meteor trails and to verify distances to the moon, the planet Venus, and the sun by timing the radar echo. As early as 1942 radar stations in Great Britain reported the discovery of radio waves emitted from the sun. In 1946 the first discrete source of radio waves from beyond the solar system was located in the constellation Cygnus.

The primary fault of early radio telescopes was that they could not separate small sources of radio waves in the sky. This was due to the fact that the reflector device of the antenna, built to collect radio waves up to 17 meters in length, could receive only a broad beam. This problem was solved with the invention of the interferometer, a device that enabled the pinpointing of signal-sending areas.

The radio telescope is analogous in function to the light-receiving telescope. Radio waves, corresponding to the light waves received by the optical telescope, are gathered by the antenna, which is generally of either the flat type or the paraboloidal type. The first consists of a vast number of collecting rods, called helices, mounted on a grid. The paraboloidal type, the commoner of the two, consists of a large concave dish of sheet metal or metal mesh.

Both of these types of antenna are usually mounted so they can be faced in the direction from which the signals are coming. In either case the energy received is concentrated and transmitted to an amplifier. Instead of a visual image, as in the optical telescope, the intensity of the radio waves is recorded on an automatic graphing device.

One of the world's major radio telescopes is located at the Jodrell Bank Radio Observatory in England. Its antenna, of the paraboloidal type, is 250 feet in diameter. Other important radio telescopes are found in Sydney, Australia, and in Green Bank, W. Va. Radio telescopes with diameters of 600 feet and more are planned.

Radio astronomers have made considerable progress in mapping the spiral arms of our own Galaxy. Many other sources of radio-wave radiation have been located in space. These include gaseous nebulae, remnants of supernovae, and external galaxies. Far less than half of the discrete radio sources coincide in location with visible objects.

Above is a Crookes radiometer that is in motion because of thermal transpiration.

RADIOMETER, an instrument used for detecting and measuring thermal (heat) radiation. Essentially, it consists of a perpendicular vane attached to each end of one or more horizontal bars, which are enclosed in a glass bulb. Radiation pressure causes the bar or bars to turn in the partially evacuated (air is removed) bulb. The two common types are the Crookes and the Nichols radiometer.

The Crookes type has a vertical pin supporting two of the bar-and-vane assemblies. The vanes have a polished metal surface on one side and a blackened surface on the reverse side, with the surfaces facing in opposite directions. When thermal radiation strikes the vanes, the bar-vane assembly rotates because of the higher heat absorption by the vanes' blackened sides. The higher temperatures of the dark surfaces cause thermal transpiration (a creeping of gas molecules) around the edges of the vanes from the brighter to the darker sides. The pressure thus built up acts against the black sides, causing the bar-vane assembly to turn.

The Nichols radiometer measures radiation pressure by means of two mirrors attached to a horizontal bar suspended by a quartz fiber from a movable scale. A beam of light is directed first on one mirror and then on the other. Radiation pressure causes the bar to turn a certain distance in one direction and then in the other, thereby twisting the quartz fiber. The torque (degree of twisting) is measured on the scale, indicating the beam's thermal content. Other instruments for measuring radiation pressure are the bolometer and pyrheliometer. Radiation pressure has been proposed as a means of spaceship propulsion.

This is the Jodrell Bank radio telescope, completed in 1957, by the University of Manchester, in England. Even larger paraboloid radio telescopes are planned.

RADIUM

RADIO-RANGE SYSTEM, an instrument-flying aid that is one of the systems that made blind flying possible. The radio-range system is a network of radio stations that broadcasts signals for the guidance of airplanes. Each station establishes four courses of flight, usually referred to as beams. An airplane on its correct course is said to be on the beam. The beams of each station meet beams from other stations and thereby establish long-distance flight courses.

The range-system signals are occasionally interrupted for station identifications, weather reports, and other items of information that may be important to airplane pilots. Stations are usually located near a terminal airport or an intermediate landing field and whenever possible are so located that the beam follows the course of the airfield's principal runway. The radio-range system is operated by the Civil Aeronautics Administration.

RADIOSONDE, an instrument that collects accurate information on the humidity, pressure, and temperature of air at various heights above the ground. These data are automatically translated by the measuring instruments into electrical im-

This repeater tower is part of a radio-relay long-distance telephone system. Directional radio waves from a sending station are picked up by the antenna of the tower. The signals the radio waves carry are amplified. Then the signals are sent on radio waves to the next station. The signals are representations at radio frequencies of the frequencies of human voices. Radio transmitters and receivers translate voice frequencies to radio frequencies and the reverse.

pulses. The electrical impulses are broadcast by a small radio transmitter. The radio waves are picked up on the ground by a radiosonde receiver and recorded by a weatherman. Large gas-filled balloons carry the radiosondes aloft to heights of 15 to 20 miles. When the balloons burst, the instruments are lowered harmlessly to the ground by means of parachutes.

RADIOTELEPHONE, the apparatus used for two-way voice communication by means of radio, from either a fixed or a movable location. A radiotelephone is the wireless counterpart of a telephone, but unlike a telephone it permits no interruption of one speaker by another.

Radiotelephony is widely used today, particularly in situations where communication by regular telephone is impractical or impossible. Both private and government agencies employ radiotelephones, particularly in communication with automobiles, ships, aircraft, spacecraft, and inaccessible exploration and development expeditions and in military communication and intercontinental public telephone communication.

In many radiotelephone systems all stations on a given frequency are normally set to receive. A station switches from receiving to sending only while the sender is talking. In such a system only one station can transmit at a time, and thus a receiving station cannot interrupt. Many such stations can occupy one frequency if none of the stations is used excessively. Radiotelephone for intercontinental public telephone systems requires two frequencies, each available full time. The system will connect with ordinary telephones, but interruption of one speaker by another is impossible.

At the far left is a radiosonde transmitter attached to a balloon. At the near left is a special radiosonde receiver and recorder. Signals from the radiosonde transmitter are automatically recorded and then translated into measurements of temperature, humidity, and pressure at different heights.

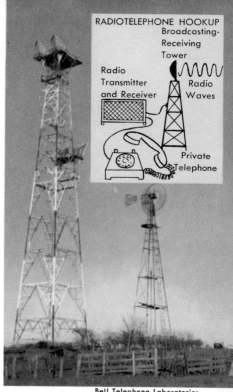

Bell Telephone Laboratories

RADIUM, symbol Ra, is a radioactive element that was discovered in 1898 by Pierre and Marie Curie, the famous husband-and-wife team of Nobel-prize-winning physicists. Radium, a member of the alkaline-earth group of metals, is formed by the radioactive disintegration of uranium and in nature is always found associated with uranium. Radium itself disintegrates to form radon, one of the inert gases. Radon is also radioactive. As radium decays to radon, it emits alpha particles (helium ions) and gamma rays (high-energy X-rays). The half life of radium, the time it takes for one-half of the radium present to disintegrate to other elements, is 1,620 years.

Radium is found in the uranium ores pitchblende and carnotite. The Great Bear Lake region of Canada and the Congo Republic are important producers of radium.

The unit of radioactive change, the curie, named in honor of Madame Curie, is defined as the number of alpha particles one gram of radium in any form emits in one second. Radium's rate of radioactive disintegration is also the standard of comparison for gamma radiation.

Radium salts (radium combined with nonmetallic elements) are used in luminous paints and in radiotherapy, the treatment of diseases by radiation. (See RADIATION.) The salts most often used in radiotherapy are radium sulfate and radium chloride. Radon is also used in radiotherapy.

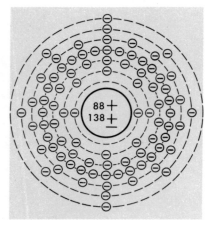

Radium (at. no. 88, at. wt. of most abundant isotope 226) has 88 electrons (−) around a nucleus of 88 protons and 138 neutrons.

Radium salts are stored in sealed glass tubes to prevent the radioactive radon gas formed during disintegration from escaping into the air. The glass tubes are kept in lead shields to absorb gamma radiation from the radium and radon.

RAFFIA, a commercial fiber obtained from the raffia palm. It is indigenous to Madagascar and is found along the coast in great abundance. The thin fiber is obtained from the under part of the leaves and can be peeled off straight to the tip without breaking. When first taken from the leaf, the fiber is pale green but turns to a light straw color when dried in the sun. The natives weave raffia to make clothing and sacking. In the United States raffia is used by nurserymen and gardeners for tying up bushes and vines, as it is pliable and does not injure the plant. Raffia was introduced into the public schools for use in kindergarten and manual training work, especially for making baskets, trays, and other articles.

RAFFLES OF SINGAPORE (1781-1826). Sir Thomas Stamford Raffles in a short life of 45 years established a noble tradition of humane colonial administration, a sound foundation for investigation of problems of living in the tropics, and a shrewd policy of naval bases at strategic points. He was a constructive builder of the British Empire.

Raffles was born at sea on his father's trading ship in the British West Indies. At the age of 14 he went to work as a clerk in the London office of the British East India Company, which then administered most of the British possessions in India and areas farther east. After ten years in London Raffles was sent by the company to the Malay Peninsula, where he rapidly learned the native language and gained the esteem of his English superiors.

In 1811 Raffles persuaded the English to conquer Java from the Dutch, who at the time were allied with Napoleon. The British took over the island without fighting and made Raffles governor. He distinguished himself by his friendliness, justice, and wisdom in dealing with the natives. After the final defeat of Napoleon Java was restored to the Dutch, so Raffles returned to England, where he was knighted.

He went out again to the East Indies in 1818 as an administrator, scholar, and humanitarian. With rare strategic foresight he saw that the growing Dutch monopoly of trade could be checked by buying an almost uninhabited swampy little island at the tip of the Malay Peninsula and erecting on it a British city and naval base. This became the colony of Singapore.

After six years, worn out by work and study and efforts to protect the natives from the greed of the East India Company, he left behind him the graves of four of his five children and returned to England. His manuscripts and thousands of his specimens were destroyed in a ship's fire. Even then his spirit was not broken. For two years of ceaseless toil he fought off the diseases he had contracted in the tropics.

RAFTER, one of the interior supporting beams of a roof. Rafters extend from the ridgepole down to the outside edge of the floor of the attic, and generally about a foot farther out to provide the supporting framework for the eaves. The upper ends of the rafters are sawed at an angle in order to make a solid connection with the ridgepole, to which they are fastened with nails. The lower ends of the rafters may be notched to receive the top plate of the attic floor and are then nailed to it. Very rarely the rafters are nailed flat against the attic floor joists and are not notched. Sound construction requires rafters to be laid 16 inches on centers, and a great deal of bat and roll insulation is made to fit neatly between rafters so laid. On the upper surface of the rafters are nailed the roof sheathing and onto the roof sheathing, the shingles or other outside surface covering.

Determining the angle at which the rafter should meet the ridgepole is not a simple matter. The size of the angle should not be left to the carpenter or contractor but should be detailed by the architect with the consent and the understanding of the owner. The appearance of a house or barn in terms of pleasing proportions is largely set by this angle. The angle cannot be specified by rule of thumb but rather by an intuitive artistic sense born of long training and experience.

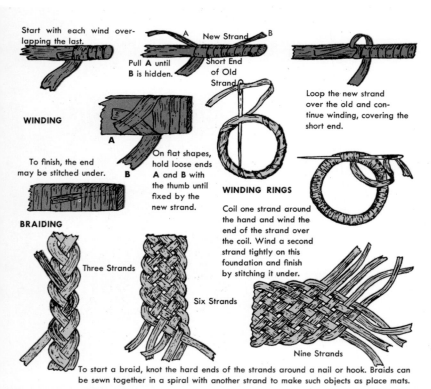

Start with each wind overlapping the last.

New Strand

Pull **A** until **B** is hidden.

Short End of Old Strand

Loop the new strand over the old and continue winding, covering the short end.

WINDING

To finish, the end may be stitched under.

On flat shapes, hold loose ends A and B with the thumb until fixed by the new strand.

WINDING RINGS

Coil one strand around the hand and wind the end of the strand over the coil. Wind a second strand tightly on this foundation and finish by stitching it under.

BRAIDING

Three Strands

Six Strands

Nine Strands

To start a braid, knot the hard ends of the strands around a nail or hook. Braids can be sewn together in a spiral with another strand to make such objects as place mats.